PATRISTIC MONOGRAPH SERIES, NO. 8

A HISTORY OF NEO-ARIANISM

Volume I

by

Thomas A. Kopecek

Published by

The Philadelphia Patristic Foundation, Ltd.

1979

To my teacher in patristics,

William R. Schoedel

Library of Congress Catalogue Number: 79-89557

ISBN: 0-915646-07-2

TABLE OF CONTENTS

Volume I

Volume II

PREFACE

In 1973 I was awarded a fellowship from the American Council of Learned Societies to research a biography of the Cappadocian Fathers of the fourth century A.D. As I pursued my study I found myself feeling time and time again the need for more precise historical and theological information about the Cappadocians' theological adversaries than was available. I especially felt the lack of studies treating the Neo-Arians Aetius and Eunomius. As a result, my research during 1973 and 1974 was divided between the Cappadocians and the Neo-Arians. The present volume is the final product of the latter focus. Although I originally became interested in the Neo-Arians because of their relationship to the Cappadocian Fathers, I have striven throughout to view them sympathetically and on their own terms, not as foils for their more famous and influential adversaries. Whether I have succeeded is for my readers to judge.

Two groups have generously provided funds for the production of this volume: The American Council of Learned Societies and the Research Council of Central College, Pella, Iowa. I am most grateful to both groups. I am also grateful to Professor Michael Schrier of Central College's History Department for reading the entire manuscript and to Ms. Evelyn Loynachan of the college's clerical staff for devoting herself with such good grace to the tedious task of typing the lengthy manuscript, mostly during overtime hours. Finally, I wish to acknowledge my debt to the Mid-West Patristics Seminar. If it were not for its existence, I doubt I could have convinced myself, as I taught a heavy load of introductory undergraduate courses and tried to tend a family in a small midwestern town, that anyone really cared about the latter half of the fourth century A.D.

May 24, 1979

T.A.K.
Pella, Iowa

CHAPTER 1:
INTRODUCTION--THE
EARLY ARIAN CONTROVERSY,
TO A.D. 328

Commenting on the late A.D. 350s, Henry Chadwick noted that "it was only at this stage of the Arian controversy that the really serious and hard thinking began to be done."[1] The stimulus for this thinking, according to Henri Marrou, was "the rise . . . of a kind of neo-Arianism more radical than that held by Arius himself: the Anomoeism of Aetius and his disciple Eunomius."[2] Despite the obvious historical importance of Neo-Arianism, scholarship has devoted scant attention to it. What attention has been paid has focused primarily on describing Eunomius' formulation of its theological system, usually as background for understanding the thought of Eunomius' committed enemies, the Cappadocian Fathers. The origins and history of Eunomius' variety of Arianism have been virtually ignored, as have its fascinating non-theological dimensions. The aim of the present volume is to begin to give the Neo-Arian movement of Aetius and Eunomius the kind of concentrated study it deserves. The volume's scope, however, is limited. It does not seek to assess the influence of the movement on the broad development of theological thought in the later fourth century A.D. While this influence defines its lasting historical significance, one can accurately assess influence only after one is clear about the nature and development of the influencing force. Thus, the present study concentrates on seeking to clarify the history of Aetius' and Eunomius'

---

1. Henry Chadwick, The Early Church (Baltimore, 1967), p. 144.
2. Jean Daniélou and Henri Marrou, The First Six Hundred Years, Vol. 1 of Louis J. Rogier, et. al., ed., The Christian Centuries: A New History of the Catholic Church (London, 1964), p. 259.

brand of Arianism in and for itself; other fourth century Christian movements are treated only as they
directly impinge on this history. Our study is also
limited in that it is not exhaustive. It does not
pretend to consider every document which may bear on
Neo-Arian history and thought, nor does it extend
beyond the death of Eunomius ca. A.D. 394. For instance,
the Contra Eunomium 4-5 of Pseudo-Basil, the De Sancta
Trinitate, Dial. 1-2, of Pseudo-Athanasius, and the
Constitutiones Apostolorum are not treated, nor are
the scattered bits of information about Neo-Arianism
which date from after A.D. 394. Our goal is simply to
provide a chronicle of the main lines of Neo-Arian
history and thought during the lifetimes of Aetius,
Neo-Arianism's founder, and Eunomius, its most famous
theologian.[1] Even so the volume has turned out to be
much longer than one perhaps would wish. Hopefully,
we will at some other time be able to provide sequels
which deal with our movement's influence and with sub-
sidiary documents which may serve to illuminate the
historical reconstruction provided in the present
study.

Aetius of Antioch and Eunomius of Cappadocia did
not emerge as significant ecclesiastical figures until
the A.D. 350s, over twenty-five years after Arianism
was defined by Arius of Alexandria. Compared with
Arius' theological claims, those of the younger Arians
were often expressed in a unique way. Hence, the
ecclesiastical movement dominated by Aetius and

---

1. Because the present volume is fundamentally
a chronicle, we have not even sought to treat every
extant fragment which may be attributed to Aetius
or Eunomius, our two main subjects. A number of the
extant fragments are difficult to date and, in a
number of cases, possibly inauthentic. For lists
and discussions of most of the fragments, see Richard
Paul Vaggione, Aspects of Faith in the Eunomian
Controversy, unpublished Ph.D. dissertation (Oxford,
1976). Vaggione also provides a helpful discussion
of Eunomius' view of Christian faith (see 121-280).

2

Eunomius has been termed "Neo-Arian" to distinguish it
from Arius' earlier movement. But one would be mistaken in differentiating too sharply between the new
movement and its theological ancestor. B.J. Kidd was,
in part, right when he characterized Neo-Arianism,
despite its uniqueness, as "a protest in favor of
original Arianism."[1] The protest was able to be particularly effective because Aetius, the founder of
Neo-Arianism, had intimate personal connections with
a number of Arius' earliest champions, most notably,
Paulinus of Antioch (formerly of Tyre) and the
Lucianists Athanasius of Anazarbus, Antonius of
Tarsus, and Leontius of Antioch. In order to assess
these connections and their influence, a history of
Neo-Arianism must be introduced by a narrative sketch
of the early Arian controversy. Unfortunately, to
provide a narrative of the progress of the early Arian
debate is far from an easy task. Some would even say
it is impossible, because, as Jaroslav Pelikan has put
it, "the transmission of the documents of early
Arianism is even more confused than that of other
heretical literature."[2] Most discussions have skirted
the difficulties by tending toward a topical rather
than a chronological treatment. Such a treatment,
however, would be of little value for determining the
historical and biographical origins of Aetius' thought.
Aware of the obvious risks, we must try to sketch
chronologically the early Arian debate. The remainder
of our introductory chapter is devoted to this task.

If we may believe Epiphanius, the Arian controversy began when the Egyptian schismatic Meletius
denounced the Alexandrian presbyter Arius to his
bishop.[3] Although Arius had backed the Meletian

---

1. B.J. Kidd, A History of the Church to A.D.
461 (Oxford, 1922), 2:151.
2. Jaroslav Pelikan, The Emergence of the Catholic
Tradition, Vol. 1 of The Christian Tradition: A History
of the Development of Doctrine (Chicago and London,
1971), p. 193.
3. Epiphanius, Haer. 69:3.

3

schism in the first decade of the fourth century,[1] by
early A.D. 322[2] he had articulated a theological position which Meletius found to be totally unacceptable.
Our scarce primary source material imperfectly informs
us about the issues at stake between Meletius and
Arius. Only one is attested: whereas Meletius was
convinced that the Son is hardly at all subordinate to
God, Arius saw the Son's subordination as great and
significant.[3] If Constantine was right when he said
that the disagreement in the Alexandrian church had to
do with "a certain passage in divine Scripture,"[4] perhaps the passage under debate was Prov. 8:22-31, which
was to become one of the Arians' favorite subordinationist texts.[5] We cannot be at all certain, however,
that the extent of the Son's subordination to God was
the central issue dividing Arius and Meletius. While
modern scholarship has consistently described the
core of Arius' thought as transcendent monotheism,
which logically implies the demotion of the Son to
the realm of the creatures, Drs. Robert C. Gregg and
Dennis E. Groh have recently argued that the heart of
Arius' thought was not theology (to which the issues
of monotheism and subordination most directly belong)
but soteriology.[6] Their interpretation is most convincing and will inform our narrative's orientation
toward early Arianism. Whatever were the major issues
at stake between Arius and Meletius, we know that
Bishop Alexander of Alexandria took them seriously

---

1. See Hans Lietzmann, A History of the Early
Church (New York, 1961), 3:103-6.
2. For the date, see Éphrem Boularand, L'Hérésie
d'Arius et la Foi de Nicée (Paris, 1972), 1:21-4.
3. Sozomen, H.E. 1:15. The details of Sozomen's
account are probably anachronistic and not to be trust-
ed, but see Lietzmann, 3:107-8.
4. Constantine, apud Eusebius of Caesarea, V.C.
69:1.
5. Pelikan, p. 193.
6. Robert C. Gregg and Dennis E. Groh, "The Cen-
trality of Soteriology in Early Arianism," Anglican
Theological Review 59 (1977): 260-78.

enough to hold two hearings at which both men presented
their cases. After the hearings Alexander decided
against Arius. This decision cast the die of the
early Arian controversy, for Arius could not be persuaded to agree with his bishop.[1] He felt compelled
to accuse Alexander of Sabellianism[2] and to look about
for support among the Egyptian bishops and clergy.[3]
Since Arius was a popular figure among the people of
his parish, the Baucalis, and especially among Alexandria's lauded "seven hundred" virgins,[4] when Alexander
decided to excommunicate the presbyter and his clerical
supporters,[5] he found himself in a situation that
quickly got out of control. According to Socrates,
sympathy for Arius spread immediately across Egypt,
Libya, and Upper Thebes.[6] Encouraged, Arius began an
active resistance in Alexandria. Alexander told about
this in a letter written much later but clearly referring
to an earlier period:

> But they [Arius and a supporter named Achillas] . . .
> refused to remain any longer in subjection to the
> Church; but built for themselves caves, like rob-
> bers, and constantly assembled in them, and day
> and night plied slanders there against Christ and
> against us . . . . Everything which outsiders
> ridicule in us they officiously practiced. They
> daily excited persecutions and seditions against
> us. On the one hand, they brought accusations
> against us before the courts, suborning as witness-
> es certain unprincipled women whom they have
> seduced into error. On the other hand, they

---

1. Sozomen, H.E. 1:15; Hans-Georg Opitz, ed.,
"Urkunden zur Geschichte des Arianischen Streites,"
Vol. 3, Part 1 of Athanasius Werke (Berlin, 1934),
Urk. 4a.
   2. Socrates, H.E. 1:5.
   3. Sozomen, H.E. 1:15.
   4. Epiphanius, Haer. 69:3.
   5. Sozomen, H.E. 1:15.
   6. Socrates, H.E. 1:6.

5

dishonored Christianity by permitting their young women to ramble about the streets.[1]

Faced with intense resistance, Alexander felt he had no choice but to convene a council of Egyptian and Libyan bishops to counteract it. The council met in Alexandria and voted to condemn and depose Arius and his clerical partisans: five priests, six deacons, and two Libyan bishops--Secundus of Ptolemais and Theonas of Marmarica.[2] Judging from the claim of Alexander that the council was composed of nearly one hundred bishops,[3] Egypt and Libya might seem to have belonged completely to their metropolitan, especially given Epiphanius' report that Arius' supporters among the virgins and laity were also excommunicated.[4] But Arius still was not defeated in Egypt, for Alexander's own Deposito Arii claimed that even after the council Arius gained the support of six more clerics in Alexandria and the Mareotis.[5] And Sozomen noted that Alexander's treatment of Arius aroused a considerable amount of sympathy for the presbyter among the Alexandrian laity.[6] Schisms continued in Alexandria until Bishop Alexander was forced to eject Arius from the city.[7]
Like Origen before him, Arius travelled to Palestine/Syria, where he found refuge with three bishops,[8] apparently to be identified with Eusebius of Caesarea, Theodotus of Laodicea, and Paulinus of Tyre.[9] Safe now from Alexander, Arius sought to enlist his new partisans in a campaign to gain support for his theological position.[10] The campaign was carried

---

1. Opitz, Urk. 14 (trans. from NPNF 3:35). The women mentioned were Christian virgins.
2. Opitz, Urk. 4b.
3. Ibid.
4. Epiphanius, Haer. 69:3.
5. Opitz, Urk. 4a.
6. Sozomen, H.E. 1:15.
7. Epiphanius, Haer. 69:4.
8. Opitz, Urk. 14.
9. Opitz, Urk. 1.
10. Epiphanius, Haer. 69:4.

6

out very systematically: legations bearing written
statements of the Arian doctrine were sent to bishops
all over the eastern empire; the recipients were requested either to signify their support of Arius or to
correct those doctrines with which they disagreed.
This procedure disseminated the Arian position widely
and made it a matter of debate and controversy.[1]

Of Arius' champions in Syria/Palestine who took
part in the campaign, Eusebius of Caesarea was the most
powerful and seemingly the most energetic. Though only
fragments remain of a letter which he wrote on Arius'
behalf to Bishop Euphration of Balanea,[2] they allow us
to form some notion of the issues Eusebius believed
were involved in the disagreement between Arius and
himself on the one side and Alexander of Alexandria on
the other. To Eusebius, the primary issue was whether
Father and Son co-exist or whether the Father pre-exists
the Son. Alexander took the first option, whereas
Arius and Eusebius took the second. Eusebius reacted
to Alexander's position in the first instance by showing the unacceptable consequences of co-existence:

> For if they co-exist, how will the Father be
> Father and the Son be Son? Or who will one
> be first and the other second? And one ungen-
> erated and the other generated (καὶ ὁ μὲν
> ἀγέννητος, ὁ δὲ γεννητός)? For two beings
> equally co-existing in a similar way with one
> another should be thought to be equal in honor,
> and either both, as I have said, are ungenerated
> or both are generated. But neither of these
> two statements is true, for both could not be
> the ungenerated nor could both be the generated.

Whether this fragment from Eusebius' letter set forth
the Caesarean bishop's perception of the main issue
separating the Arians and Alexander cannot be determined for certain, but it does prove that Eusebius believed
at least one of their significant disagreements concerned

---

1. Sozomen, H.E. 1:15.
2. Opitz, Urk. 3.

the problem of Christian monotheism. Eusebius thought Alexander's position made nonsense of the biblical language of Father and Son, which for the Caesarean prelate signified the notion of priority: the Father is first, the Son is second. The passage also makes clear that Eusebius conceived the primary characteristic of the Father to be the fact that he is ungenerated (ἀγέννητος) and the primary characteristic of the Son the fact that he is generated (γεννητός). In appealing to the ungenerated/generated distinction to define the nature of God and the Son, Eusebius was making use of Platonic language popular among Christian theologians since Justin Martyr. As we shall see, the distinction was central not only to Eusebius but also to nearly every Arian sympathizer in the fourth century, including Arius himself, the Lucianists Athanasius of Anazarbus, Theognis of Nicaea, and Asterius the Sophist, and, especially, the Neo-Arians Aetius and Eunomius. It was central, in fact, to Alexander of Alexandria, Arius' great ecclesiastical opponent. We shall have occasion to investigate the use of the distinction periodically as our study proceeds; at this point all we need to keep in mind is that the term ungenerated meant to early Christian theologians approximately what the terms absolute and ultimate mean to us. For nearly every one of these theologians, since they were monotheists, there could be only one ungenerated, absolute, ultimate being--God the Father. All other beings, including the Son, must in one manner or another be generated. Therefore, Eusebius was using the accepted terminology of early Christian philosophic theology when he appealed to the ungenerated/generated distinction to bear the major weight of his logical demonstration that the co-existence of Father and Son destroys monotheism and implies either polytheism (two ungenerateds) or atheism (no ungenerateds). Having disposed of the notion of co-existence, Eusebius proceeded to state his understanding of the remaining--and true-- alternative, pre-existence: "But that which is first precedes as superior the second both in rank and in honor on the ground that it has become the cause of the second's being and manner of being." For Eusebius,

not only does the ungenerated Father precede the
generated Son but also the first is in every way the
cause of the second. Christianity's peculiar form
of monotheism must be preserved: God the Father is
the one God. But Eusebius did not rest his defense
of monotheism on such theological formulations; he
backed up his argument with a series of appeals to
scripture. First, quoting a conflation of Jn. 14:28
and 6:44 ("The Father who sent me is greater than I"),
the Caesarean bishop argued that the Son, who completely
understood all things, showed by this saying that he
knew himself to be "different from, less than, and
inferior to the Father." Eusebius feared that Alexander's position endangered all subordination; he was
worried that it might end in Sabellianism. Second,
appealing to Jn. 17:3 ("And this is eternal life, that
they know you the only true God, and Jesus Christ whom
you have sent"), the bishop noted that this verse did
not mean that Christians must hold that there is only
one God but merely that there is only one "true" God.
He is one "because he does not have anyone before him";
the priority of the "true" God, the Father, must be
maintained. Eusebius buttressed his exegesis with
allusions to Col. 1:15 and Jn. 1:1. The Son is "true"
only in the sense that he is the image of the true
God, because, as Jn. 1:1 put it, the Logos is God-
without-the-article and not only-true-God-with-the-
article.[1] Drawing out the implications of the Son as
image, Eusebius made it very plain that he was concerned
about Alexander's position leading to Sabellianism:
"The image and that of which he is the image are not
indeed thought to be one and the same thing, but they
are two essences and two realities and two powers, as
also this many appellations." Finally, the prelate
quoted the credal statement in 1 Tim. 2:5 and suggested
that the Apostle implied the priority of the Father to

---

1. Notice how Athanasius, Syn. 17, misrepresented
Eusebius' claim by stating that in his letter to
Euphration he was not afraid to say clearly that
"Christ is not true God." Eusebius was simply using
the language of scripture.

the Son by first saying, "there is one God," and only afterwards adding, "there is one mediator between God and men, the man Christ Jesus."

With the entrance of Eusebius of Caesarea and his Syrian/Palestinian colleagues into the ranks of Arius' active supporters, Alexander of Alexandria decided that the Arian letter campaign had become much too successful for comfort. So he embarked upon a campaign by mail of his own, one letter of which is extant, namely, Alexander's letter to Bishop Alexander of Thessalonica.[1] From this document we learn that the Egyptian prelate's own efforts were as ambitious as his opponents'; he contacted bishops in the following areas: Egypt and the Thebaid, Libya, the Pentapolis, Syria, Lycia, Pamphylia, Asia, and Cappadocia-- to which we may add Macedonia, where Thessalonica was located. Though Alexander's letter was rather lengthy, it would repay us to give it close consideration, for the letter was intended to define comprehensively the major differences between Alexander and the Arians. The bishop began by warning his colleague to be on his guard against Arian legations and letters entering his diocese. Then he reviewed the events in the controversy which had occurred up to the time of his writing: the formation of what was characterized as the Arians' "conspiracy" against the divinity of Jesus Christ, the Arians' "schismatic" activities, their "shameful" use of Alexandria's virgins, and finally, Alexander's excommunication of Arius and his supporters. The excommunication led to what Alexander termed the Arians' "cabals" in Syria/Palestine and to their letter-writing campaign. Next, in order that Alexander of Thessalonica know precisely the theological issues at stake, his Egyptian namesake enumerated the fundamental Arian claims as he understood them,

---

1. Opitz, Urk. 14. This letter antedated Alexander's encyclical, as Gustave Bardy has convincingly shown. See "Saint Alexandre d'Alexandria a-t-il connu la 'Thalie' d'Arius?," Revue des Sciences Religieuses 6 (1926): 527-30.

probably from listening in person to Arius.[1] According
to Alexander, the Arian assertions were basically three.
The first was that "there was when the Son of God was
not." This was construed to imply that (1) "he who
previously did not exist, subsequently came into
existence" and (2) "when he came into existence, he
became such as every man has the nature to be [that is,
generated]." Second, "God made all things from nothing,"
including, Alexander added, the Son of God. The third
Arian assertion cohered with the first two. It maintained that the Son, like all other generated persons,
always has had a nature liable to change and thus has
been capable of both virtue and vice (καὶ φασὶν αὐτον
τρεπτῆς εἶναι φύσεως, ἀρετῆς τε καὶ κακίας ἐπιδεκτικόν).
The Arians' first corollary of this was based on
Ps. 45:7, which said, "You have loved righteousness and
hated iniquity; therefore God, your God, anointed you
with the oil of joy above your fellows." This verse
was interpreted to mean that the Son was not the Son of
God by nature but was chosen for the honor from all men
"because, in his attention to his ways and in his
discipline, he did not turn to what was worse." He
became God's adopted Son. A second corollary was that
"we [men] are also able to become, like him, the sons
of God," for Is. 1:2 said, "I have begotten and raised
sons." Professors Groh and Gregg have argued that
these two corollaries are not corollaries at all but
the heart of early Arianism: the Son is "the pioneer"
of men's salvation, "the pioneer" of their adoption as
God's sons.[2] Their interpretation presumes that if men
imitate the first adopted Son's persistent choice of
virtue, they too may become adopted as sons of God.
On the other hand, Alexander was as interested in
Arius' theological claims as in his soteriological
contentions--in fact, more so.

---

1. There is no evidence that Alexander at this
point was following any written document of Arius.
See Bardy, pp. 529-30.
    2. Gregg and Groh, pp. 268-72.

11

In refutation of his presbyter, Alexander appealed
primarily to the Gospel of John, as did Eusebius of
Caesarea in Arius' defense. He began with an exegesis
of Jn. 1:18 and 1:1-3 intended to prove that the Son of
God was not created out of nothing but rather was
always "in the bosom of the Father." On the basis of
Jn. 1:18 Alexander concluded that "the two realities,
Father and Son, are inseparable from one another" and
on the basis of Jn. 1:13 that there is "no interval at
all" between them, not even in thought. Yet, he added,
the Son has "his own distinctive hypostasis." Having
claimed both the Son's identity with the Father and
his distinction from the Father, Alexander was at a
loss how to explain the seeming paradox. Perhaps
stimulated by Eusebius' letter, he did mention that
the Father is ungenerated while the Son is μονογενής
(only-begotten or, perhaps more accurately, uniquely-
generated), but he did not develop the theme, content-
ing himself with pointing out that "the most pious
apostle John" did not presume to speak about the
"Son's generation and creation." The hypostasis of
the μονογενής is "indescribable."

Turning to the Arian notion of God's pre-existence
of the Son expressed in the formula, "there was when
the Son of God was not," Alexander responded that the
formula presupposed the reality of time. But since
scripture said in Col. 1:16 that all things were
created by the Son, this must include time itself. So
"the Father is always Father" and "is so because the
Son is always present, on account of whom he is called
Father." In order to substantiate this argument,
Alexander appealed to Heb. 1:3 and Col. 1:15, "To say
that the brightness of his glory is not, obliterates
also the prototypical light, of which it is the
brightness; and if the image of God was not always,
it is plain that he of whom the image is, is not
always." Only after he established to his satisfaction that the Son is co-eternal with the Father and
indescribably generated from him did Alexander feel
he was in a position to deal with the Son's relation
to man. Since the Son is generated from God, while
men are not, his sonship to God must differ fundamentally from man's. Simply stated, the Son is son of

12

God "by nature," whereas men are adopted as sons of
God "by ordinance." Only men, God's adopted sons,
are liable to change and advance in virtue; God's
natural son is not. Alexander sought to support both
of these points by reference to scripture, employing
Rom. 8:32, Mt. 3:17, Ps. 2:7, and Ps. 110:3 to back up
his first point and 2 Cor. 6:14-15, Prov. 30:19 (along
with 1 Cor. 10:4), Gen. 6:2, and Is. 1:2 to establish
the second. He insisted that Arius was thoroughly
heretical in his adoptionist Christology, just as were
his antecedents: Ebion, Artemas, Paul of Samostata,
and Lucian of Antioch. It was such a brand of Christianity that the "three bishops of Syria" (namely,
Eusebius of Caesarea, Paulinus of Tyre, and Theodotus
of Laodicea) were promoting when they aided and abetted
Arius. To wrap up this sequence, Alexander appealed
to Jn. 10:30 ("I and my Father are one") and Jn. 14:9
("He who honors the Son honors the Father"). He was
probably attempting to counter Eusebius' use of the
Johannine subordinationist texts, Jn. 14:28 and 17:3.
But because he was conscious of Eusebius' charge of
Sabellianism, he added in explication of Jn. 10:30,
"The Lord says this, not proclaiming himself to be the
Father nor articulating that the two natures in respect
to hypostasis are one, but because the Son of the
Father has the nature accurately to preserve resemblance
to the Father, his natural likeness in all things: he
is an undeviating image of the Father and a distinct
impression of the prototype."

Alexander perhaps had avoided Sabellianism, but
he realized that he had so closely identified Father
and Son by denying the Father's priority and the Son's
generation from nothing that Eusebius' charge that he
taught two ungenerateds, two gods, appeared unanswered.
So he distinguished sharply between "the ungenerated
Father" and "the things created by him from nothing,"
adding that the uniquely-generated or only-begotten
Nature, through which the Father made all things from
nothing, stands in between (μεσιτεύουσα) the ungenerated Father and the created things, though he has been
generated from the very being of the Father. He
clarified his view in the first two articles of a
three-article creed. In the first article Alexander

13

confessed belief in an only ungenerated Father, while
in the second he confessed one Lord Jesus Christ, the
uniquely-generated Son of God, who was generated from
the being of God. The Son's generation, however, was
"not in a material way by means of severance or by
means of efflux which causes division, as Sabellius
and Valentinus taught, but in an ineffable and indescribable way." According to Alexander, the Son,
like the Father, has always been immutable (ἄτρεπτον),
unchangeable (ἀναλλοίωτον), self-sufficient (ἀπροσδεῆ),
and perfect (τέλειον). He has lacked only the Father's
ungeneratedness. This lack of ungeneratedness was the
reason why the Son said, "The Father is greater than
I," Eusebius of Caesarea's exegesis notwithstanding.[1]
Finally, Alexander argued that while the Son "always"
has existed, the word "always" is not equivalent to
"ungenerated." The meaning of the latter is a mystery
beyond human comprehension. Alexander's conclusion
was that the Father's "own individual dignity" is his
ungeneratedness, while the Son is uniquely-generated
in that he "always" exists with the Father as "the
Father's exact and precisely similar image," "the
brightness of his glory." Alexander seemed to be maintaining that the uniquely-generated Son is distinguished
from all other generated existences by being the most
accurate image of the Father and, especially, by being
eternal--that is, he "always" has existed and "always"
will exist alongside the ungenerated Father. Thus,
men must afford him "worship." The Alexandrian bishop
has come very close to asserting Origen's doctrine of
the eternal generation of the Son. Whether or not
Eusebius of Caesarea was at all intrigued with Alexander's explication of the ungenerated/generated
distinction is an open question; Arius plainly was
not, as he revealed in his first piece of writing
extant, his letter to Bishop Eusebius of Nicomedia.

Surely the reason Arius decided to solicit the
support of the powerful court prelate of Nicomedia
was because Alexander was making important gains in
his anti-Arian campaign: the prestigious sees of

---

1. See above, p. 9.

Antioch and Jerusalem, as well as the see of Tripolis, had been won over by the Egyptian metropolitan.[1] If we analyze Arius' letter to Eusebius of Nicomedia,[2] we find that in overall structure it followed the pattern of Alexander's, whereas its content was nearly identical with that of Eusebius of Caesarea's earlier letter to Euphration. Arius responded to Alexander's historical narrative of events by explaining that he had been unjustly persecuted and driven as an atheist from Alexandria. Next, like Alexander, he first outlined his opponents' position and then his own. According to Arius, Alexander publicly preached as follows:

> God is always, the Son is always, at the same time the Father is, at that time the Son is; the Son co-exists ungeneratedly with God; he is always generated, he is ungeneratedly generated (ἀγεννητογενής), neither by thought nor by any interval of time however small does God precede the Son; God is always, the Son is always; the Son is from God himself.

Both the assertion that the Son is "always" with the Father and the assertion that the Son is "from God" were explicit in Alexander's letter.[3] Only the concept that the Son is in some sense ungenerated was missing: either Arius was relying on an oral statement of Alexander made before the clarification offered in the letter to Alexander of Thessalonica or he found Alexander's clarification less than convincing. The latter seems much more probable. Arius insisted that the Egyptian bishop taught two ungenerateds, that he taught two gods. If we turn now to the theological position taken by Arius in his letter and compare it with that taken by Eusebius of Caesarea in his letter to Euphration, we see that Arius and Eusebius were in

---

1. Opitz, <u>Urk</u>. 1.
2. <u>Ibid</u>.
3. As is the detail that Father and Son are not separated even by a thought (Arius: οὔτε ἐπινοία; Alexander: οὐδ'ἄχρι τινὸς ἐννοίας).

15

fundamental agreement. Both attacked Alexander's
doctrine of co-existence and set in its place a
doctrine of pre-existence. Regarding the latter,
Arius wrote:

> And when Eusebius your brother in Caesarea,
> Theodotus [of Laodicea], Paulinus [of Tyre],
> Athanasius [of Anazarbus], Gregory [of Berytus],
> Aetius [of Lydda], and all those in the East
> say that God without beginning pre-exists the
> Son, they have been made anathema, except
> Philogonius [of Antioch], Hellanicus [of
> Tripolis], and Macarius [of Jerusalem], who
> are heretical, uncatechized men, some of
> whom say that the Son is a belch, others
> an emanation, and others a co-ungenerated.

Like Eusebius before him, Arius formulated the basic
issue separating Alexander on the one side and Eusebius
and Arius on the other in terms of co-existence versus
pre-existence, in terms of polytheism versus monotheism. This shows us that Eusebius' letter and Arius'
were parts of a synchronized campaign. Whatever differences there were between the two were more stylistic
than substantive. For instance, Arius did not attempt,
as did Eusebius, to demonstrate logically the untenable
implications of Alexander's position; he simply let its
inherent logical tensions (such as "always generated"
and "ungeneratedly generated"), as well as its implicit
polytheism, speak for themselves. And to recommend his
alternative position he resorted to a catalogue of
bishops who supported him and a gallery of rogues who
did not, the latter allegedly presenting impious (the
Son is a belch), heretical (the Son is an emanation),
or polytheistic (the Son is a co-ungenerated) formulations. But we discover at least one substantive
difference from Eusebius' letter (though comparable
passages in the Eusebius document could easily have
been lost), namely, Arius' focus on Alexander's claim
that the Son is "from God himself." This notion was
attacked in the next section of Arius' letter. The
presbyter introduced the section as presenting what
he said and thought and what he had taught and was

16

teaching. According to Arius, "The Son is not ungenerated, nor in any way part of the ungenerated, nor
from that which underlies [that is, matter], but he
has subsisted by [God's] pleasure and will before time
and before ages as full God, uniquely-generated, unchangeable; and before he was begotten (γεννηθῆ) or--
mark this (ἤτοι)--created or ordained or established,
he was not, for he was not ungenerated." Arius' assertion that the Son is not ungenerated or a part of the
ungenerated but, rather, subsists by [God's] pleasure
and will, was an explicit rejection of Alexander's
claim that "the Son is from God himself," that is,
from his essence. This rejection of essentialist
categories in favor of voluntarist ones[1] was buttressed
by an appeal to Prov. 8:22ff in the next to the last
clause of Arius' statement ("begotten . . . created
. . . established"). The claim in Prov. 8:25 that the
Son (Wisdom) is begotten must be qualified by the
additional claim in Prov. 8:22 ("mark this") that he
is created. The notion of creation went quite beyond
Eusebius' statement that the Father is the "cause" of
the Son. But though Arius yielded nothing to Alexander
on the themes of pre-existence or creation from
nothing, reiterating both at the end of his letter as
the cause of his persecution, he did take to heart
some of his bishop's criticisms by noting (1) that
the Son did subsist "before time and before ages" and
(2) that the Son is, in some sense at least, unchangeable.[2] The presbyter did not explain, however, the
relationship between his doctrine of the Son's unchangeability and Bishop Alexander's charge that he
taught the Son's capacity for ethical change. Arius
seemed to have decided not even to mention, let alone
to press, his view of the relationship of the Son to
mankind, a view which occupied a rather prominent
place in Alexander's letter and was the key to the
Gregg/Groh interpretation of his thought. Perhaps he
was unsure what Eusebius of Nicomedia's reaction to it

_____

1. See Gregg and Groh, passim, especially pp. 265-7.
2. For a discussion of Arius' attribution of unchangeability to the Son, see below, p. 37ff.

17

would be. Arius' omission of this portion of his position from his letter to Eusebius of Nicomedia suggests to us that the fragment we examined earlier from Eusebius of Caesarea, which focused on monotheism and the Son's subordination, did indeed represent the Caesarean bishop's perception of the main disagreement between Arius and his bishop Alexander. Apparently Arius found Eusebius of Caesarea particularly receptive to his views on this issue and decided to play them up to Eusebius' Nicomedian namesake, while downplaying his understanding of the Son's kindred relationship to man.

From Eusebius of Nicomedia's response to Arius' letter we learn that the court bishop agreed completely both with Arius' claim of the Father's priority and with his representation of the Son as created, for he wrote, "It is clear to everyone that that which has been made was not before it came into being."[1] Eusebius offered Arius more than just epistolary support; he also, it seems, extended to him an invitation to visit him in Nicomedia.[2] The two men had one very important thing in common: both were students of the famous Antiochene martyr Lucian.[3] Eusebius and the numerous other so-called Lucianists were soon to become the foundation of ecclesiastical support for Arius (and, we may add, the bridge to Neo-Arianism). Presumably encouraged by Eusebius, Arius wrote in

---

1. Opitz, Urk. 2.
2. Athanasius, Syn. 15; Epiphanius, Haer. 69:4-7. Though the Greek of Syn. 15 does not unquestionably support a visit of Arius to Nicomedia, and though details of Epiphanius, Haer. 69:4-7 are surely exaggerations, a visit still remains likely in my opinion. I am unconvinced by W. Telfer's view that the narrative of Epiphanius is "such a tissue of improbabilities that every assertion . . . in the passage must be under suspicion from the beginning" (W. Telfer, "Arius Takes Refuge in Nicomedia," Journal of Theological Studies 37 (1936): 63).
3. Arius referred to Eusebius as a "fellow-Lucianist." See Opitz, Urk. 1.

Nicomedia his main theological document, the Thalia,[1] of which unfortunately only fragments remain. They are numerous enough, however, to reveal to us far more detail about Arius' position than anything we have seen thus far. For convenience's sake, Arius' teaching in the Thalia can be reviewed under the three rubrics used by Alexander in his letter to Alexander of Thessalonica: (1) the priority of the Father, (2) the creation of the Son from nothing, and (3) the Son's relation to man. However, a fourth rubric must be added, namely, God's and the Son's unknowability.

In the Thalia Arius articulated his doctrine of God's priority to the Son in even stronger terms than he did in his letter to Eusebius of Nicomedia. He wrote:

> . . . [God] alone has none equal to him, or
> like him, or the same in glory with him.
> We say he is ungenerated because of him who
> is by nature generated.
> We praise him as unbegun because of the one
> having a beginning.
> We adore him as eternal because of the one
> having come into being in time.
> And the unbegun established the Son as a
> beginning of generated things . . . .
> Understand that the Monad was, but the Dyad
> was not before it came into existence.[2]

We must notice at the outset, as Professor Groh has pointed out, that although this passage certainly did argue for the priority of God to the Son, it did so by assuming the Son's essential generatedness: "We say he is ungenerated because of him who is by nature generated." That is to say, the priority of God as the ungenerated was presented as a logical deduction from the essential generatedness of the Son, not vice-versa.[3] According to Gregg's and Groh's interpretation, of

---

1. Athanasius, Syn. 15.
2. Ibid.
3. This point was brought to my attention by Professor Groh in a telephone conversation.

19

course, for the Son to be the pioneer of man's adoptive
salvation he must, like man, be generated. Arius'
motive for asserting God's priority aside, there can
be no mistaking the importance of the assertion itself
for him. He went on to note not only that the Father
was prior to the Son but also that he was not always a
father: "God was not always Father, but there was when
God was alone, and he was not yet Father; but later he
became Father."[1] Having made such an affirmation,
Arius turned to Jn. 1:1 and made a statement which seemingly contradicted the verse explicitly: "For God alone
was . . . , and the Word was not with him." This brings
us to the presbyter's first corollary to his view of
God's priority. Quite obviously the corollary was
formulated in part to deal with a number of biblical
texts used by Alexander of Alexandria to support his
view of co-existence, especially Jn. 1:1.[2] Arius'
exegetical ploy was quite simple. As reported by
Athanasius, it was as follows, "He [Arius] says that
there are two Wisdoms--that one co-exists with and is
proper to God and that the Son has come into being by
means of this Wisdom and was only named Wisdom and Word
as partaking of this . . . . So also he says that
there is another Word in God besides the Son and that,
again, the Son is named Word and even Son according to
grace."[3] Or as it was reported by Athanasius in another
place, "[Christ] is not the true and absolutely only
Word of the Father, but he is said to be Word and Wisdom
only in name and is said to be Son and Power by grace."[4]
With this distinction in hand, Arius was in a position
to say that God's true Word or Wisdom is both ungenerated and unbegun, whereas the Son Jesus Christ is a
created being who merely partakes of the true Word:
"The Wisdom of God is ungenerated and unbegun, but many
are the created powers, of which one is Christ."[5]

---

1. Athanasius, Ar. 1:5 and Ep. Aeg. Lib. 12.
See Gregg and Groh, pp. 263-5.
   2. See Alexander of Alexandria, Ep. Alex. (Opitz,
Urk. 14).
   3. Athanasius, Ar. 1:5.
   4. Ibid., 1:9. Compare Athanasius, Ep. Aeg. Lib. 12.
   5. Athanasius, Syn. 36.

In fact, not only does the Son Jesus Christ merely partake of the true Word but also he has been created through this Word: "He has come into being by means of the Word proper to God and the Wisdom in God, in which God has created all things and also him."[1] Undoubtedly one of Arius' motives for developing his doctrine of two Words of God, one ungenerated and the other generated, was to be able to explain Jn. 1:1 in a way consistent with his doctrine of God's priority. Yet, in light of the interpretation of Arius' thought forwarded by Gregg and Groh, it also is apparent that another of his motives--and perhaps a more important one--was to protect the Son's essential generatedness and, thus, his changeability and ability to serve as a model for other generated beings. If we take up Arius' second corollary to his doctrine of the Father's priority, we discover it to be one which would have particular influence on Neo-Arianism. Stated negatively, it maintained that "[the Son] is not like in essence (κατ'οὐσίαν) to the Father."[2] Or to cite a more complex passage, which used another theological catchword, "And the unbegun established the Son as a beginning of generated things, and he brought him forward as a Son to himself, having adopted him. He has nothing proper to God in his own hypostasis, for he is neither equal nor, likewise, homoousios with him."[3] Interestingly, Arius extended this corollary to cover not only Father and Son but the entire Trinity. Using the language of hypostasis, Arius said, "Now there is a Triad, not like in glories; their hypostases are not mingled with one another; one hypostasis is more glorious than another in glories to infinity."[4] Using the language of essence, he wrote, "The essences (οὐσίαι)

---

1. Alexander of Alexandria, Ep. Encycl. (Opitz, Urk. 4b). Compare also Athanasius, Ar. 2:37 and 2:38 and Decr. 6, and Marcellus of Ancyra, Ep. apud Epiphanius, Haer. 72:2:3.
   2. Alexander of Alexandria, Ep. Encycl. (Opitz, Urk. 4b).
   3. Athanasius, Syn. 15.
   4. Ibid.

of Father, Son, and Holy Spirit are by nature separated, alienated, excluded, foreign, and without participation in one another. They [that is, Father, Son, and Holy Spirit] are completely unlike one another to infinity both in essences and in glories."[1] Thus, the three beings of the Trinity are not "like in essence" but "unlike in essence."

Turning now to Arius' view that the Son was created and is not "from God," we find his phraseology much more precise and clear in the Thalia than it was in his letter to Eusebius of Nicomedia. Whereas in the latter he did not explicitly state that the Son was created from nothing, he did just that in the Thalia, thereby putting the Son on precisely the same ontological level as all other created things: "Since all things have come into being from nothing, the Son of God also is from nothing; and since all things which exist have come into being as created things, he also is a created thing."[2] And if Arius' letter to Eusebius said that the Son was made to subsist at the Father's pleasure and will, the Thalia made it crystal clear that, in this, the Son is precisely like all other created things: "Just as all things, which formerly did not exist, began to subsist because of God's will, so also [the Son], formerly not existing, has come into being because of God's will, for the Word is not the proper and natural offspring of the Father, but he also has come into being by grace."[3] Finally, as a corollary to creation from nothing Arius maintained, using the language of participation we have met before, that Christ is not true God: "He is not from the Father but has been made to subsist from nothing and is not proper to the Father's essence . . . ; and Christ is not true God but by participation has been made God."[4] What was meant by the expression "by participation" is somewhat unclear, for in one place Arius wrote that "the Son is distinct by himself and in all things

1. Athanasius, Ar. 1:6.
2. Ibid., 1:5 and Ep. Aeg. Lib. 12.
3. Ibid. Compare also Athanasius, Syn. 1:5.
4. Athanasius, Ar. 1:9.

22

without participation in the Father."[1] Presumably he meant that the Son participates only in God's eternal Word, not in God himself.[2] Perhaps Arius even went so far as to say that the Son is "God only in name,"[3] though Athanasius may not have been quoting him with precise accuracy.[4]

We must now review how the Thalia illuminates our understanding of Arius' doctrine of the Son's relation to man, a doctrine sketched by Alexander of Alexandria in his letter to his namesake in Thessalonica but totally missing from Arius' own letter to Eusebius of Nicomedia. Alexander was quite right in emphasizing that Arius taught the mutability of the Son, for Arius wrote in the Thalia, "[The Son] is not unchangeable (ἄτρεπτος) like the Father, but he is by nature changeable (τρεπτός) like created things."[5] This is so because he is by nature a created thing. Furthermore, since the Son is not a created thing like stone or wood but rather a reasonable being who possesses free will (αὐτεξούσιος), he can change by his own choice (προαίρεσει).[6] But, Arius asserted, though the Son is capable of either virtue or vice, he always in actuality has remained virtuous, a fact that God foreknew and, consequently, felt justified in rewarding with the gift of glory even before any virtuous deeds were done:

> Like all others, the Logos himself by nature
> is changeable, but by his own free will, while
> he wishes (ἕως βούλεται), he remains good.
> But when, however, he wills, he himself, like
> us, is able to change, since he is of change-
> able nature. For on account of this, having
> foreknown that he will be good, having

---

1. Ibid., 1:6.
2. See Ibid., 1:5, quoted above p. 20.
3. Ibid.
4. This comment was missing in the quotation of the fragment of the Thalia as it was found in Athanasius, Ep. Aeg. Lib. 12.
5. Athanasius, Ar. 1:9.
6. See Alexander of Alexandria, Ep. Encycl. (Opitz, Urk. 4b) and Athanasius, Ar. 1:22 and 35.

anticipated it, he gave this glory to him
which as man he later came to have from his
virtue, so that by his deeds, which God foreknew, he has made him come to be now such a
one [that is, a glorious being].[1]

The gift of glory must surely be identified with adoption as God's Son, an adoption which was unfortunately
only mentioned in passing in the extant fragments of
Arius' Thalia: "The Father advanced him as Son to
himself by adoption."[2] Presumably Arius could claim
the Son to be unchangeable, as he stated in his letter
to Eusebius of Nicomedia, yet still to be changeable,
because he maintained that the Son has the capability
of both virtue and vice. Arius appears to have been
most concerned to preserve the Son as an ethical model
for man--which certainly means that his soteriology
was based on the notion of reward for ethical activity,
as Professors Groh and Gregg have argued.[3] Such a
soteriology was nowhere developed in Arius' extant
writings, but it seems implied in his adoptionist
Christology. That man was at the center of Arius'
thought is substantiated by his subserving even the
Son to him. He wrote, "For [the Son] has been made
for our sake, in order that God might create us through
him as through an instrument (ὡς δι'ὀργάνου); and he
would not subsist unless God willed to make us."[4]
Or even more pointedly, "[God] did not create us for
his sake but him for our sake."[5]
    All three of the major themes in the Thalia which
we have met thus far were already mentioned as in-
gredients of Arius' teaching either in Alexander's

---

1. Athanasius, Ar. 1:5 and Ep. Aeg. Lib. 12.
2. Athanasius, Syn. 15. Compare Ar. 1:37.
3. See Gregg and Groh, pp. 267-72.
4. Alexander of Alexandria, Ep. Encycl. (Opitz,
Urk. 14).
5. Athanasius, Ep. Aeg. Lib. 12. The phraseology
might have been that of Athanasius, since it was missing
from the quotation of this section of the Thalia as
found in Athanasius, Ar. 1:5.

letter to Alexander of Thessalonica or in Arius' own letter to Eusebius of Nicomedia. This is not true of a fourth theme, which nonetheless is prominent, namely, the unknowability of God. The first statement made in the _Thalia_ about God was that "God himself, insofar as he is, is ineffable to all."[1] Arius meant "all" in an inclusive sense: "And there is sufficient proof that God is invisible to all, both to those who [are created] through the Son and to the Son himself he is invisible." Of course, God's unknowability to the Son and to man is not total, but it is significant. As Arius put it, "The Father is invisible to the Son, and the Word is able neither to see nor to know completely and precisely his own Father, but what he knows and what he sees, he knows and sees in proportion to his own measure, just as we also know according to our own ability."[2] Finally, presumably because God's will rather than the Son's will is responsible for the Son's coming into existence, the Son does not even know himself completely: "For the Son not only does not know the Father precisely . . . but also the Son does not himself know his own essence."[3] If we ask ourselves why Arius introduced the notion of God's and the Son's unknowability into the _Thalia_, we perhaps have only to look as far as Alexander's letter to Alexander of Thessalonica. There the Egyptian bishop argued that the Father's unique dignity, his ungeneratedness, is a mystery beyond human comprehension and that the hypostasis of the uniquely-generated Son is indescribable. Arius was expressing agreement with Alexander. But because the Son is a created being like other created beings, both the Father and the Son himself were asserted to be unknown even to the Son. Arius did not want to leave himself open for the accusation that he lacked reverence for God's transcendence and the mystery of God's creation.

---

1. Athanasius, _Syn_. 15.
2. Athanasius, _Ar_. 1:6 and _Ep. Aeg. Lib_. 12. See also Athanasius, _Syn_. 15 and Alexander of Alexandria, _Ep. Alex_. (Opitz, _Urk_. 14).
3. _Ibid_.

25

Arius wrote his Thalia in Nicomedia with the active
encouragement of the city's Lucianist bishop Eusebius.
Eusebius, however, did not content himself with providing encouragemerc; instead, he took the ominous step of
assuming the direction of Arius' letter campaign.[1] The
court bishop of Nicomedia had many friends throughout
the eastern empire, especially among his fellow students
of Lucian, the martyr of Antioch. Judging from an
encyclical letter later penned by Alexander of Alexandria, these friends were quickly contacted by Eusebius
and asked to support the Arian cause.[2] One of those
who responded spiritedly was an early supporter of
Arius[3] and fellow-Lucianist,[4] Bishop Athanasius of
Anazarbus in Cilicia, an individual who later became
a teacher of the Neo-Arian Aetius. In a letter to
Alexander of Alexandria he vigorously defended Arius'
assertion that the Son of God was "made as a created
being from nothing" and, therefore, is "one of all
things."[5] Athanasius gave this assertion scriptural
support by appealing to the gospel parable of the
hundred sheep. His exegesis was developed as follows:

> For since all things which have been made are
> represented by the hundred sheep, also the Son
> is one of them. Now if the hundred are not
> created and generated things, or if there
> exists something besides the hundred, clearly

---

1. See Alexander of Alexandria, Ep. Encycl.
(Opitz, Urk. 4b).
2. Ibid.
3. See Arius, Ep. Eus. (Opitz, Urk. 1).
4. Philostorgius, H.E. 3:15. The history of Philostorgius has been preserved only in an epitome by
Photius and in other fragments. I have used the edition
of Joseph Bidez, Philostorgius Kirchengeschichte: mit
dem Leben des Lucian von Antiochien und den Fragmenten
eines Arianischen Historiographen, 2nd ed., revised by
Friedhelm Winkelmann, in Die Griechischen Christlichen
Schriftsteller (Berlin, 1972).
5. Athanasius, Syn. 17.

let the Son not be a created thing and one
of all things. But if the hundred are all
generated things, and if there is nothing
besides the hundred except God alone, why do
Arius and his followers say something absurd
if, including and numbering Christ as one
thing among the hundred, they say that he is
one of all things.[1]

This argument was equivalent to Arius' affirmation in
his Thalia, "Since all things have come into being from
nothing, the Son of God also is from nothing; and since
all things which exist have come into being as created
things and things made, he also is a created thing and
thing made" (see above, p. 22). Athanasius' exegetical
syllogism assumed that the Son is one of the hundred
sheep and would be unsound if that assumption were not
granted. The Anazarban bishop presumed that Bishop
Alexander would be compelled to grant the assumption.
He had good grounds for the presumption, since scripture did speak of the Son as the "lamb of God" and
"Christ our passover." Athanasius was arguing that
logic would persuade any Christian, and especially any
bishop, who believed the word of scripture that the
Arian assertion of the Son's creation was true. The
logical alternatives--either (1) that the hundred sheep
are ungenerated like God (a polytheistic notion) or
(2) that the Son is not one of the hundred (an unscriptural notion)--were impermissible.

Joining Athanasius of Anazarbus in writing to
Bishop Alexander was another Lucianist, Theognis,
bishop of Nicomedia's neighboring see of Nicaea. Though
only fragments remain of his letter, and these in Latin
translation, we see that Theognis was convinced by the
fundamental Arian position. After noting that God is
properly ineffable to man ("For to speak justly concerning Father and Son, as you know, is to walk on a cloud"),
he appealed to the Son's scriptural statement that the
Father is greater than himself (Jn. 14:28) to prove that
the Father alone is God, "not only by reason of his

---

1. Ibid.

creating but also because he is ungenerated (ingenitus)."[1]
We are struck that Theognis, like Arius, Eusebius of
Caesarea, Athanasius of Anazarbus, and, indeed, their
opponent Alexander himself, conceived God's unique characteristic to be his ungeneratedness; everyone in the
debate seemed simply to have assumed this, as they
assumed its correlative, the generatedness of the Son.
Theognis wrote, "Therefore we say that the Son is generated (genitum), for the Son is never able to become
ungenerated."[2] We are also struck by the appeal to
Jn. 14:28, which we found previously both in Eusebius
of Caesarea's letter to Euphration and in Alexander's
letter to his Thessalonian namesake. But there is something unique, and rather fascinating, in Theognis'
letter, namely, a hint that Arians like Theognis did
not worship the Son. The bishop wrote, "Knowing from
the holy scriptures that the Father alone is ungenerated, him alone we adore . On the other hand we
venerate (veneramur!) the Son, because among us it is
certain that his glory ascends to the Father."[3] Perhaps
statements like this convinced Alexander and his successor Athanasius that at stake in the Arian controversy
was not theological nicety but popular piety itself.

While we possess only a few short fragments from
the documents penned in support of Arius' cause by
Theognis of Nicaea and Athanasius of Anazarbus, when
we turn to Asterius the Sophist, a third Lucianist,
we find more numerous and lengthy fragments. Like
Athanasius of Anazarbus (who was to become Aetius'
teacher), Asterius is of more than passing interest for
historians of Neo-Arianism, for he was both a native of
Cappadocia and a theological advisor to Cappadocia's
metropolitan at the time of the famous Council of
Antioch in A.D. 341--at which time a young countryman
of his, Eunomius, was being educated in their homeland.

---

1. Sermones Arianorum, Fr. 16. The text was reproduced by Gustave Bardy, Recherches sur Saint Lucien
d'Antioche et son Ecole (Paris, 1936), p. 212.
2. Ibid.
3. Ibid.

This young man was to become Aetius' successor as the head of Neo-Arianism and the movement's most aggressive writer. That he was influenced by Asterius to espouse Arianism cannot be ruled out. Unlike the three Lucianists we have met thus far (Eusebius, Athanasius, and Theognis), Asterius was not a bishop. He was not even a cleric, having been made ineligible because he sacrificed to the pagan gods during one of the early fourth century persecutions. He became, nonetheless, one of Arius' most tireless champions, travelling from church to church armed with introductions from Eusebius of Nicomedia and with a short treatise on theology. He read the latter publicly.[1] A considerable number of extracts from this treatise--his Syntagmation--have been preserved; they reveal to us early Arianism's most original thinker, save Arius himself.

Asterius' original contributions in the Syntagmation were basically five. First of all, he saw very clearly that for Arianism to remain theologically legitimate the Thalia's doctrine of two Words or Wisdoms of God was indispensable. If this distinction could not be maintained, Alexander would be able to marshal numerous scriptural passages for his cause, and the Son's capacity for ethical change would have to be surrendered. The Arian diligently sought to show that the doctrine had firm scriptural support.[2] Second, Asterius seemed to have been uneasy with Arius' strong stand in the Thalia that neither God nor the Son could be fully known, for he said nothing at all in this vein in the extant fragments of the Syntagmation. Arguing in diametrically the opposite direction, the Sophist offered a precise definition of the meaning of the term "ungenerated," which all parties to the controversy admitted to be the principal characteristic of God. According to Asterius, "The ungenerated is that which has not been created but always is."[3] No doubt Asterius was afraid of the manner in which Arius had

---

1. Athanasius, Syn. 17.
2. Ibid., 18 and Athanasius, Ar. 1:5, 1:32, 2:37-8 and 2:40.
3. Athanasius, Ar. 1:30.

developed God's and the Son's unknowability primarily
because of the way Arius' opponent Alexander had discussed God as ungenerated. Alexander had said that
neither "was" nor "always" nor "before the ages" gives
the meaning of "ungenerated," for "no name which the
mind of men endeavors to invent conveys the meaning of
ungenerated." It remains "the mystery."[1] Asterius
apparently thought that if Alexander were allowed to
appeal to mystery at the crucial point in his theology,
the Arians would have no grounds upon which to criti-
cize him for confusing the ungenerated and the generated. Arius' views on divine unknowability seemed to
allow such an appeal. Therefore, Asterius agreed with
Alexander that the word "always" by itself does not
convey the meaning of ungenerated, but he added that
its combination with "that which has not been created"
defines the concept precisely.

The Syntagmation's third original contribution to
the development of Arian theology concerned the status
of the Son in relation to other created things. Whereas both Arius' Thalia and Athanasius of Anazarbus'
letter to Alexander posited a sharp dualism between
God and "all things" and proceeded to include the Son
solidly among "all things,"[2] Asterius was seemingly
concerned that such a view, baldly maintained, might
call into question the Johannine/Pauline dogma of the
demiurgic Son/Word through whom the world came into
being.[3] So he refined the Arian view by claiming that
while the Son is truly one of "all things," he is
decidedly the "first" of generated things.[4] In an
attempt to explain his position Asterius compared the
Son of God with the physical sun. Just as the sun,
although it is "one of the things that appear," is
preeminent because it shines upon the "entire" physical
cosmos, so the Son, being one of the intelligible
natures, is preeminent because "he illuminates and

---

1. Alexander of Alexandria, Ep. Alex. (Opitz,
Urk. 14).
2. Athanasius, Ar. 1:5 and Ep. Aeg. Lib. 12;
Athanasius, Syn. 17.
3. Jn. 1:1-3; 1 Cor. 8:6.
4. Athanasius, Syn. 19.

shines upon all those that are in the intelligible
cosmos."[1] In another passage Asterius explicated his
position by developing in Arian fashion the concept of
mediation which had been used by Bishop Alexander in
his letter to Alexander of Thessalonica. Alexander
had argued, we remember, that the Son stands "in-
between" the ungenerated Father and the things created
from nothing, though as one generated from the very
being of the Father.[2] Similarly, Asterius wrote,
"God, wishing to create generated nature, when he saw
that it was not able to endure the untempered hand of
the Father and fabrication by him, makes and creates
first and alone one only, and calls him Son and Word,
in order that, this one having been generated as an
intermediary, thereupon also all things might be able
to be generated through him."[3] This statement preserved Alexander's concept of mediation and the demiurgic uniqueness of the Son without sacrificing
fundamental Arian beliefs. Finally, we must add
another phrasing by Asterius of this same point, for
we will find it to be an important assertion of the
Neo-Arians. He said that "the Son alone is generated
by God alone, but the other things are generated
through the Son as an underworker and helper (ὡς
δ'ὑπουργοῦ καὶ βοηθοῦ)."[4] This language connected the
Son rather more closely to God, given Arian presuppo-
sitions, than the language of the intermediary.
Apparently even Arius was pleased with it, for Athanasius noted that Arius transcribed the statement from
Asterius and presented it to his followers.[5]

The final two contributions of Asterius' Syntagmation to Arian theology concerned the creedal and
exegetical foundations of Arianism. In his Thalia
Arius had argued that God was not Father before the
generation of the Son--which, according to the

---

1. Ibid.
2. Alexander of Alexandria, Ep. Alex. (Opitz,
Urk. 14).
3. Athanasius, Ar. 2:24.
4. Athanasius, Decr. 8.
5. Ibid.

presbyter, meant that "God was not always Father."[1]
Asterius held that Arius had been too bold, perhaps
feeling this way because of the creedal tradition
that confessed faith in God the Father before speaking of the generation of the Son: "Before the generation of the Son, the Father possessed pre-existing
knowledge how to beget, since a physician also has
the knowledge how to cure before he cures."[2] This
view was shared by the Lucianist Theognis of Nicaea,
whom we have already met. The Neo-Arian historian
Philostorgius remarked that Theognis "maintained that
God was the Father even before he begat the Son, inasmuch as he had the power of begetting him."[3] We come
now to the last contribution of Asterius' Syntagmation
to Arian theology, namely, a series of exegetical
undergirdings for Arian adoptionism and soteriology.
Alexander, we recall, had buttressed his rejection of
Arian adoptionism and his assertion that the Son is
son of God by nature by appealing to three Johannine
passages, including Jn. 10:30 ("I and my Father are
one") and the response of Jesus to Philip in Jn. 14:9
("He that has seen me has seen the Father").[4] With
regard to Jn. 10:30, Asterius followed Origen[5] in
arguing that the text did not deal with a natural
relationship between Son and Father but merely with
a oneness of will, thought, and teaching; only in this
sense is there identity. Asterius wrote, "The things
which the Father wishes, these things also the Son
wishes, and he is opposed to him neither in thoughts
nor in judgments but in agreement with him in all
things, exhibiting identity of doctrines and discourse
in conformity with and closely joined to the teaching
of the Father--on account of this, he and the Father
are one (Jn. 10:30)."[6] A comparable Origenist

---

1. Athanasius, Ar. 1:5 and Ep. Aeg. Lib. 12.
2. Athanasius, Syn. 19. See Gregg and Groh, p. 261
3. Philostorgius, H.E. 2:15.
4. Alexander of Alexandria, Ep. Alex. (Opitz,
Urk. 14).
5. Origen, Jo. 13:36.
6. Athanasius, Ar. 3:10. See Origen, Cels. 8:12.

interpretation was given of Jn. 14:8-11, a passage
which included Jesus' response to Philip, "He that
has seen me has seen the Father," as well as Jesus'
words, "I am in the Father and the Father is in me."[1]
A modern reader would probably incline to favor
Asterius' Origenist interpretation of the passage over
Alexander's, since Origen and Asterius took the entire
pericope rather more seriously than did Alexander,
especially Jesus' explanation, "The words that I speak
to you I do not say from myself, but the Father who
remains in me does his works (Jn. 14:10)." As Asterius
phrased it, "For it is clear that on account of this
has he said that he himself is in the Father, and again
that the Father is in himself, since he says that the
discourse which he was relating in detail is not his
own, but the Father's, who has given him the power."[2]
Finally, Asterius took up one by one characteristics
which Alexander attributed to the Son to indicate his
difference from created things, especially his difference from man.[3] The Arian's procedure was intended
to demonstrate that each of the characteristics was
explicitly attributed to man in scripture; therefore,
none could define the Son's unique status. Alexander
said that the Son possesses "likeness in all things"
to the Father; Asterius countered with 1 Cor. 11:7,
"Man is the image and the glory of God." Alexander

---

1. Asterius quoted only the latter statement in
(the preserved fragments of) the Syntagmation, whereas
Alexander did not mention the line in his letter to
Alexander of Thessalonica. But in others of his letters
penned at the same time as the document to the Thessalonian bishop, Alexander of Alexandria may very well
have also quoted "I am in the Father and the Father is
in me," for we find this line cited later in his encyclical. Perhaps Asterius had read the proof-text in
one of these other letters and, therefore, decided to
quote it himself in his Syntagmation.
2. Athanasius, Ar. 3:2.
3. That is, in his letter to Alexander of
Thessalonica and, perhaps, other letters written at
the same time.

attributed the adverb "always" to the Son; Asterius pointed to 2 Cor. 4:11, "For we the ones who live are always." The Egyptian bishop termed the Son "unchangeable (ἄτρεπτον)"; Asterius responded with Rom. 8:35, "Nothing will separate us from the love of Christ"; etc., etc. Though it was probably Arius who first devised these exegetical maneuvers, Athanasius of Alexandria remarked that Asterius "wrote them," presumably in his Syntagmation;[1] the ploys worked so well that the Arians later used them at the Council of Nicaea.[2] So we see that the Cappadocian layman, sophist, and Lucianist was determined both to refine Arius' position wherever he thought it required refinement and to develop its exegetical underpinnings wherever possible.

We have no precise information about Asterius' success in representing the Arian cause throughout the eastern empire, but judging from the venom directed toward him by Athanasius of Alexandria,[3] it probably was significant. Given the solid support afforded Arius by Lucianists like Asterius, Theognis of Nicaea, and Athanasius of Anazarbus, not to mention non-Lucianists such as the Alexandrian presbyter George,[4] it is abundantly clear that Arius' new patron and champion, Bishop Eusebius of Nicomedia, was having no trouble whatsoever rallying his friends to enthusiastic support of Arianism. Arius could only have been gratified with the outpouring of sympathy for his position. But surely he must have been encouraged most by the vigor which Eusebius of Nicomedia displayed in marshalling forces for his cause.

Faced with letters pouring into Alexandria on Arius' behalf, with the propaganda activities of Asterius, and with the publication of Arius' Thalia, Bishop Alexander became alarmed. Therefore, he wrote a terse encyclical to all Catholic bishops "everywhere."[5]

---

1. Athanasius, Decr. 20.
2. Athanasius, Ep. Afr. 5.
3. Athanasius, Syn. 18-20.
4. Ibid., 17.
5. Opitz, Urk. 4b.

34

It accused Eusebius of Nicomedia of ambition in thinking himself qualified to run the affairs of the Catholic
Church and denounced him for becoming the leader of the
"apostates." After warning his readers against Eusebius, Alexander listed the Egyptian and Libyan clerics
who agreed with Arius, outlined the Arian theology
with a series of extracts from the Thalia,[1] and noted
that the council of Egyptian and Libyan bishops he
called soon after the outbreak of the controversy
"anathematized Arius for his shameless avowal of these
heresies, together with all such as have countenanced
them." He added pointedly, "Yet the partisans of
Eusebius have received them," indicating that Eusebius
and all those who had given Arius asylum and support
were acting against a properly constituted ecclesiastical synod. Then, in order to refute the Arian claims,
he again enumerated them, this time adding short scriptural quotations chosen to contradict them. Rejecting
the procedure he employed in his letter to Alexander
of Thessalonica, Alexander did not include in his
encyclical a positive explication of his own theology,
probably because he realized that it would only lead
to further controversy. He rested his case on (1) the
authority of the Egyptian council which anathematized
the Arians and (2) the authority of scripture. The
document concluded with an assurance to Alexander's
fellow-bishops that the Egyptian Arians had been previously instructed in the doctrines of the church,
especially the doctrine of the Word's divinity, but had
willfully chosen to apostasize. Plainly the bishop
was concerned to demonstrate that none of what had
happened was his own fault. He quoted both Jesus and
Paul as predicting such apostates as the ones who had
emerged from his diocese.

Eusebius of Nicomedia's response to Alexander's
encyclical was predictable. He quite got the point
of Alexander's claim that proper ecclesiastical authority was on his side because an Egyptian council had
supported him. So Eusebius took the grave step of
countering Alexander's Egyptian council with a Bithynian

---

1. Compare Bardy, "Saint Alexandre," pp. 527-9.

council of his own, which also issued an encyclical.
To cite Sozomen, the encyclical was sent "to all the
bishops, desiring them to hold communion with the
Arians, as with those making a true confession, and
to require Alexander to hold communion with them likewise."[1] What had been primarily a theological controversy had now developed into a serious ecclesiastical
power-struggle between two of the most well-placed and
influential bishops in Christendom, the court prelate
of Nicomedia and the pope of Alexandria. Each could
now claim conciliar backing.

Except for the report in Sozomen, we know nothing
for certain about the Bithynian council, but it is
likely that Sozomen's "true confession" is to be
identified with the so-called "profession of faith"
penned by Arius and his Egyptian presbyters and deacons.
This document has been preserved by Athanasius and
Epiphanius in a version sent directly to Bishop Alexander of Alexandria.[2] The profession was a crisply
written statement probably meant to be read not only
by Alexander but also by the bishops of the Catholic
Church who had just received Alexander's encyclical.
Confronting directly Alexander's assertion that the
Arians had apostasized after having been correctly
instructed by him in the church's doctrine, the profession introduced itself as "our faith from our fore-
fathers which we have also learned from you, blessed
pope." Alexander's attempt to shift responsibility
for Arianism away from himself was rejected out of
hand; Arius' doctrine was presented as having been
taught by the Alexandrian bishop himself. From him
the Arians said they learned to "know one God, alone
ungenerated, alone everlasting, alone unbegun, alone
true, alone having immortality, alone wise, alone good,
alone sovereign; judge, controller, administrator of
all things, unchangeable and immutable . . . who generated an uniquely-generated Son before eternal times,
through whom he made the ages and the universe and
generated him not in semblance but in truth, having

---

1. Sozomen, H.E. 1:15 (trans. from NPNF 2:252).
2. Athanasius, Syn. 16 and Epiphanius, Haer. 69:7.

36

made him to subsist by his own will as unchangeable
and immutable, a perfect created thing, but not as one
of the created things . . . ." This statement empha-
sized the sovereign transcendence of the Father, yet
sought--probably following the suggestion of Asterius[1]--
to define a mediating position for the Son between God
and the created universe. Strikingly, the passage
backed off Arius' claim in his Thalia that the Son is
changeable. Just why is not entirely clear, though
probably this claim, central as it seems to have been
to Arius' soteriology and Christology, was questioned
by more persons than just Alexander of Alexandria and
his sympathizers. Indeed, as influential a person as
Eusebius of Caesarea was probably one of the question-
ers. J.N.D. Kelly has rightly remarked that Eusebius'
"overriding interest" was "cosmological rather than
soteriological,"[2] and, as we shall see when we consider
Eusebius' reaction to the Arians' profession, the
Caesarean bishop was very favorably impressed with the
profession's assertion of the Son's cosmological status
as God's unchangeable and immutable agent of creation.
In any case, the Arians at the Bithynian council decided
to emphasize Christ's cosmological role as God's unchangeable agent of creation rather than his soteriological role as man's changeable ethical model.[3] Arius
seems to have been nervous from the start about baldly
affirming the Son's changeability: he had termed him
unchangeable as early as in his initial letter to
Eusebius of Nicomedia (see above, p. 17). The profession presented the Son as an unique and "perfect"

---

1. See above, p. 31.
2. J.N.D. Kelly, Early Christian Doctrines, 4th
ed. (London, 1968), p. 225. Compare H. Berkhof, Die
Theologie des Eusebius von Caesarea (Amsterdam, 1939).
3. Gregg and Groh, p. 267, explain the profession's attribution of unchangeability to the Son
by arguing that when "Arius applies the term ἄτρεπτος
to the Son, he has in mind that ultimate perfection
of willing which the creature achieves through
obedience."

created thing. Then, admitting the Son to be an offspring (γέννημα), the profession quickly added, "Just
as he is a created thing unlike all other created
things, so he is an offspring unlike all other offspring (γέννημα, ἀλλ'οὐχ ὡς ἓν τῶν γεγεννημένων)."
The Arians argued that this claim was endorsed by
Bishop Alexander himself, for he was said to have renounced both in church and in council (1) the view of
Valentinus that the offspring of the Father is an
emanation, (2) the view of Manichaeus that the offspring is a part homoousios with the Father, (3) the
view of Sabellius that the divine monad, being divided,
is Son/Father, (4) the view of Hieracas which used the
images of torch from torch and "lamp becoming two,"
and (5) the view that "the one who was before, later
was begotten or created again into a Son." The positions renounced, it was implied, could be avoided only
by the Arian formula of the Son's creation and his subordination and secondariness to the Father--a formula
which thereby was, by implication, taught by Bishop
Alexander. One who renounced the views of Valentinus
and Manichaeus was forced to reject the notion that
the Father devoided himself of what he possessed ungeneratedly in himself. Alexander was also precluded
from interpreting such expressions as "from him"
(Rom. 11:36), "from the womb" (Ps. 109:3), and "I have
come forth from God and am present" (Jn. 16:28) as
signifying a homoousian partition of the Father or an
emanation from him. Otherwise, God would be "composite,
divisible, changeable and a body . . . , a bodiless God
suffering things appropriate to body." The bishop's
renunciations forced him to agree that the Son was
created by the will of God and was made to subsist as
a hypostasis, having received his life, his being, and
his glories as gifts from the Father. Furthermore,
since Alexander had denounced Manichaeus, Sabellius,
and those who held that "the one who was before, later
was begotten or created again into a Son," he was compelled to affirm the priority of the Father as the only
unbegun being and to agree that the Son was not before
he was begotten (although the time in question is to
be construed as a kind of "pre-temporal" time).
Alexander's own denunciations implied the view that

the Son is not eternal and co-eternal or co-ungenerated
with the Father. Not even the philosophical doctrine
of relations (τὰ πρός τι)[1] could be evoked, since it
introduced two ungenerated first principles (δύο
ἀγεννήτους ἀρχὰς). Yet, though the Son must be
secondary to the Father, the profession of faith
represented him--perhaps again influenced by Asterius--
as prior to all other things, for "he alone was made
to subsist by the Father."

This profession of faith formulated at Eusebius
of Nicomedia's Bithynian Council was sent to Alexander,
but it perhaps was also distributed widely as a response
to Alexander's encyclical. Probably a version was included in the synodical letter issued by the council.
In any case, Bishop Alexander had been put on the
defensive. Nonetheless, he would still not extend
communion to Arius and his Egyptian adherents. Sens-
ing it to be important to preserve momentum, the
Arians in Nicomedia quickly moved to continue applying
pressure on Alexander. Arius sent a letter to his
supporters in Syria--to Paulinus of Tyre, Eusebius of
Caesarea, and Patrophilus of Scythopolis--and, according to Sozomen,

> solicited permission for himself and his
> adherents, as they had previously attained
> the rank of presbyters, to form the people
> who were with him into a church. For it
> was the custom in Alexandria, as it still
> is in the present day, that all the churches
> should be under one bishop, but that each
> presbyter should have his own church in
> which to assemble the people. These three
> bishops, in concurrence with others who
> were assembled in Palestine, granted the
> petition of Arius, and permitted him to
> assemble the people as before; but enjoined
> submission to Alexander, and commanded

---

1. The view that held, for instance, that
'Father" necessarily implies "Son," since they are
related realities.

Arius to strive incessantly to be restored
to peace and communion with him.[1]

Apparently to supplement the decisions of this Palestinian council, Eusebius of Caesarea penned a rather
blunt letter to Alexander.[2] Remarking that he came to
his decision to write only "with much agony and much
thought," Eusebius referred to Alexander's accusation
(in his encyclical) that Arius claimed the Son to have
come into being from nothing as one of all things.
The accusation was, of course, well founded, for Arius
did say precisely that in his Thalia. Eusebius quoted
in Arius' defense the passage in the Bithynian profession of faith which confessed the Son's uniqueness:
he was begotten before eternal times, was the agent of
the creation of all things, was generated "not in
semblance but in truth," and was "made to subsist by
[God's] own will as unchangeable and immutable, a
perfect created thing of God but not as one of the
created things." Just to make sure Alexander got the
point, when Eusebius came to the clause that claimed
the Son to be the agent of creation, he changed Arius'
τὰ ὅλα to the more technical τὰ πάντα. Eusebius' conclusion was plain:

> Your letter accuses them as though they were
> saying that the Son has come into being as
> one of the created things. Since they do
> not say this, but clearly determine that he
> is "not as one of the created things," see
> if it cannot be that their home base (ἀφορμή)
> be again given to them so that they may
> begin to obtain and dispense whatever they
> wish. You censure them for saying that 'he
> who is' has begotten 'he who is not'. I
> marvel that someone is able to say otherwise.

---

1. Sozomen, H.E. 1:15 (trans. from NPNF 2:252).
2. Eusebius of Caesarea, Ep. Alex. (Opitz,
Urk. 7).

40

Eusebius not only saw no sense at all in Alexander's
objections but also strongly endorsed the decision of
the council of Palestine which allowed Arius to re-
establish a congregation in Alexandria.

Perhaps present at the Palestinian Council was
the Lucianist bishop of Anazarbus, Athanasius, for we
learn from some fragments in the Latin Sermones
Arianorum[1] that he, like Eusebius of Caesarea, was
impressed with Arius' recent profession of faith.
The fragments were not introduced as having come from
a letter of Athanasius to Alexander of Alexandria,
but they well may have. Be that as it may, the fragments contained an implied attack on the Alexandrian
prelate, as we shall see. Athanasius was less concerned than Eusebius that the Son's uniqueness and difference from all other created things be preserved. He
rather focused on the Bithynian profession's strong
defense of the Father's sovereignty and priority.
Alluding to the phrasing of the profession, Athanasius
confessed that "God is the controller, judge, and
administrator of all things (provisor omnium, iudex,
et dispensator = the profession's πάντων κριτὴν,
διοικητὴν, οἰκονόμον), who created and constructed all
things (omnia), who made all things (omnia) from
nothing." Again here, as in his earlier letter to
Alexander,[2] Athanasius stressed a radical dualism
between God and "all things." And he had no qualms
about including the Son among the latter: "In this
way is he Father, Father and not Son; not because he
has been made, but because he is; not subsisting from
another but in himself; on the other hand, the Son is
also not the Father; not because he was, but because
he had been made; not from himself, but from him who
made him has he received the dignity of the Son."
Unlike Eusebius, Athanasius did not play up the
Bithynian profession's qualifications concerning the
relation of the Son to "all things." But the most
interesting thing about these lines is that they were

---

1. Fr. 16 of the Sermones Arianorum, reproduced
by Bardy, St. Lucien, pp. 207-8.
2. See above, pp. 26-7.

presented under the authority of Dionysius, the third-century bishop of Alexandria. The Sermones Arianorum introduced the passage as follows, "Again also Athanasius himself brings forth the memory of the ancients and particularly Dionysius the bishop in order that he might show that the Father exists before the Son is generated." Gustave Bardy went so far as to suggest that the passage was a quotation from Dionysius.[1] However this may be, clearly Athanasius was seeking to put Bishop Alexander in the uncomfortable position of having abandoned the view of an ecclesiastical predecessor in the Alexandrian see. Responding to the charge made in Alexander's encyclical that the Arians were apostates, Athanasius was accusing Alexander of being the true apostate. Finally, the Anazarban prelate implied that Alexander was not only an apostate from his ecclesiastical ancestors but also from scripture itself. He wrote:

> For the Son did not rise against the Father
> nor did he think equality with God was a thing
> to be grasped (Phil. 2:6), but he submitted
> to his Father and confessed him . . . ,
> teaching everyone that the Father is greater
> [than himself (Jn. 14:28), but greater]
> neither in vastness nor in magnitude, which
> indeed are properties of bodies, but in
> perpetuity and in his indescribable father-
> ly and generating strength, so that,
> because he himself is indeed eternal and
> has completeness in himself and life from
> no one . . . .

What differentiates Father from Son is his sovereign authority and power, and especially his priority.

Backed by the endorsement of the councils of Bithynia and Palestine and armed with epistolary support from Eusebius of Caesarea and, perhaps, Athanasius of Anazarbus, Arius and his Egyptian clergy felt in strong enough a position to return to Egypt. When they

---

1. Bardy, St. Lucien, p. 209.

did, Egypt was thrown into such turmoil that the emperor was forced to intervene. To quote Bardy's vivid description:

> [The Arians'] arrival led to an extraordinary agitation, for Arius was able to arouse the interest of all in his cause. He even composed songs which the sailors, millers, travellers and merchants repeated over and over again in the streets and on the quay. In the theaters the spectators quarrelled over theology; in public places blows were exchanged, and the pagans ridiculed all these discussions . . . . It was in these circumstances that Constantine, having become master of the whole East by his victory over Licinius, entered Nicomedia . . . . When he learnt, as he soon did, of the religious situation in the East, he was deeply chagrined thereby.[1]

Having already called a general council to meet at Ancyra,[2] probably to deal with the fact that Easter was not celebrated on the same date throughout the empire,[3] the emperor asked Eusebius of Nicomedia about the problems in Egypt. Because the bishop apparently replied that it was an arcane dispute over the

---

1. Gustave Bardy, "The Arian Crisis," in J. R. Palanque, G. Bardy, P. de Labriolle, G. de Plinval and Louis Bréhier, The Church in the Christian Roman Empire, trans. by Ernest C. Messenger (London, 1949), pp. 82-3.
2. Otto Seeck, Geschichte des Untergangs der antiken Welt, 2nd ed., (Stuttgart, 1921), 3:405ff. Compare Henry Chadwick, "Ossius of Cordova and the Presidency of the Council of Antioch, 325," Journal of Theological Studies, New Series, 9 (1958): 301-3.
3. See J. R. Nyman, "The Synod at Antioch (324-25) and the Council of Nicaea," Studia Patristica IV (Berlin, 1961), pp. 488-9.

interpretation of scripture,[1] Constantine sent a letter
to Arius and Alexander asking them to stop their bick-
ering and to consider Christian and imperial unity.[2]
The letter was carried by Constantine's western
ecclesiastical advisor, Ossius of Cordova.[3] It was
to no avail; the two parties in Egypt would not be
reconciled. Presumably on the way back to Nicomedia,
Ossius passed through Antioch and found the city in a
crisis. Because Antioch's anti-Arian bishop Philogonius had died on 20 December 324, Antioch, like
Alexandria, was in an uproar over the Arian question;
Arian and anti-Arian vied for the prize of the diocese.[4]
Intent on solving the problem, Ossius summoned a council
and "threw in his weight decisively on the side of the
anti-Arian faction,"[5] having effected the translation
to the Antiochene see of the anti-Arian bishop of
Berea, Eustathius. Under Ossius' aggressive presidency
the council was moved to issue a synodical letter
(reminiscent of Alexander's encyclical) sharply condemning Arian theology.[6] The Son, it said, was

---

1. Eusebius of Caesarea, V.C. 2:69; Constantine,
Ep. ad Eccl. Nic. apud Gelasius, H.E. 3. Compare
Nyman, p. 483.
2. Opitz, Urk. 17.
3. Socrates, H.E. 1:7.
4. Chadwick, "Ossius of Cordova," p. 301.
5. Ibid.
6. The synodical letter is extant only in a Syriac
translation, but it has been translated back into Greek
by Eduard Schwartz. Both the Syriac and Schwartz's
Greek rendition have been reproduced as Opitz, Urk. 18.
On the Antiochene Council, see Erich Seeberg, Die
Synode von Antiochien in Jahr 324-5 (Berlin, 1913);
F. L. Cross, "The Council of Antioch in 325 A.D.,"
Church Quarterly Review 128 (1938):49-76; Chadwick,
"Ossius of Cordova," pp. 292-304; with which must be
compared the critical comments of David Larrimore
Holland, "Die Synode von Antiochien (324/325) und ihre
Bedeutung für Eusebius von Casesarea und das Konzil
von Nizäa," Zeitschrift für Kirchengeschichte 81 (1970):
163-81, and "The Creeds of Nicaea and Constantinople

begotten not from nothing, but from the Father,
not as a created thing, but as something
properly begotten . . . who always is, and
did not at one time not exist . . . an image,
not unbegotten . . . immutable and unchangeable . . . begotten . . . neither by will nor
by adoption . . . begotten from the unbegotten Father . . . the image not of the will
or of anything else but of the very hypostasis
of the Father.

Those who thought the contrary were anathematized.
Although such former defenders of Arius as Gregory of
Berytus and Aetius of Lydda were cowed into signing
the synodical letter, three bishops--Eusebius of
Caesarea, Theodotus of Laodicea, and Narcissus of
Neronias--stolidly refused to go along with Ossius
and Eustathius. They were excommunicated, though with
the proviso that they would be given a chance to repent
and to recover their position at "the great and
hieratic synod of Ancyra."[1]

    Conspicuously absent from the Antiochene Council
were Paulinus of Tyre and Patrophilus of Scythopolis.
Both men--along with Eusebius of Caesarea--had been
leading figures at the earlier council of Palestine
which had so strongly supported Arius against Alexander.
They had undoubtedly been invited to Antioch, but, to
quote Chadwick, "They had the good sense to stay
away . . . ."[2] News of what had transpired at the
council travelled quickly to Eusebius of Nicomedia.
He was pleased with Eusebius of Caesarea's zeal in
resisting Ossius but so incensed with the absence and
silence of Paulinus of Tyre that he wrote the latter
a scolding letter encouraging him to write immediately

Revisited," Church History 38 (1969):255-8. I am
unpersuaded by Holland's arguments that the synodical letter is not authentic and accept the majority
position that it is.
    1. Opitz, Urk. 18.
    2. Chadwick, "Ossius of Cordova," p. 301.

to Bishop Alexander in Arius' behalf.[1] "I have faith,"
he said, "that if you should write to him, you would
turn him." And to insure that the bishop of Tyre
would discharge his obligation properly, Eusebius
provided an outline of points which Paulinus should
include in his letter. Apparently the Nicomedian's
ploy worked, given a notice in Athanasius and two
fragments preserved by Marcellus of Ancyra which seem
to come from a letter of Paulinus to Alexander.[2] Since
Eusebius' letter quickly became considered a classic
statement of early Arianism, we are bound to consider
it; and since Paulinus was the first teacher of the
Neo-Arian Aetius, it is important that we also review
the fragments of his response to Eusebius' scolding.

Eusebius' effort, while not exceedingly original,
was a forceful statement of the early Arian position.
As had become customary, Eusebius rejected the view
that the Father had become divided into two and that
the Son is "from him" (since this, he said, would mean
the Son is a corporeal part of the Father or the result
of a corporeal efflux of his essence). He asserted
that there is only one ungenerated ("we believe that
the ungenerated is one") and that the Son was generated
by his agency, not from his essence, though his beginning is both indescribable and incomprehensible.
Eusebius was insistent that nothing exists from God's
essence, for "all things" are generated by his will,
and only in this sense are "from God." Thus, the Son
must have been "generated as utterly different in

---

1. Eusebius of Nicomedia, Ep. Paulin. (Opitz,
Urk. 8).

2. Athanasius, Syn. 17; Paulinus of Tyre apud
Marcellus of Ancyra, Frr. 37 and 40 (the fragments of
Marcellus were collected and edited by Erich Kloster-
mann in Eusebius Werke, Vol. 4, in Die Griechischen
Christlichen Schriftsteller der Ersten Jahrhunderte
(Berlin, 1972), pp. 185-215). That the fragments of
Paulinus were from one of his letters was explicitly
stated by Marcellus; Fr. 87; that the letter was sent
to Alexander is merely a probable conjecture.

nature and power" from God. This corresponded to Arius'
claim in the Thalia that the Son is "unlike" God in
essence. For Eusebius, as for Arius, the Son is "like"
God only in will: "[The Son] has developed into perfect likeness of the disposition and power of the one
who made him." Furthermore, like Arius (in his letter
to Eusebius), the Nicomedian prelate appealed to
Prov. 8:22 as the basis of the Arian position that
when scripture spoke of the Son as "generated" or
"begotten," this must be interpreted as meaning he
has been "created." And he argued, if someone should
use the fact that the word "generated" or "begotten"
was used of the Son as a pretext for asserting his
"identity of nature" with the Father, that person
would be clearly contradicting scripture. Eusebius
wrote, "We know that scripture says not about him only
that he is that which is begotten, but also about those
by nature unlike him in all things. For also in the
case of man it says, "I have begotten and raised sons,
and they have denied me" (Is. 1:2), and "you have for-
saken God who has begotten you" (Deut. 32:18), and in
other places "who, he says, is the one who has borne
the drops of dew?" (Job 38:8) . . . ."
   If we turn now to the few extant fragments of
Paulinus' response to Eusebius' prodding, we learn
that the bishop of Tyre, like his friend Eusebius of
Caesarea, was more explicitly an Origenist than most
other early Arians. After having agreed that the Son
is a created being Paulinus went on to say that Christ
is a "second God" and "was generated as a more human
God,"[1] both of which claims were also set out in the
writings of his Origenist friend Eusebius of Caesarea.[2]
And more tellingly, Paulinus backed up his assertion
that the Son is a created being rather than a begotten
being with an actual quotation from Origen's De Principiis:

---

   1. Paulinus of Tyre apud Marcellus of Ancyra, Fr.
40.
   2. On the notion of Christ as a "second God," see
Eusebius of Caesarea, D.E. 1:5, 4:6, 5:3, 5:4:9-14,
5:8:2, 5:30, P.E. 7:12, 7:13, and H.E. 1:2:5; on Christ
as a "more human God," see D.E. 4:10:165a-c.

It is time, in reiterating concerning Father,
Son, and Holy Spirit, to go through thoroughly
a few things which were formerly passed over;
concerning the Father, how, being undivided
and indivisible, he became Father of a Son,
not bringing him forth, as some suppose. For
if the Son is something of the Father brought
forth and something begotten from him, of a
sort like the begotten things of earthly
living beings, it is necessary that the one
bringing forth and the one brought forth be
corporeal.[1]

Like Eusebius of Caesarea, Paulinus of Tyre clearly believed that Arius had far the better case than Bishop
Alexander. Hence, he supported the Egyptian presbyter
from the beginning and perhaps now, at Eusebius of
Nicomedia's prodding, so informed Alexander directly,
for Marcellus of Ancyra remarked that Paulinus had the
boldness personally to announce in Ancyra that the Son
is a created being. This presumable occurred when
Paulinus was travelling to the ecumenical council at
Nicaea, to which city the proposed Council of Ancyra
had been transferred by Emperor Constantine.[2]

With the meeting of the Nicene Council, the early
Arian controversy entered a new phase. A decision one
way or the other was inevitable. For the first time
virtually all the contestants were gathered in one
room--under the watchful eye of the emperor. Perhaps
even Arius himself was there, despite not being a
bishop: according to Rufinus, Constantine had commanded his presence.[3] From a variety of sources we
may reconstruct the contingent of those present who
supported his cause. Extant, though defective, Latin
lists of the participants included the following
avowed Arians as having been present: Secundus of

---

1. Paulinus of Tyre apud Marcellus of Ancyra,
Fr. 37. Compare Origen, Princ. 4:1:28.
2. Opitz, Urk. 20. Compare Chadwick, "Ossius of
Cordova," pp. 301-3.
3. Rufinus, H.E. 1:1.

Ptolemais (Egypt); Eusebius of Caesarea, Aetius of Lydda,[1] Patrophilus of Scythopolis (Palestine); Gregory of Berytus[1] (Phoenicia); Theodotus of Laodicea (Syria); Narcissus of Neronias (Cilicia); Menophantus of Ephesus (Asia); Eusebius of Nicomedia, Theognis of Nicaea, Maris of Chalcedon (Bithynia).[2] The Arian historian Philostorgius added: Theonas of Marmarica, Sentianus of Boraeum, Dachius of Berenice, Secundus of Teuchira, Zopyrus of Barca (Libya);[3] Melitus (the Thebaid); Paulinus of Tyre,[4] Amphion of Sidon (Phoenicia); Narcissus of Irenopolis,[5] Athanasius of Anazarbus, Tarcodemantus of Aegae (Cilicia); Leontius, Longianus, Eulalius (Cappadocia); Basil of Amasea, Melitius of Sebastopolis[6] (Pontus).[7] Finally, Epiphanius claimed the presence of the Cappadocian Sophist Asterius and the Antiochene presbyter Leontius (who,

---

1. In view of his signing the synodical letter of the Council of Antioch, perhaps his support was now less than enthusiastic.
2. Cuthbertus Hamilton Turner, ed., Ecclesiae Occidentalis Monumenta Iuris Antiquissima (Oxford, 1899), pp. 36-91.
3. The last three were included also in the lists reproduced by Turner, Ibid. That they inclined toward Arianism, however, cannot be substantiated.
4. Regarding evidence which calls into question Paulinus' presence at Nicaea as bishop of Tyre, see the discussion of Gustave Bardy, "Sur Paulin de Tyr," Revue des Sciences Religieuses 2 (1932):39-41, 44-5. Bardy concluded, no doubt rightly, that Paulinus was present.
5. Identical with Narcissus of Neronias. Both were noted in the Latin lists. See Turner, pp. 56-7.
6. There is some question whether Philostorgius was right in listing the Cappadocians Leontius and Longianus and the Pontans Basil and Meletius as Arian sympathizers, for Athanasius claimed all four to be "orthodox" (Ep. Aeg. Lib. 8). Perhaps they came to the council as Arians and left as Nicenes, convinced Nicenes, unlike numerous others.
7. Philostorgius, H.E. 1:8-9 and 8a.

like Athanasius of Anazarbus, was both a Lucianist and a future teacher of the Neo-Arian Aetius).[1] It is unclear whether these were joined by two more Lucianists, Eudoxius (who is probably not to be identified with the Neo-Arian champion of the same name)[2] and Antonius (who, like Athanasius and Leontius, would later instruct Aetius), for neither seem to have been bishops in A.D. 325. Impressive as this list of Arian adherents was, the Arians numbered less than thirty out of a council of well over two hundred bishops. Posed against them was a formidable array of powerful princes of the church: Ossius of Cordova, Alexander of Alexandria, Eustathius of Antioch, Macarius of Jerusalem, and Marcellus of Ancyra. The Arian leaders--the two Eusebii, of Nicomedia and Caesarea--were on the defensive from the very outset. The Caesarean prelate was, of course, still stigmatized by what had transpired at the Council of Antioch, so Eusebius of Nicomedia was tapped to explain and defend the Arian position.[3] After a number of documents were read to the council (including a piece penned by the Nicomedian Eusebius, probably his letter to Paulinus of Tyre;[4] parts of Arius' Thalia;[5] and perhaps Alexander's encyclical and the synodical letter of the Antiochene council),[6] a consensus quickly emerged. It was decidedly anti-Arian.[7] The most offensive Arian claims were

---

1. Epiphanius, Haer. 69:4.
2. See Bardy, St. Lucien, p. 194.
3. Athanasius, Decr. 3-5, 18-20, Ep. Afr. 5; Eustathius of Antioch apud Theodoret, H.E. 1:7.
4. See Eustathius of Antioch apud Theodoret, H.E. 1:7.
5. Athanasius, Ep. Aeg. Lib. 13; Sozomen, H.E. 1:21.
6. Suggested by Victor C. De Clercq, Ossius of Cordova: A Contribution to the History of the Constantinian Period, No. 13 of Johannes Quasten, ed., The Catholic University of American Studies in Christian Antiquity (Washington, D.C., 1954), p. 253.
7. See the synodical letter of the council apud Socrates, H.E. 1:9; Athanasius, Ep. Aeg. Lib. 13; and Eustathius of Antioch apud Theodoret, H.E. 1:7.

undoubtedly those finally anathematized by the council:[1]
"Regarding those who say: There was when he was not,
and before he was begotten he was not, and that he was
generated from nothing, or who affirm that the Son of
God is from a different hypostasis or essence or
created or changeable or mutable--these the Catholic
Church anathematizes."[2] Serious problems arose, however, when the gathering turned to drawing up a new
creed which would express the faith of the church yet
exclude Arianism. Traditional scriptural language
was found to be inadequate,[3] as were traditional
baptismal creeds.[4] What resulted was a creed containing four pointedly anti-Arian descriptions of the Son:
(1) only-begotten, that is from the essence of the
Father, (2) true God from true God, (3) begotten, not
made, and (4) homoousion with the Father. Arius was
defeated: his primary claims were contradicted by
the largest and the most authoritative Christian
council the church had ever held. Nor could his
Libyan supporters, Secundus of Ptolemais and Theonas
of Marmarica, agree with the creed; they courageously
refused to subscribe it.[5] Constantine moved quickly
against them and banished them to Illyricum[6] (where
Arius instructed two young men, Valens and Ursacius,[7]
who were later to play crucial roles in the Neo-Arian
controversy of the A.D. 350s). According to Philostorgius, all the remaining Arian devotees did subscribe
the creed.[8] Although they were embarrassed (witness

---

1. See De Clercq, pp. 253-4.
2. The text of the creed and anathemas of Nicaea
are conveniently reproduced by J.N.D. Kelly, Early
Christian Creeds, 3rd ed., (London, 1972), pp. 215-6.
3. Athanasius, Decr. 20 and Ep. Afr. 5.
4. See Eusebius of Caesarea, Ep. Caes.
5. Socrates, H.E. 1:8; Philostorgius, H.E. 1:9.
6. Philostorgius, Ibid.
7. Athanasius, Ep. Aeg. Lib. 7.
8. Philostorgius, H.E. 1:9. Surely Philostorgius'
additional claim that Eusebius of Nicomedia, Theognis
of Nicaea, and Maris of Chalcedon signed a text in
which homoiousios had been substituted for homoousios

the letter of Eusebius of Caesarea to his home church explaining his action),[1] the imperial presence was too overpowering to resist. Yet, interestingly, the signatures of the two bishops present at the council who are of the most importance for historians of Neo-Arianism--namely, Paulinus of Tyre and Athanasius of Anazarbus, the first two teachers of Neo-Arianism's founder Aetius--were missing from the subscription lists. Not too much can be made of this, since our lists are surely incomplete, and the Neo-Arian historian Philostorgius said nothing of the two men's resistance. But it is at least possible that they found some unobtrusive way to avoid signing, perhaps by arranging not to be present at subscription time or, in the case of Paulinus, by letting an extremely old bishop named Zeno, to whom Paulinus may have been technically an adjutant-bishop, sign for the see of Tyre.[2]

Although the Arian party was now in serious disarray, matters soon became even worse. Within three months of the conclusion of the Nicene Council, Constantine felt constrained to order Eusebius of Nicomedia and Theognis of Nicaea into exile; they had conspired with some Alexandrian priests of Arian inclination whom Constantine had ordered deported to Nicomedia.[3] And when the Arian Theodotus of Laodicea also began overtly to lobby for the anathematized Arian cause, his attention was drawn to the fate of Eusebius and Theognis by a warning letter from the emperor himself.

---

is to be ascribed to Neo-Arian legend intent on saving some face for its theological ancestors (compare Bardy, The Church in the Christian Roman Empire, pp. 97-8 and Boularand, 2:240).

   1. Eusebius of Caesarea, Ep. Caes.
   2. The suggestion that Paulinus was adjutant-bishop to Zeno was made by Eduard Schwartz, Nachrichten der Kgl. Gesellschaft der Wissenschaften zu Göttingen, 1905, p. 259, n. 1.
   3. Theodoret, H.E. 1:19; Gelasius, H.E. 3, Appendix; Philostorgius, H.E. 1:10 (the continuation in Philostorgius, H.E. 2:1 is surely a piece of Arian

Despite the discouraging course of events, Arianism was not yet finished. In response to an accusation
of the rabid anti-Nicene bishop, Eustathius of Antioch,
that Eusebius of Caesarea was trying to pervert the
Nicene Creed, Eusebius accused Eustathius in turn of
Sabellianism.[1] Distressed by the exile of their
Bithynian colleagues and harassed by Eustathius,
Eusebius and Paulinus of Tyre soon were provided with
an opportunity to strike back effectively at their
opponents. During the summer and autumn of A.D. 326,
the year after the Council of Nicaea, the queen mother
Helena was making a pilgrimage to Jerusalem when
Eustathius sarcastically insulted her.[2] That was all
Eusebius and Paulinus needed. A council at Antioch
was summoned in autumn A.D. 326 under Eusebius of
Caesarea's presidency; it deposed Eustathius and his
strong supporter, Bishop Asclepas of Gaza. Furthermore, sweet revenge, Paulinus of Tyre was translated
to Antioch to be its new bishop.[3] The Arians had
captured one of the two most honored sees in the East!
Unfortunately for the momentum of the Arian counter-
attack, however, after only six months in office
Paulinus died and was replaced by a cleric named
Eulalius, who apparently was less devoted to the Arian
cause than was Paulinus.[4] Eulalius' episcopate turned
out to be as short as Paulinus'; he too soon died.[5]

---

legend). See also the report of agitations in Egypt
after Nicaea in Socrates, H.E. 1:23.
    1. Socrates, H.E. 1:23.
    2. See Henry Chadwick, "The Fall of Eustathius of
Antioch," Journal of Theological Studies 49 (1948):
32-4.
    3. Philostorgius, H.E. 3:15 and 15b; Eusebius of
Caesarea, Marcell. 1:4:2. See also Chadwick, "The Fall
of Eustathius of Antioch," pp. 30 and 35 and compare
Ferdinand Cavallera, Le Schisme d'Antioche (Paris,
1905), pp. 66-70.
    4. Philostorgius, H.E. 3:15. Compare Theodoret,
H.E. 1:21.
    5. Theodoret, Ibid.: "since he survived only a
short time (τούτου ὀλίγον ἐπιβιώσαντος χρόνον) . . . ."

According to a letter written by Constantine and preserved by Eusebius of Caesarea, the new vacancy was
the motive for yet another council at Antioch, again
dominated by Arians, namely, by Theodotus of Laodicea,
Theodorus of Heraclea, Narcissus of Neronias, Aetius
of Lydda, and Alphaeus of Apamea.[1] The bishops, who
probably met in summer or early autumn A.D. 327,
wanted Eusebius of Caesarea to be the new Syrian metropolitan. One would think that Eusebius would have
leaped at the opportunity of occupying a see which
easily could develop into a major Arian base of opera-
tions. He did not, citing the canons of Nicaea which
outlawed translations from one see to another.[2]
Perhaps Paulinus had been criticized for his translation, even though he may have only been adjutant-
bishop of Tyre. Moreover, since the time of the
deposition of Eustathius the church at Antioch had
experienced schism; it had polarized into two distinct
and hostile factions, an Arian faction and one loyal
to the memory of Eusathius. Upon the death of Eulalius
the hostilities had become so fierce that even the
magistrates of Antioch, not to mention its soldiers
and masses, had been so drawn into the fray that
Constantine was forced to send a count to calm things
down.[3] In refusing the see of Antioch, Eusebius was
no doubt being careful not to undermine his own
strength; an uncanonical translation was all his
opponents needed. Therefore, he supported the election of a Cappadocian presbyter named Euphronius,[4]
who probably, to quote Gustave Bardy, "was a follower
of the ideas set forth by Eusebius of Nicomedia"[5] and
perhaps was a friend of the Cappadocian Arian Asterius.
Though somewhat weakened by the Eustathian schism,
which was to continue for decades, the see of Antioch
was preserved for Arianism.

---

1. Eusebius of Caesarea, V.C. 3:62.
2. Ibid., 3:60-2.
3. Ibid., 3:59.
4. Ibid., 3:62.
5. Bardy, The Church in the Christian Roman Empire,
p. 117. Compare Theodoret, H.E. 1:21 and Socrates,
H.E. 1:24.

Meanwhile, Eusebius of Nicomedia and Theognis of Nicaea remained in exile. Banishment was bitter medicine for the Nicomedian prelate. First his letter to Paulinus had been read and condemned at Nicaea; now he was without a see. But while he was in exile, his condemned letter was vigorously defended by the Arian sophist Asterius, probably in late A.D. 327.[1] The Arians were fighting back not only ecclesiastically (by deposing opponents and filling the vacancies with sympathizers) but also theologically (by writing defenses of the Arian position). Asterius was obviously an excellent choice for carrying on the theological battle; he was not a cleric, let alone a bishop, and thus had no special obligation toward the symbol of Nicaea, which "was first and foremost a definition of orthodox faith for bishops."[2] Although Asterius' defense of Eusebius of Nicomedia is not extant in full, there are enough bits and pieces quoted in fragments of Marcellus of Ancyra to give us a taste of his approach. Since Marcellus also quoted passages from Paulinus of Antioch and referred to both Eusebius of Nicomedia and Paulinus as the "fathers" of Asterius, perhaps we should conclude that Asterius wrote not only in defense of Eusebius' letter to Paulinus but also of Paulinus' letter to Alexander.[3]

The Cappadocian sophist began his defense of Eusebius by saying that the bishop's letter was not written as dogma in his capacity as teacher, nor was it addressed to the church or to uneducated Christians. It was, rather, an unofficial, personal letter to Paulinus.[4] The implication was that the Council of Nicaea was wrong in considering it dogma and, therefore, condemning it. Asterius then launched into theology and argued that the "main point" of Eusebius

---

1. The defense must post-date the death of Paulinus in early A.D. 327, for Asterius refers to Paulinus as dead, that is, as μακάριος (Asterius apud Marcellus of Ancyra, Fr. 87).

2. Kelly, Creeds, p. 255.

3. Compare above, pp. 47-8.

4. Asterius apud Marcellus, Fr. 87.

of Nicomedia's letter was "to ascribe the generation of the Son to the will of the Father and not to represent God's act of begetting as a passion."[1] Clearly he thought that the Nicene Creed, with its notions of the Son being begotten "from the Father's essence" and homoousion with the Father, did the latter. He was concerned, he asserted, about the nature of God and "the nature of the generated one."[2] The one generated "out of the Father" is different from him,[3] so that one must believe that there are two hypostases of Father and Son,[4] not one hypostasis, as the Nicene anathemas implied. Or, to use other words, there are "two separate persons"[5] and even "two gods separate in hypostasis."[6] Scripture itself affirmed this when it said in Jn. 17:5 that the Son is the Father's "pre-cosmic glory,"[7] as did the creed which expressed the Christian's belief "in the Father, God Almighty, and in his Son, the uniquely-generated God, our Lord Jesus Christ, and in the Holy Spirit." For if one takes the creed seriously, Asterius argued, "it is necessary to think that the Father is truly Father and the Son truly Son and the Holy Spirit likewise."[8] That meant difference in hypostasis, two separate persons. The creed, in fact, drove Asterius to affirm that there are three separate persons. There are "three hypostases,"[9] with the third, the Holy Spirit, conceived as "proceeding from the Father."[10] But since Asterius was a Lucianist and since Lucian's creed affirmed not only difference between Father and Son but also likeness, the sophist followed suit, at least to the extent of quoting the portion of the creed which confessed faith in "the

---

1. *Ibid.*, 34.
2. *Ibid.*, 35.
3. *Ibid.*, 96, 3, and 90.
4. *Ibid.*, 63. Compare *Fr.* 76.
5. *Ibid.*, 67.
6. *Ibid.*, 76.
7. *Ibid.*, 104.
8. *Ibid.*, 65.
9. *Ibid.*, 69.
10. *Ibid.*, 67.

Father who generated from himself the uniquely-generated
Word and first-born of all creation, one only (who
generated) one only, perfect (who generated) perfect,
King King, Lord Lord, God God, an unchanging image of
his essence and will and glory and power."[1] Father and
Son are two in essence or hypostasis, but the Son's
essence is the perfect "image" of the Father's. Inci-
dentally, in the course of his defense of Eusebius,
Asterius articulated once again a number of themes he
struck in his earlier writing, the Syntagmation--for
instance, the distinction between God's proper Word
and the Son and the claim that Jn. 10:30 enjoined
belief in the harmony of the Father's and Son's words
and deeds, not belief in their oneness of essence.[2]

If we return now to our historical narrative, we
may say that Asterius' defense of Eusebius of Nicomedia
prepared the way for the latter's reinstatement as
bishop of the imperial seat. But this way was even
more smoothly paved by Arius himself. Encouraged by a
presbyter in the imperial entourage who said that Arius
was now ready to affirm the Nicene faith, on November
23, 327 Constantine invited him to court. He was asked
to accept the Nicene formulation of the faith and to
present a written statement of his beliefs.[3] He did
both. Arius' profession of faith, while perfectly
traditional, was obscure and evasive on all the crucial
points upon which Nicaea had pronounced clearly and
decisively.[4] Yet Constantine was probably moved more
by the last paragraph of the profession than by its
theological claims. The paragraph read as follows:

> We beseech your God-fearingness, most God-
> beloved Emperor, we being ecclesiastically
> legitimate, holding the faith and having
> the mind of the church and the Holy Scrip-
> tures, that we be united through your peace-
> making and God-fearing piety to our mother

---

1. Ibid., 96.
2. Ibid., 36 and 72.
3. Opitz, Urk. 29 (= Socrates, H.E. 1:25).
4. Opitz, Urk. 30 (= Socrates, H.E. 1:26).

the church, controversies and superfluous
words having been set aside, so that both
we and the church, having begun to live
peacefully with one another, may all in common make our accustomed prayers on behalf
of your pacific reign and on behalf of your
whole family.[1]

These statements could only have pleased the emperor.
Arius' word that he assented to the Nicene Creed was
accepted. It was late November or early December
A.D. 327.

Soon after Arius' recantation, what was, in effect,
a second session of the Nicene Council, a session composed of 250 bishops, met in Bithynia in the emperor's
presence.[2] Perhaps the most important event which
transpired was the reinstatement of the exiled Eusebius
of Nicomedia and Theognis of Nicaea. The two bishops
wrote a letter to the council[3] which argued that since
Arius himself had been recalled from exile, there was
no sense in the continuation of their own banishment.
They also sought to justify their conspiring with
Alexandrian Arians in the months following Nicaea, 325.
While they had subscribed the faith of Nicaea, including
the homoousion, they asserted that they had never

---

1. Ibid.
2. Philostorgius, H.E. 2:7; Athanasius, Apol. c.
Ar. 59; Eusebius of Caesarea, V.C. 3:32; Hieronymus,
Dial. c. Lucif. 19-20. Gustave Bardy has argued at
length against the meeting of this council ("Sur la
Reiteration du Concile de Nicée," Recherches de Science
Religieuse 23 (1933):430-50), but his objections, ignor-
ing as they do much evidence, are not persuasive, not
the least because they require a rejection of Opitz,
Urk. 29 and 31 as spurious. For an excellent discussion
of the evidence, which establishes the existence of this
council, see Hans-George Opitz, "Die Zeitfolge des
arianischen Streites von den Anfängen bis zum Jahre 328,"
Zeitschrift für die neutestamentliche Wissenschaft 33
(1934):155-9.
3. Opitz, Urk. 31.

intended to subscribe the anathemas, which they believed to be based on inaccurate accusations. The
council accepted their petition, as did the emperor;
Eusebius and Theognis were reinstated as bishops of
Nicomedia and Nicaea in early A.D. 328.[1] Eusebius,
joined by Emperor Constantine himself, immediately
began to seek the return of Arius to Egypt.[2] Within
three years of the Nicene Council of 325, all the
important Arians were back in the good graces of Constantine and the majority of Christendom's bishops.
Of course, in order to achieve this, Arius, Eusebius
of Nicomedia, and the others had been forced to sur-
render their principles and to assent, at least verbally, to the Nicene formula, an assent they maintained
as long as Constantine lived.

So ended the initial stage of the Arian controversy.
As we shall see when we follow the early life of Aetius,
the original Arians had a profound impact on their Neo-
Arian descendants. Aetius learned his Christianity from
them and throughout his life sought consistently to
champion what he believed to be their central theological affirmations. Our sources prevent us from knowing
as much as we would like about Aetius' theological
development, but as our next chapter proceeds, we will
be able to glean enough to assess with reasonable
assurance not only Aetius' personal connections with
early Arianism but also his intellectual connections.

---

1. Sozomen, H.E. 2:16; Philostorgius, H.E. 2:7.
2. Athanasius, Apol. c. Ar. 59; Opitz, Urk. 32.

CHAPTER 2:
THE EARLY YEARS OF
AETIUS

If chronicles of groups are the meat of history, biographies of the groups' distinctive personalities are its spice; man may be by nature an animal compelled to live on the meat, as it were, of society, but he is also an animal who has evolved to relish individuality. Modern histories of Christianity's early "heresies" are forced by the extant sources to provide a substantial diet of history's meat. A narrative of Neo-Arianism can be no exception: our first chapter has chronicled the early Arian movement; our last five will be organized around a similar chronicle of the Neo-Arian movement. The present chapter, however, focuses on the intriguing early biography of Neo-Arianism's founding father Aetius, a person who made his way from dutiful student of the early Arians to demanding patriarch and doctor of Neo-Arianism and from the lower to the very upper reaches of the fourth century's social hierarchy.

Aetius was a native of Antioch who was born toward the beginning of the second decade of the fourth century, in roughly A.D. 313.[1] Although he in time became an intimate of such princes as Gallus, Julian, and Procopius, he began life not on the top but near the bottom of fourth century society. Our knowledge of his early life is surprisingly detailed, yet we can with assurance determine only within relatively broad limits the social class to which he and his family belonged. Gregory of

---

1. The first secure date which we have for the life of Aetius is autumn/winter A.D. 326/327, when he studied with Paulinus, who had just been translated from Tyre to Antioch (Philostorgius, H.E. 3:15 and 3:15b; see Chadwick, "The Fall of Eustathius of Antioch," pp. 30 and 35). Since, as we shall see, Aetius was in A.D. 326/327 considered young by fellow theological students, of whom most were undoubtedly in their late teens, a birth date ca. A.D. 313 would seem justified.

Nyssa implied it was the lowest when he stated that
Aetius began his life's trek as a slave to a woman
named Ampelis and then escaped to take up the "filthy"
trade of a "smith."[1] Theodore of Mopsuestia, on the
other hand, claimed that Aetius' father was "free,"
though added that he was a "goldsmith" who "taught
[his son] his minor craft (τεχνήδριον)."[2] Theodore
went on to say that the father was eager for the son
to learn his letters only so that Aetius could write
up business contracts.[3] We may suspect the orthodox
Gregory and Theodore of some slander against an Arian
opponent, but their story was in essentials not much
different from that of the Neo-Arian historian Philostorgius. Like Theodore, Philostorgius said nothing
about Aetius or his father having been in slavery, but
he did claim that Aetius' parents were "poor and
humble." According to the Neo-Arian, the father was
employed in the office of a provincial governor when
he misconducted himself and was punished by having his
property confiscated; since he died soon afterward,
his youngster and wife were left in a state of such
extreme poverty that Aetius himself was forced to take
up the trade of goldsmith as a means of family support.[4]
If we compare Theodore's and Philostorgius' reports, we
see that they are easily harmonized: Aetius' father
could very well have been forced into the trade of goldsmithing after his property was confiscated. Of all
this information, our best clue to Aetius' social class
membership is his father's initial employment. A.H.M.
Jones has cited evidence indicating that service in
fourth century provincial offices was generally limited
to plebeians and to the humbler members of the curial
class.[5] Aetius' father could have been either a poor

---

1. Gregory of Nyssa, C. Eun. (Werner Jaeger, ed.,
Gregorii Nysseni Opera (Leiden, 1960), 1:35).
2. Theodore of Mopsuestia apud Nicetas, Thes. 5:30.
3. Ibid.
4. Philostorgius, H.E. 3:15 and 3:15b.
5. A.H.M. Jones, The Later Roman Empire, 284-602
(Norman, Oklahoma, 1964), p. 595, with p. 1246 n.
76.

curial or an ambitious plebeian. The fact that relatives did not find a way to save him or his son from the disgrace of becoming artisans suggests to us that the family was not wealthy. In light of Aetius' intense interest in educating himself, an interest we shall document in detail, the likelihood is that he came from one of the poorer curial families of Antioch, since it is well known that the eastern curials, as a class, were famous for their devotion to education. However, even if the young man had been born a curialis, he was treated as an artisan as he worked in Antioch at his trade of goldsmithing.

Philostorgius implied that Aetius was not a normal artisan. His mind would not be limited to goldsmithing; it yearned for more. According to Photius' epitome, Philostorgius wrote of him, "Practicing his trade enough [to support his mother and himself], he turned, because of his natural ability, to logical studies (ἐπὶ τὰς λογικὰς μαθήσεις)."[1] Or, to quote the comparable passage in Philostorgius apud Suidas, "Having arrived at the extreme of poverty, he withdrew to goldsmithing, and became excellent at it. But since his nature yearned for greater learning (μειζόντων . . . μαθημάτων), he turned to logical studies (πρὸς λογικὰς θεωρίας)."[2] Unfortunately, Philostorgius gave no explicit details about the content of these "logical" studies. He seemed to be using the adjective "logical" as merely expressive of intellectual as opposed to manual endeavors. But two pieces of evidence strongly suggest that Aetius pursued specifically theological studies. First, the teacher to whom he repaired was Bishop Paulinus of Antioch, the Arian champion recently translated from Tyre.[3] Second, in a paraphrase of Philostorgius, Suidas wrote that as Paulinus' pupil, Aetius showed "much power of impiety (πολλὴν . . . τῆς ἀσεβείας τὴν ῥώμην)."[4] We may conclude that he was studying Arianism. Aetius as a teenager probably became fascinated

---

1. Philostorgius, H.E. 3:15.
2. Ibid., 3:15b.
3. Ibid., 3:15 and 3:15b.
4. Ibid., 3:15b.

63

with the Arian cause during the years from A.D. 322 to
326, at which time Arianism occupied the attention of
the bishops of his native city (Bishops Philogonius
and Eustathius) and was debated both in the Antiochene
Council of 324/325 and in the great Council of Nicaea,
325. Then, when Paulinus of Tyre was translated to
Antioch in autumn, 326 to replace Eustathius, the
young artisan began to study theology with the new
bishop, presumably during the time he could spare from
his trade. Paulinus was without a doubt a learned man,
for he was both a devotee of Origen and a friend of the
scholarly bishop of Caesarea, Eusebius.[1] He apparently
was also an excellent teacher. After the death of his
mother (sometime during the six month episcopacy of
Paulinus) Aetius began to devote full time to his
study[2]--being supported, it seems, out of episcopal
resources.[3] Soon he was even engaging in public debates. Both Photius' and Suidas' versions of the
report in Philostorgius are extant. The two men wrote,
respectively, "Soon he appeared as the victor over the
crowd (τῶν πλειόνων) in disputations (περὶ λόγων
ἁμίλλαις), and because of this kindled not a little
envy"; "He was his [Paulinus'] pupil, revealing
much power of impiety in controversies with those debating with him (εἰς τὰς πρὸς τοὺς διαφορουμένους
ζητήσεις), and he was already not to be withstood by

---

1. Eusebius praised him highly in an oration addressed to him on the occasion of Paulinus' building a
new cathedral in Tyre. See Eusebius of Caesarea, H.E.
10:4.

2. Philostorgius, H.E. 3:15.

3. There is no direct evidence that Aetius at this
juncture was supported by the church, but Theodore of
Mopsuestia noted that before the young man began to
study full time "the Steward of the church was feeding
him" (C. Eun., as quoted and translated by Vaggione,
pp. 79* and 84*). If Aetius was fed by the church even
while he was working as a goldsmith, most probably he
was supported by the church after he became a theological student. Theodore's claim, however, was included in
an exceedingly slanderous passage; the claim may itself
have been part of the bishop's invective.

64

the crowd (τοῖς πολλοῖς)."[1] These passages did not
mention, of course, with whom Aetius debated or what
the debates were about. The word ζητήσεις, however,
was often used in early Christianity specifically of
exegetical controversies.[2] It may well have been used
in this sense here: after he was no longer associated
with Paulinus, Aetius appealed to scriptural interpretations he had apparently learned from the bishop.[3]
If our view is accurate, the persons with whom Aetius
debated were most likely pupils of other Antiochene
clerics studying theology; many of them surely represented the anti-Arian theological position of the
former Antiochene bishops, Philogonius and Eustathius,
rather than the pro-Arian stance of Paulinus. Aetius'
prowess in debate with them netted him much envy.
Our information about Aetius' study with Paulinus,
then, suggests to us that our young Arian learned at
least two things from the bishop: (1) Arian doctrine
and exegesis and (2) techniques of dialectic debate.
Aetius would continue to work diligently to improve his
abilities in both of these areas, especially the latter;
throughout his life perhaps his favorite activity would
be dialectic theological debate.

In connection with Aetius' first disputations in
Antioch, it is interesting to note Philostorgius'
report that the resentment of those conquered by him
was especially deep because he was so young and because he was an artisan (δεῖνον ποιησάμενοι πρὸς
ἀνδρὸς δημιουργοῦ καὶ νέου).[4] The talented orphan's
involvement in theological study had brought him face
to face not only with theological hostility but also
with social prejudice. Antioch's theological students
were seemingly not of plebeian backgrounds[5] and resented

---

1. Philostorgius, H.E. 3:15 and 3:15a.
2. G.W.H. Lampe, A Patristic Greek Lexicon (Oxford, 1961), see under ζήτησις.
3. See below, the episode of Aetius' study with
the grammarian of Anazarbus, p. 67.
4. Philostorgius, H.E. 3:15b.
5. Compare Frank Daniel Gilliard, The Social
Origins of Bishops in the Fourth Century (Diss.,

an artisan's intrusion into their ranks. As for Aetius'
youth, our evidence indicates that he probably was
young in comparison with other theological students.
Most theological students, like John Chrysostom, had
undoubtedly attended rhetorical school or, at least,
grammar school, and thus were between fifteen and
twenty years old; at the time of his first disputations
Aetius was about thirteen years old.[1] Aetius did not
study with a grammarian until after Paulinus' death
and the young artisan's departure from Antioch. It
seems his father had died while he was in elementary
school; grammar school--which cost four or five times
as much as elementary school[2]--was out of the question.
Since theological study with Bishop Paulinus was free,
it was for Aetius an opportunity to gain an education
which was otherwise out of his financial reach. But,
of course, it also gained him hostility from his peers,
an hostility which was so strong that it was able to be
checked only by the influence of Bishop Paulinus himself.[3] Paulinus died, however, after only six months
as bishop of Antioch. Aetius' opponents then prevailed
upon Eulalius, Paulinus' successor, to rid himself of
the ambitious young goldsmith--which he did.[4] Eulalius
must have been concerned about the deepening schism
between the Eustathians and the Arians in the metropolis and must not have wanted to add Aetius to his
troubles.

With his mother dead and Eulalius unwilling to
continue his tutoring, there was nothing for Aetius in
Antioch. In the spring of A.D. 327 he travelled to
Anazarbus in Cilicia, began there to ply his trade of

University of California, Berkeley, 1966), pp. 8-66 and
77-86, which demonstrated that the overwhelming majority of bishops in the fourth century were members of
the curial or "middle" class.

    1. Concerning John Chrysostom's education, see
Chrysostomus Baur, John Chrysostom and his Time, tr. by
Sr. M. Gonzaga (London and Glasgow, 1959), 1:22-8.

    2. Jones, p. 997.

    3. Philostorgius, H.E. 3:15.

    4. Ibid., 3:15 and 3:15b.

goldsmithing to pay his bills, and engaged in disputations with any individuals who happened to be interested.[1] Surely he went to Anazarbus (or was sent)
because Athanasius, the city's bishop, was an ardent
champion of Arianism, perhaps even more ardent than
his original mentor Paulinus. He probably hoped that
Anazarbus would be more hospitable to him than tension-
filled Antioch. It was: Aetius' public disputations
brought him to the attention of a grammarian who offered
to enroll him as a student. Since the young artisan
was still unable to afford such a luxury, the grammarian agreed to allow him to perform the tasks of a
household slave (τὰς οἰκετικὰς . . . λειτουργίας) in
return for his room, board, and grammatical education.[2]
Bishop Paulinus' tutoring had served Aetius well: it
had enabled him to develop his intellectual abilities
to the point that even the conventionally-trained
recognized his potential. Aetius was on the way to
becoming an educated man; according to Philostorgius,
his new teacher "taught him the grammatical art zeal-
ously."[3] But whereas study with Paulinus had made
Aetius' grammatical education possible, it also served
to undermine it. Philostorgius wrote, "Aetius, having
once fallen publicly into a refutation of his teacher
because he did not give the correct interpretation
(διηγήσις) of the Holy Scriptures and having showered
much shame on him because of his ignorance of such
matters (ἐπ'ἀμαθείᾳ τοιούτων), found as his reward ex-
pulsion from the house which was benefitting him."[4]
Paulinus had taught Aetius exegesis and debating techniques, but he had not taught him tact and restraint.
Nor would Aetius ever learn these; he tended throughout
his life to be both enthusiastically aggressive and outspoken. For his display of disrespect Aetius was sum-
marily expelled by the grammarian. Never would he
resume formal grammatical study, let along go on to the
highest level of fourth century education, the rhetorical
school.

---

1. Ibid.
2. Ibid., 3:15.
3. Ibid.
4. Ibid.

67

Once again Aetius sought tutelage under an Arian bishop, this time the Lucianist bishop of Anazarbus, Athanasius. Apparently the outraged grammarian had the sympathy of many Anazarbans in expelling the arrogant young Antiochene, for Philostorgius wrote, "Without being observed (ἐλαθεὶς) he [Aetius] became a student of Athanasius." Athanasius probably was as apprehensive about Aetius as was Eulalius of Antioch before him. Because we do not know how long Aetius studied with the Anazarban grammarian, it is impossible to date with certainty the inception of his study with Athanasius, but it probably was in A.D. 328 or 329,[1] around the time of Arius' and Eusebius of Nicomedia's reconciliation with the emperor and the majority of the church. If we may trust reports in Socrates, Sozomen, and Rufinus, Aetius was not at all pleased with the dissembling displayed by Arius and Eusebius in their bids for reconciliation. Socrates and Sozomen wrote that he "separated himself from the Arian party" because of Arius' hypocrisy, while Rufinus claimed that he maintained close associations with intransigent Arians who opposed Arius' and Eusebius' actions.[2] That

---

1. This dating would be nearly assured if Gustave Bardy were right in his claim that Antonius, Aetius' next teacher after Athanasius, was raised to the episcopate ca. A.D. 330 (St. Lucien, p. 197 n.21), since Aetius studied with Antonius while the later was still a presbyter (Philostorgius, H.E. 3:15). But, as far as I can determine, Bardy was merely guessing.

2. Socrates, H.E. 2:35 and Sozomen, H.E. 4:12; Rufinus, H.E. 1:25. These reports are unsubstantiated by more contemporary authors, but they are plausible, for later on in the A.D. 340s Aetius opposed Arians who concealed their theological positions in order to remain in communion with Nicenes (see Nicetas, Thes. 5:30 and Philostorgius, H.E. 3:19). John Chapman has suggested another example of Neo-Arian hostility toward Arians who dissembled by verbally accepting Nicaea ("On the Date of the Clementines," Zeitschrift für die neutestamentliche Wissenschaft 9 (1908):21-34). He argued that the Neo-Arian editor of the (Pseudo) Recognitiones

Athanasius of Anazarbus was one of these intransigents was never stated in our sources, but it is a possibility in light of his rather radical Arian stance. In any case, unwillingness to compromise would become Aetius' style throughout the rest of his life.

Aetius resumed with Athanasius the exegetical studies he began with Paulinus of Antioch. Philostorgius claimed that Aetius "read with him the gospels, having devoted himself to them one by one."[1] Although this is the extent of the detail provided us by the Neo-Arian historian, we are fortunate that there is extant a sample of Bishop Athanasius' exegetical technique--and happily that technique was brought to bear on a passage in the gospels. We recall that in a letter to Alexander of Alexandria written soon after the publication of Arius' _Thalia_, Athanasius defended Arius' assertion that the Son was "created from nothing" as "one of all things" by appealing to an exegesis of the parable of the hundred sheep.[2] This exegesis, quoted in full and discussed on pages 26-7 above, is especially fascinating because of its syllogistic procedure: since scripture calls the Son a "lamb" and "our passover," one must take this seriously and include him among the hundred sheep of the parable, which stand for "all things"; if this be granted, then one must conclude that the Son is created, lest one end up with the polytheistic notion of an hundred ungenerateds--which for a Christian is absurd. We shall see in later chapters that Aetius, as a Neo-Arian, became famous for his syllogisms and, in fact, published his only extant work in the form of a collection of syllogisms. If Athanasius' use of syllogism in his parabolic exegesis was at all characteristic of his intellectual method, he may well have been a major influence on Aetius to

---

Clementinae polemized against "the writing of an Arian who . . . invented a way of accepting the Nicene decision so far as words go"; he even speculated that the Arian writing in question dated from around A.D. 330 (_Ibid._, p. 30).

   1. Philostorgius, _H.E._ 3:15.
   2. Athanasius of Anazarbus _apud_ Athanasius, _Syn._ 17.

develop and perfect syllogistic techniques. That Athanasius, in addition, introduced Aetius to a more radical form of Arianism than he had learned at the feet of Paulinus is also probable. As we remarked in our introduction, Paulinus' theological affirmations resembled more the thought of Eusebius of Caesarea than that of other early Arians.[1] Therefore, Paulinus, like Eusebius, most likely welcomed the clarifications of Arius' "profession of faith" which served to protect the uniqueness of the Son by distinguishing him from "all things."[2] Athanasius' response to the profession was much different.[3] He was more impressed with its statements about the Father's uniqueness than those about the Son's; that is, he was concerned about the Father's sovereignty, priority, and distinction from "all things." It was to this more stringent brand of Arianism that Aetius was introduced when he read the gospels and studied their meaning with the Anazarban bishop.

Apparently the gospels were Athanasius' specialty, since the bishop did not instruct Aetius in other parts of scripture. For his study of Paul's epistles Aetius travelled to the Cilician town of Tarsus; he was taught there by a second Lucianist, presbyter Antonius.[4] We know next to nothing about Antonius save that he was secretary to his master Lucian and the martyr's most beloved disciple.[5] Our lack of information is most unfortunate, for Philostorgius claimed that Aetius "spent an ample period of time with him while he [Antonius] was filling the rank of presbyter."[6] When Antonius was elevated to bishop of Tarsus, he found that he no longer had the time to devote himself to the instruction and education of his young pupil.

---

1. See above, pp. 47-8.
2. See above, pp. 40-1.
3. See above, pp. 41-2.
4. That Antonius was a Lucianist was claimed by Philostorgius, H.E. 2:14.
5. Vita Luciani 10 and 14 (Bidez, pp. 192, 15 and 196, 15).
6. Philostorgius, H.E. 3:15.

Consequently, he seems to have arranged to have Aetius' education continued by a third Lucianist, a presbyter of Antioch named Leontius.[1] So, sometime in the A.D. 330s Aetius returned to his native city of Antioch.

With Leonius in Antioch, Aetius completed his theological education by studying the prophets, especially the prophet Ezekiel. Reflecting upon Aetius' study of gospels, epistles, and prophets with three different Lucianists in turn, Gustav Bardy suggested that the erstwhile artisan had followed a well-organized "cours d'exégèse" which may well have been that of the famous Lucian of Antioch himself: " . . . l'on échappe difficilement à l'impression que ces leçons s'organisent suivant un plan assez rigoureux: ce sont d'abord les Évangiles, les livres les plus faciles et en même temps les plus indispensables au chrétien, ceux qui contiennent l'authentique enseignement du Seigneur; puis viennent les Épîtres, plus compliquées déjà, mais où la doctrine est présentée sous une forme plus nette, mieux définie. Les prophetès terminent la série, bien que leurs oeuvres aient été composées les premières; c'est qu'on les interprète de manière plus exacte lorsqu'on sait déjà l'histoire de celui qui les a réalisées."[2] In support of his suggestion Bardy noted that essentially the same order was recommended by Jerome in two of his epistles; moreover, Origen remarked about a Jewish tradition which reserved the beginning of Genesis, the beginning and end of Ezekiel, and the Song of Songs for the conclusion of a student of scripture's instruction.[3] Leontius, of course, concluded Aetius' exegetical training with Ezekiel. Although there is no evidence that Aetius, as a Neo-Arian, was particularly concerned about exegetical problems per se, we have every reason to believe that he had undergone rigorous and thorough exegetical training. On the other hand, Aetius and his disciple Eunomius did articulate a sophisticated theory regarding the nature

---

1. Ibid.
2. Bardy, St. Lucien, pp. 197-8.
3. Ibid., p. 198 n. 22a.

of language, especially biblical language. It is very
possible that this theory was, in part, an outgrowth
of Aetius' long years in scriptural study with his
Lucianist mentors.

Of the three Lucianists--Athanasius, Antonius,
and Leontius--Aetius spent the shortest amount of
time with Athanasius, a longer period with Antonius,
and the most time with Leontius. He was associated
with Leontius first as a student (apparently in the
middle and late A.D. 330s) and then (during later
decades) in other capacities. But as is the case with
Antonius, we know very little about Leontius' theological position. Yet, if we may trust Philostorgius,
Antonius and Leontius shared one important theological
conviction which was of crucial importance for Neo-
Arianism, namely, the conviction that God could be
known and comprehended by the human mind. Whereas the
Neo-Arian historian criticized Arius for asserting
God's unknowability, he praised five men for holding
the opposite point of view: the two Libyan Arians
Secundus and Theonas and the three Lucianists Leontius,
Antonius, and Eusebius of Nicomedia.[1] Regrettably
for our faith in the reliability of Philostorgius'
list, we remember that Eusebius of Nicomedia (in his
letter to Paulinus) affirmed both the indescribability
and the incomprehensibility of the Son's generation.[2]
However, it must be added that Eusebius did limit
himself to claiming incomprehensibility for the
"beginning" of the Son's generation. He was asserting that the Son was generated during a "pretemporal
time" which is, strictly speaking, indescribable and
incomprehensible; he did not go so far as Arius, who
claimed that God the Father is himself almost completely unknowable.[3] With some hesitation, therefore,
we may accept Philostorgius' assertion regarding
Antonius and Leontius and trace to them Aetius' distinctive attitude toward the ability of the human mind
to understand God. Most probably these two men, in

---

1. Philostorgius, H.E. 2:3, compare 2:15.
2. Eusebius of Nicomedia, Ep. Paulin. (Opitz,
Urk. 8).
3. See above, pp. 24-5.

turn, derived their view of God's comprehensibility
from Asterius the Sophist, for he, we remember, had
forwarded in his Syntagmation a precise definition of
God's principal characteristic, his ungeneratedness.[1]

Surely Leontius influenced Aetius in many ways
of which we are not aware. Besides the information
just discussed from Philostorgius, the only other
things we know about the cleric's early days are that
he was a native of Phrygia and that he was once deposed from the Antiochene presbyterate, perhaps by
Bishop Eustathius, for mutilating himself.[2] The mut-
ilation was Leontius' response to a charge that he
had been living with a virgin. The virgin was probably a relative, and the deposition was only temporary.
In any case, Philostorgius claimed that Aetius' study
with Leontius in Antioch was cut short because "envy
again drove him away from there."[3] It is probable
that again on this occasion, as after the death of
Bishop Paulinus in A.D. 327, Aetius' tendency towards
outspoken public defense of stringent Arianism made
him persona non grata in Antioch, especially among
the so-called Eustathians, who still continued their
hostility to Arianism and, indeed, their schism.[4] If
this supposition is correct, perhaps a likely date for
Aetius' second withdrawal from his native city would
be late A.D. 341 or early 342. At this time the
eastern church, after the famous Council of Antioch
in summer, 341, decided to seek conciliation with the
supporters of Nicaea (by means of the so-called
"fourth" creed of the Antiochene council). We shall
review the Council of Antioch and its creeds in more
detail directly. Suffice it to say here that since
rapprochement with the adherents of Nicaea was the new

---

1. See above, pp. 29-30.
2. Athanasius, Fug. 26 and H. Ar. 28. Compare
Archibald Robertson, Select Writings and Letters of
Athanasius, Bishop of Alexandria, Vol. 4 of Philip
Schaff and Henry Wace, ed., Nicene and Post-Nicene
Fathers (1892), p. 279 n. 1.
3. Philostorgius, H.E. 3:15.
4. Cavallera, pp. 42-7.

eastern policy, a one-time student of Bishops Paulinus
and Athanasius of Anazarbus who, as we have seen, was
hardly diplomatic and restrained about his theological
convictions may well have proved to be an embarrass-
ment to the now concilatory Antiochene clergy.

Pressured once again to leave Antioch, Aetius
returned to Cilicia and there continued his favorite
activity of public debating. But he was so roundly
defeated in a disputation with a member of the Gnostic
sect of the Borboriani[1] that it took a vision from
God to convince him that life was worth living. Then
he travelled to Alexandria and won a disputation
against a Manichaean named Aphthonius.[2] Aetius' stay
in Alexandria marked yet another milestone in his long
and varied education, for Sozomen claimed that he
frequented there the Aristotelian schools, probably
to perfect his logical and dialectical techniques.[3]
And Philostorgius--supported by Gregory of Nyssa--
reported that he took up the study of medicine under
a man named Sopolis.[4] Aetius, now around thirty years
old, obviously had an intensely inquisitive mind.
How he was able to afford these studies, especially
the medical, is unclear. Philostorgius claimed that
he worked nights as a goldsmith,[5] but that could hardly have defrayed all the expenses of a medical education, unless Sopolis was an official public physician
who not only took students, as seemingly was normal,[6]
but did not charge healthy fees, a much less likely

---

1. See F. J. A. Hort, "Borboriani," in W. Smith
and H. Wace, ed., Dictionary of Christian Biography,
Literature, Sects, and Doctrines (London, 1877-87),
1:331.

2. Philostorgius, H.E. 3:15.

3. Sozomen, H.E. 3:15. Compare, however, Socrates, H.E. 2:35.

4. Philostorgius, H.E. 3:15; Gregory of Nyssa,
C. Eun. (Jaeger, 1:36-7). Compare Sozomen, H.E.
3:15.

5. Philostorgius, H.E. 3:15.

6. Jones, p. 1013, which was based on Codex
Theodosianus, 13:3:3.

possibility. The probabilities are that Gregory of Nyssa was right when he implied that Aetius became once again a household servant--this time to Sopolis.[1] He stayed in Alexandria, working primarily in medicine, for approximately three or four years, during the time that a Cappadocian Arian, Bishop Gregory, occupied the Alexandrian see. Aetius' medical activities did not mean, however, that he had at all abandoned his devotion to Arianism, for Gregory of Nyssa wrote that even the Alexandrian "schools of medicine were echoing at that time with uproars about this question [Arianism]."[2] Apparently Bishop Gregory's presence in Alexandria had caused Arianism to become the issue of the day in the city. But not long after Aetius' mentor Leontius was raised to the episcopate of Antioch, Aetius again returned to his native city; he was subsequently offered a clerical post as deacon by the new bishop.[3] We will consider this development in detail later in this chapter.

At this point, however, we must interrupt our narrative of Aetius' early life to review some wider ecclesiastical history of the A.D. 330s and 340s. Events took place in these decades which seriously affected the eastern church's attitude toward Arianism and spawned Aetius' theological competitors of the A.D. 350s, the Homoousians and the Homoiousians. It was in debate with men devoted to these slogans that Aetius articulated his distinctive brand of Arianism. So, in order to sketch the evolving eastern attitude toward Arianism and to provide necessary background for an understanding of the consolidation of the homoousian and homoiousian positions, we resume the

---

1. Gregory of Nyssa, C. Eun. (Jaeger, 1:37).
2. Ibid.
3. Philostorgius, H.E. 3:17. Philostorgius' report in H.E. 3:16 that between Aetius' study in Alexandria and his return to Antioch he engaged in a disputation with Basil of Ancyra and Eustathius of Sebaste was surely an anachronistic doublet, see Johannes Schladebach, Basilius von Ancyra: Eine historisch-philosophische Studie (Leipzig, 1898), pp. 14-6 and below, pp. 107-8.

outline of the Arian controversy which our introductory chapter left off at A.D. 327/328.

As a result of the "second" session of Nicaea held in winter, A.D. 327/328, the three leading Arian exiles--Arius himself, Eusebius of Nicomedia, and Theognis of Nicaea--returned from banishment and were reconciled with Constantine. From this time until Constantine's death there were few confessedly Arian bishops; nearly everyone formally accepted the Nicene definition. Those bishops who had supported Arian theology turned their attention to realizing two practical goals, namely, the reinstatement of Arius to the Alexandrian priesthood and the deposition--on non-theological grounds--of Nicaea's defenders. Athanasius of Alexandria, who had succeeded Alexander as bishop on June 8, 328, dubbed these bishops "Eusebians," since they were led by Eusebius of Nicomedia. The first Eusebian goal was never achieved. When Arius died in A.D. 336, he was still excluded from Egyptian communion.[1] The Eusebians were far more successful in achieving their second goal--deposing the champions of Nicaea. Eustathius of Antioch and his friend Asclepas of Gaza had, we remember, been deposed as early as A.D. 326/327; they were soon joined by a host of others, including the equally as prominent Athanasius of Alexandria and Marcellus of Ancyra.[2] In order to achieve the ouster of Athanasius, the Eusebians formed an alliance with the schismatic Meletians of Egypt; the latter had accused the Alexandrian bishop of wrongdoing during the course of his election in A.D. 328 and during the early 330s.[3] The alliance achieved Athanasius' deposition at the Council of Tyre in A.D. 335. The Alexandrian bishop did not have a chance; the gathering was against him nearly two to one. Constantine was at first hesitant about the deposition, but after Athanasius' opponents accused him (at the Council of Constantinople, A.D.

---

1. Rufinus, H.E. 10:11-2; Socrates, H.E. 1:37; Sozomen, H.E. 2:29.
2. See Athanasius, H. Ar. 5 and 7.
3. See Lietzmann, 3:129-32 and Kidd, 2:56-9.

336) of threatening to stop the annual export of corn
from Alexandria to Constantinople, the emperor was
persuaded to exile the bishop to Trier in Gaul. As
important as the ouster of Athanasius was that of
Marcellus of Ancyra. Outraged by the Council of
Tyre's treatment of the Alexandrian bishop, Marcellus
refused to take part in eastern conciliar proceedings--
which led to his being accused by the Eusebians of
disrespect for the emperor.[1] More offensive than
Marcellus' ecclesiastical actions were his theological
convictions. Indignant at Asterius the Sophist's
defense of Eusebius of Nicomedia and Paulinus of
Antioch, Marcellus penned a refutation which was so
Sabellian that Eusebius of Caesarea devoted two
treatises--the Contra Marcellum and the De Ecclesiastica Theologia--to exposing his thought. To Eusebius,
Marcellus was proof of what theological horrors the
Nicene position was breeding.[2] When Marcellus was
deposed at Constantinople in A.D. 336,[3] his see was
given to a man named Basil. This new Ancyran bishop
was to become the main organizer and proponent of the
homoiousian party of the A.D. 350s. He turned out to
be one of Aetius' bêtes noires.

Although he had given his all to realizing his
dream of a unified church, Constantine died on May 22,
337 with his dream as unfulfilled as ever. The formula

---

1. Sozomen, H.E. 2:33; Socrates, H.E. 1:36.
2. For an outline of Marcellus' thought, see
Henry Melville Gwatkin, Studies of Arianism, 2nd ed.
(London, 1900), pp. 79-87 and T. E. Pollard, Johannine
Christology and the Early Church (Cambridge, 1970),
pp. 246-57; for an extended discussion, see Wolfgang
Gericke, Marcell von Ancyra: Der Logos-Christologe und
Biblizist (Halle, 1940).
3. The date of Marcellus' deposition has been a
matter of some controversy. I have followed the dating
of the ancient historians Socrates and Sozomen. For
another possibility, see Edward Schwartz, Nachrichten
der Kgl. Gesellschaft der Wissenschaften zu Göttingen,
Philol. histor. Klasse, 1911, pp. 400-7 and Bardy, The
Church in the Christian Roman Empire, pp. 118-9.

of Nicaea he had hoped would provide the theological touchstone of unity failed to live up to his expectations. The Eusebians pretended adherence, but their actions revealed that they mistrusted everyone who was committed to it--especially Eustathius, Athanasius, and Marcellus. The deposition of these was a sign that when Constantine's presence was removed as a guarantee of the Nicene formula, it would have a difficult time remaining the official "bishops' creed."

Upon Constantine's death the empire was divided among his sons: Constantine II took the far western provinces, Constans received Italy, Africa, and Greece, whereas Constantius ruled the eastern provinces and the Danubean region. Exiled bishops were immediately allowed to return to their cities. The return of Athanasius, however, initiated a series of events which had momentous consequences. After effecting a second exile for Paul of Constantinople, Eusebius of Nicomedia was translated to his see and began to move against Athanasius.[1] Because the Egyptian prelate had not bothered to seek synodical restitution to his see (even though he had been deposed by an official synod), the Eusebians declared his see vacant and elected in council an old Arian named Pistus to be his successor.[2] Then Eusebius made a fatal mistake. Knowing of the close ecclesiatical relationship between Alexandria and Rome, he wrote to Bishop Julius of Rome and explained the case against Athanasius and for Pistus.[3] Athanasius countered by calling an Alexandrian synod (A.D. 338), which sent an encyclical to Julius detailing and refuting every charge, supported by all sorts of records.[4] Now determined to adjudicate the dispute, Julius requested the presence of both parties.[5] He quickly discovered that the Eusebians were not awaiting a reply to their

---

1. Socrates, H.E. 2:7.
2. Athanasius, Apol. Sec. 19, 24 and Ep. Encycl. 6.
3. Athanasius, Apol. Sec. 22.
4. Ibid., 3-19.
5. Athanasius, H. Ar. 9 and Ep. Encycl. 7.

letter. Rather,[1] they had abandoned Pistus, had con-
secrated a Cappadocian named Gregory to be bishop of
Alexandria, and had sent Gregory to the Egyptian
metropolis. Gregory was strongly supported by his
Cappadocian countryman Philagrius, the new Egyptian
prefect; clearly Emperor Constantius was now on the
Eusebians' side. Gregory's entrance into Alexandria
stimulated weeks of riots and bloodshed and led
Athanasius voluntarily to abandon the city and travel
to Rome. There he completely won over Bishop Julius
and penned his massive refutation of Arianism, the
Orationes Contra Arianos.[2] The impact of this polemical series on the development of eastern Christian
theology, including Neo-Arian theology, was, as we
shall see, considerable.

Athanasius was soon joined in Rome by Marcellus
of Ancyra; like the Egyptian prelate, Marcellus had
also been once again driven from his see. The eastern
bishops most vigorous in their support of Nicaea were
as one in recognizing Rome as their best hope against
the Eusebians. They were not disappointed. Julius
again invited the Eusebians to a council to examine
the Athanasian and Marcellan cases. When they treated
his envoys with disrespect and responded with a hostile
letter defending their authority to sentence the two
eastern bishops, Julius convoked without them a synod
in Rome (A.D. 340). It exonerated Athanasius and
declared Marcellus orthodox on the strength of his
acceptance of the so-called "old Roman Creed."[3] The
results of the council were then reported to the
easterners in a long letter written by Julius himself.[4]

---

1. See Lietzmann, 3:188-90 and Kidd, 2:72-3.
2. The traditional date assigned to the Orationes
has been A.D. 356-362 (Montfaucon), but Loofs and Stül-
cken have argued persuasively for A.D. 338/339, though
they have not been universally followed. For good re-
views of the debate and defenses of the A.D. 338/339
date, see Jaakko Gummerus, Die Homousianische Partei
bis zum Tode des Konstantius (Leipzig, 1900), pp. 186-
96.
3. See Kidd, 2:75 and Lietzmann, 3:191-2.
4. Julius, Ep. apud Athanasius, Apol. Sec. 20-35.

Among other things, the letter accused the Eusebians of showing disloyalty to Nicaea by receiving Arians; the implication was that they were themselves Arians.

The Eusebian response came in the form of a council held at Antioch on the occasion of the dedication in A.D. 341 of a new cathedral. Emperor Constantius was present,[1] as were ninety-seven bishops, including Eusebius of Constantinople, Flacillus of Antioch, George of Laodicea, Gregory of Alexandria, Dianius of Cappadocian Caesarea (accompanied by his countryman Asterius the Sophist[2]), and two new faces-- Eudoxius of Germanicia (later to become a champion of Aetius and the Neo-Arians) and Acacius of Palestinian Caesarea (successor to Bishop Eusebius, now deceased).[3] The events of this council were of pivotal significance, for the eastern prelates present, hesitant about the creed of Nicaea because it smacked too much of Sabellianism and the thought of Marcellus, began to develop an opposing but non-Arian theology. How Bishop Dianius of Cappadocia's associate at the Antiochene council, Asterius the Sophist, reacted to this development is unknown to us; our sources simply fail us at this point. In any case, the emerging eastern theology was a conservative theology of conciliation. It would inspire, first of all, the development of the so-called Macrostich creed of A.D. 344, which was hostile toward Arianism but equally as hostile toward at least portions of Athanasius' Orationes Contra Arianos; it would also inspire the formation of the homoiousian ecclesiastical party of the A.D. 350s. The East was on its way toward articulating a position neither Arian nor Nicene. Hence, when Aetius emerged as a champion of Arianism during the A.D. 350s, he faced two foes--the Nicene devotee Athanasius and the Homoiousians who were heir to Antioch, 341 and the Macrostich.

---

1. Athanasius, Syn. 25.
2. Libellus Synodicus (J.D. Mansi, Sacrorum Conciliorum Nova et Amplissima Collectio (Florence, 1758-1798), 2:1350).
3. Sozomen, H.E. 3:5.

The first action of the Council of Antioch was
to draw up an encyclical letter to be sent to Julius.[1]
In it the easterners protested that they were decidedly not Arians: "We have not been followers of Arius--
how, being bishops, should we follow a presbyter?--nor
did we receive any other faith beside that which has
been handed down from the beginning. But after taking
on ourselves to examine and to verify his faith, we
admitted him rather than followed him . . . ." This
statement was followed by a creedal profession of
faith which, though not as sharply anti-Arian as the
creed of Nicaea, was, nonetheless, pointedly so. The
easterners at Antioch were seeking to claim a middle
ground between the extremes of Arianism on the left
and Marcellus' thought on the right. This came out
even more clearly in the so-called "second" and "third"
creeds of Antioch, 341 (the one we have just considered
is reckoned as the "first"). Apparently a Cappadocian
bishop named Theophronius of Tyana was accused at
Antioch of favoring Marcellus' brand of Sabellianism;
to defend himself he offered a baptismal confession
remodelled in both an anti-Marcellan and anti-Arian
way.[2] It is normally called the "third" creed of
Antioch, 341. Stimulated by the case of Theophronius,
the Council of Antioch decided to promulgate an
official creed, its so-called "second creed,"[3] alleged
on good grounds to be substantially the creed of the
Eusebian hero Lucian of Antioch.[4] Perhaps the Lucianists Asterius the Sophist and Eusebius of Constantinople first suggested it. The creed[5] was both scriptural in language and tone and anti-Arian and
anti-Marcellan in content. Although its anti-Arian
statements were not as strong as those of Nicaea,
they were clearly present. Especially anti-Arian were

---

1. Athanasius, Syn. 22.
2. Hilary of Poitiers, Syn. 29; Athanasius, Syn.
24. Compare Kelly, Creeds, pp. 267-8.
3. Compare Lietzmann, 3:196-7 and Kelly,
Creeds, p. 268.
4. See Bardy, Saint Lucien, p. 85ff.
5. Athanasius, Syn. 23.

the creed's concluding anathemas: "If anyone teaches contrary to the sound and right faith of the scripture, that time or season or age either is or has been before the generation of the Son, let him be anathema. Or if anyone says that the Son is a created thing as one of the created things, or an offspring as one of the off-spring, or a thing-made as one of the things-made . . . , let him be anathema." The Son was confessed as "begotten before all the ages from the Father, God from God, whole from whole, sole from sole, perfect from perfect . . . ." But however anti-Arian the "second" creed was, it was even more anti-Marcellan. Kelly's characterization is hard to improve upon:

> In its main drift, . . . the creed is reso-
> lutely anti-Sabellian, anti-Marcellan. This
> comes out forcibly in the exegesis attached
> to the baptismal command of Mt. 28:19. With
> its insistence on the separation of the three
> hypostases and on the fact that they are not
> just three names, it re-echoes teaching which
> Eusebius of Caesarea had put forward at
> Nicaea and which he later repeated specifi-
> cally against Marcellus. The latter had
> taken Asterius the Sophist, the disciple of
> Lucian, to task for precisely this teach-
> ing. The string of descriptive phrases
> from the Bible (God from God . . . exact
> image), not to mention a number of other
> passages, is strongly reminiscent of
> language which Asterius had used and
> Marcellus had vigorously denounced . . . .
> Positively it has a markedly Origenist
> flavour . . . . Its guiding conception
> is of three quite separate hypostases,
> each possessing its own subsistence and
> rank and glory, but bound into a unity by
> a common harmony of will. This reproduces
> exactly what Origen had taught . . . .
> Nothing could be more opposed than this
> hierarchically constructed trinity to the
> Monarchianism recently approved at Rome

and represented in its extreme form by
Marcellus.[1]

In time this creed was to be called "the faith of the
fathers" by the Homoiousians and to be considered by
them the touchstone of orthodoxy, especially its
notion that the Son is "the exact image of the divine,
of the Father's essence, will, power, and glory (τῆς
θεότητος οὐσίας τε καὶ βουλῆς καὶ δυνάμεως καὶ δόξης
τοῦ πατρὸς ἀπαρράλλακτον εἰκόνα)." Yet, while the
creed was anti-Marcellan and to that extent represented a criticism of both Julius' council of A.D. 340
and his explanatory letter, it was clearly a move in
the direction of conciliation with the champions of
Nicaea, for it was explicitly anti-Arian--and to that
extent represented the intention of the council of
Nicaea.

The easterners' process of conciliation moved
forward even further in the months following the
Antiochene council. Presumably because of the death
of their leader Eusebius of Constantinople soon after
the council and because of the increased power of
Emperor Constans, who was taking an active interest
in eastern church affairs after having won in battle
the western realms of Constantine II, a deputation of
four eastern bishops arrived at the western court of
Constans in late 341 or early 342.[2] The deputation
was bearing an extremely concilatory confession, the
so-called "fourth" creed of Antioch. It was obviously
designed to demonstrate how anti-Arian the easterners
really were. To quote Gwatkin:

> . . . its form is a close copy of the Nicene
> . . . . Upon the whole it might fairly pass
> for such a revision as Eusebius of Caesarea
> might have been glad to see. On the one side
> it omitted Lucian's controversial clauses
> and dropped the word οὐσία;[3] on the other

---

1. Kelly, Creeds, pp. 270-1.
2. Lietzmann, 3:198-9.
3. The anathemas of Nicaea, we remember, spoke

it left out the offensive reference to the unity of will.[1]

Gone were statements confessing an hierarchically ordered Trinity of three hypostases. And the anathemas against Arianism were phrased considerably more strongly than those in the "second" creed of Antioch, 341: "Those who say that the Son is from nothing or is from another hypostasis and is not from God, and that there was a time when he was not, the Catholic Church knows as aliens."[2] Even though this confession did not insist on a Trinity of three hypostases as a protection against Marcellus, it did have one, but only one, anti-Marcellan clause.

Unfortunately, Constans and the western church would not be conciliated so easily. They insisted on forcing Constantius to agree to a general council to iron out the differences between East and West.[3] It met at Sardica in A.D. 343. The easterners, now led by Acacius of Caesarea and Stephen of Antioch, continued to be interested in rapprochement on doctrinal issues, while they were adamant that Athanasius and Marcellus should not be seated at the council. They argued that seating the two exiles would void the depositions of Tyre, 335 and Constantinople, 336 and, indeed, beg one of the most important questions which Sardica was to discuss.[4] When the bishops of the West resisted them, the easterners left Sardica and retired

---

against "those who assert that the Son of God is of a different hypostasis or essence (οὐσίας)." The "second" creed of Antioch, 341 affirmed precisely that when it spoke of the Son as the ἀπαράλλακτον εἰκόνα of the Father's οὐσία and of Father, Son, and Holy Spirit as three in hypostasis (τῇ ὑποστάσει τρία). The Nicene Creed and the "second" creed of Antioch have been conveniently reproduced in Kelly, Creeds, pp. 215-6 and 268-70.

1. Gwatkin, pp. 123-4.
2. Athanasius, Syn. 25.
3. Athanasius, H. Ar. 15.
4. Hilary of Poitiers, Fr. 3:14.

to Philippopolis. The two portions of the council met separately and mutually excommunicated and deposed their respective leaders.[1] Yet, even at this stage the easterners maintained their conciliatory theological stance, reissuing as they did the "fourth" Antiochene creed; it obviously represented their heartfelt theological convictions. However, to the two anti-Arian anathemas of the "fourth" Antiochene formula the eastern bishops added six new anathemas, five of them directed against their conceptions of Marcellus' position.[2] They were signalling to the West and to Athanasius that while they were not sympathetic to Arianism, neither did they want any part of Marcellus. Regrettably, the West was completely uninterested in docrinal rapprochement. It issued an encyclical[3] which defined Arianism so broadly that nearly every easterner who had ever heard of Origen was considered Arian: not only did it rule as heretical those who believed the Son to be made and secondary to the Father but also those who maintained that

---

1. Philippopolis renewed the depositions of Athanasius and Marcellus and added the names of Julius of Rome, Ossius of Cordova, Protogenes of Sardica, and a number of other western leaders (Hilary of Poitiers, Fr. 1:23-9); Sardica deposed the "intruding" bishops Gregory of Alexandria, Basil of Ancyra, and Quintianus of Gaza, as well as the eastern leaders Stephen of Antioch, Acacius of Caesarea, George of Laodicea, Ursacius of Singidunum, and Valens of Mursa (Athanasius, Apol. Sec. 36, 43, 49; Theodoret, H.E. 2:6).

2. For a discussion of the five anti-Marcellan anathemas, see Kelly, Creeds, p. 276. The anathema against "those who say that there are three gods" was aimed at western worries about the notion of three hypostases set forth in the "second" creed of Antioch but omitted from the "fourth." On the tendency of the council of Sardica (and Athanasius?) to define Arianism itself as adherence to three hypostases, see below.

3. Theodoret, H.E. 2:6.

Father, Son, and Holy Spirit are three hypostases or three essences. In fact, to quote Kelly, it anathematized any "who ascribed to the Logos or Son of God an independent personal existence side by side with the Father."[1] Furthermore, the positive definitions of the encyclical looked to an easterner like barely disguised Marcellan theology. The definitions were: the Father and Son are one and the same in hypostasis and essence; the only difference between them is one of name--the Son is not the Father but his Son, his word, his power, and his wisdom. Sardica's only acknowledgement of eastern worries was its anti-Marcellan statement that "the Son reigns with the Father without end . . . ."

The eastern leaders were understandably bitter about what had transpired at Sardica, yet Constantius' involvement in Persian wars during A.D. 344-350, pressure from Constans in support of Sardica, and an ecclesiastical scandal in Antioch prevented them from doing very much about their feelings. Although some in the East may have wanted to give up their policy of conciliation, the situation precluded such a move; the tension had to be endured. But however distressing the developing differences between East and West were for the church as a whole, it was a period of hope for Aetius, since the scandal in Antioch led to the elevation of his teacher Leontius to the Antiochene episcopate and to Leontius' subsequent offer to Aetius of an ecclesiastical post. On the other hand, the period after Sardica also led to the first conciliar formulation of a clearly identifiable homoiousian theological definition--the Macrostich of A.D. 344. To this development we now turn.

Around Easter A.D. 344 two western bishops arrived in Antioch, accompanied by an imperial magister militum. They brought to Constantius a letter from Sardica, a supporting document from Constans, and Constans' request that Athanasius be reinstated in Alexandria.[2] When one of the bishops

---

1. Kelly, Creeds, p. 277.
2. Athanasius, H. Ar. 20 and Apol. Const. 4; Socrates, H.E. 2:22.

86

retired to his bedroom, he found a prostitute awaiting
him. It was obviously a plot intended to compromise
the cleric's moral reputation, but the prostitute
played her part badly (she was aghast that the bishop
was so old). The plot failed. A full investigation
demanded by the magister militum revealed behind the
affair Bishop Stephen of Antioch, one of the two most
important church leaders of the East (along with
Acacius of Caesarea).[1] The eastern church was disgraced, especially in the eyes of its emperor, Constantius, who invited all exiled supporters of Nicaea--
including Athanasius--to return to their sees.[2]

Though disgraced, the eastern church was not
ready to retire from the ecclesiastical and theological arena. A council was convoked at Antioch in
summer, A.D. 344; it replaced Stephen with the
Lucianist and erstwhile supporter of Arius, presbyter
Leontius of Antioch. This election was surely intended as a signal to Athanasius, Marcellus, and the
West that the East's policy of conciliation did not
mean it had no deep-seated convictions. The see of
Antioch was now occupied by a man with the same
theological background as Eusebius of Constantinople,
Asterius the Sophist, and Arius himself. And the
council composed a most fascinating document intended
for the reading of the West,[3] the so-called Ekthesis
Macrostichos. Although the Macrostich was basically
composed of (1) the "fourth" creed of Antioch, its
two anti-Arian anathemas, and (3) the six additional
anti-Marcellan anathemas appended at Philippopolis,
the eight anathemas were explained at such length
for the West's benefit[4] that the document turned out

---

1. Athanasius, H. Ar. 20; Theodoret, H.E. 2:7-8.
2. Athanasius, H. Ar. 21.
3. It was carried to the western Council of Milan
(A.D. 345) by four bishops, namely, Demophilus, Macedonius, Eudoxius, and Martyrius (Liberius of Rome apud
Hilary of Poitiers, Fr. 5:4).
4. Anathema number 7--which cursed those who say
that the Son is ungenerated--was not separately explained, but it was explicated at great length in explanations number 1 through number 4.

to be more a short theological treatise than a confession of faith.[1] A most complex document, it was resolutely anti-Arian and anti-Marcellan, slightly less resolutely anti-Athanasian, and throughout conciliatory and respectful of western sensibilities, especially in its concluding, ringing declaration of God's unity. A theological position distinctly eastern was articulated.

The intention of the Macrostich's first four explanations was multiple. Explanations numbers 1 and 2 were in the first place meant to convince the West that the eastern bishops were not Arian: the bishops explicitly denied that the Son is "from nothing" and that "there was when he was not." But while these explanations were clearly directed against Arianism, they were also directed against Athanasius, specifically against his argument concerning God's ungeneratedness developed in Orationes Contra Arianos 1:30-34. In order to understand the Macrostich's polemic, we must consider rather carefully the paragraphs in question from Athanasius' Orationes. These paragraphs, as well as the Macrostich's response, are of particular importance for a history of Neo-Arianism: as we shall see, the keystone of Neo-Arian theology was God's ungeneratedness. In Orationes 1:30-34 Athanasius was responding to the early Arians' use of the concept ungenerated (ἀγέννητος). The early Arians asked, wrote Athanasius, whether the Ungenerated were one or two; when church people, committed to monotheism, instinctively answered "one," the Arians would conclude, "thus the Son is one of the generated things," and would add that they were correct in their claim that "he was not before he was generated." Moreover, the Arians were apparently quoting early Christian creedal formulations in their defense, such as "One is the Ungenerated, the Almightly God, and one is the first generate (τὸ προγεννηθέν or τὸ γέννημα) from him, his Image."[2] Athanasius' reaction to the Arian

---

1. The text of the Macrostich was reproduced by Athanasius in Syn. 26.
2. This quotation is a reconstruction based on Athanasius, Ar. 1:31 and Syn. 47 and Clement of

position was twofold: first, he argued against the
Arians on their own ground, and second, he tried to
cut this ground from under them. Arguing in Arian
terms, Athanasius stated that the word ungenerated
could be used in four different ways: the first three
ways were philosophic, the fourth that of Asterius the
Sophist. To Athanasius' mind, 'ungenerated' meant
either (1) what is not yet generated but is able to be
generated, or (2) what is not generated and is not
ever able to be generated,[1] or (3) what exists but has
not been generated from anything and has no father at
all, or (4) what has not been made but always is. If
definition (1) should be taken, there would be many
(πολλά) ungenerateds; if definition (2), there would
be none (οὐδέν). If, however, the Arians should prefer
Asterius' view, then they must be told that the Son as
well as the Father is in this sense ungenerated, for
he always exists but has not been made. In order to
back up this response, Athanasius quoted two passages
from Asterius in which the Arian claimed that God's
Wisdom and Power are ungenerated. Athanasius was
arguing that the famous Cappadocian Arian himself
believed in two ungenerateds. This, of course, was a
total misrepresentation of Asterius' view, for the
Arian distinguished, as we have seen, between God's
Wisdom and Power, which are God's inherent attributes,
and the Son, who is God's creation. Athanasius had
the most difficulty with the third definition. Judging from the way the bishop singled it out in his
De Decretis of ca. A.D. 350,[2] it must have been the
one the Arians used most often. According to this

Alexandria, Strom. 6:7. It was probably a statement
very much like Clement's (ἓν μὲν τὸ ἀγέννητον, ὁ
παντοκράτωρ θεὸς, ἓν δὲ καὶ τὸ προγεννηθὲν δι'οὗ
τὰ πάντα ἐγένετο, καὶ χωρὶς αὐτοῦ ἐγένετο οὐδὲ ἕν)
that the Arians were quoting. When Athanasius reported
the statement, he seems to have changed it somewhat so
that it would sound more favorable to his theological
position.

    1. Definitions numbers 1 and 2 were offered first
by Aristotle in Cael. 11 (280b).

    2. Athanasius, Decr. 29, compare 28.

definition, the ungenerated is that which has not been generated from another. Athanasius' response was that there is in this sense only one ungenerated, but that does not mean that the Son is generated:

> We shall tell them that the ungenerated in this sense is only one, namely the Father; and they will gain nothing by their question [that is, whether the ungenerated is one or two]. For to say that God is in this sense ungenerated does not show that the Son is a generated thing, it being evident from the above proofs [in preceding sequences of the Orationes] that the Word is such as is He who begot him. Therefore, if God be ungenerated, his image is not generated but is an offspring (οὐ γενητὴ, ἀλλὰ γεννημά ἐστιν ἡ τούτου εἰκὼν), which is his Word and his Wisdom. What likeness has the generate to the ungenerated? For if they will have it that the generate is like (ὅμοιον) the ungenerated [a deduction from the Arian admission that the Son is God's image], they are not far from saying that the ungenerated is the image of created things, the end of which is a confusion of the whole subject, an equalling of generate things with the ungenerated . . . .[1]

In other words, Athanasius was arguing that, given the third definition of the term ungenerated, the Father is the only ungenerated, the Son is the Father's offspring and is like him in every way save that he is his offspring, and the generated things of the world are essentially different from both Father and Son. Athanasius was thereby well on his way toward distinguishing between the Greek word for ungenerated spelled with two "ν"s (ἀγέννητος) and the word spelled with one "ν" (ἀγένητος). Before Athanasius made this

---

1. Athanasius, Ar. 1:31 (trans. from NPNF 4:325, slightly altered).

90

distinction the terms were simply identified by Christian authors; in fact, the bishop himself generally confused them.[1] In the passage just quoted, however, Athanasius implied that they differ. Correlative to God as ἀγέννητος is the begotten Son, τὸ γέννημα; correlative to God as ἀγένητος are all generated things, τὰ γένητα. This threefold ontology of God ὁ ἀγέννητος/ἀγένητος, his Son τὸ γέννημα, and his creations τὰ γένητα would later come into its own with the Cappadocian Fathers.[2] So much for Athanasius' attempt to argue on Arian ground. His attempt to cut this ground from under them was introduced by the following words: "When they were no longer allowed to say 'from nothing' and 'he was not before his generation', they hit upon this word 'ungenerated', that, by saying among the simple that the Son was 'generated', they might imply 'from nothing' and 'he once was not', for, in such expressions, generated and created things are implied." But, said Athanasius, while it is permissible to use the term ungenerated in contrast with generated things, it is not permissible to use it in contrast with the Son; in fact, one should employ the scriptural term Father of God rather than the term ungenerated, "for the latter is unscriptural and suspicious." If we return now to the Macrostich, we find that its first two explanations were in direct defiance of Athanasius, even while they rejected the Arian claims that the Son is "from nothing" and "once was not":

---

1. See G.L. Prestige, "ἀγέν[ν]ητος and γεν[ν]ητός and kindred words in Eusebius and the Early Arians," Journal of Theological Studies 24 (1923): 486-96 and "ἀγέν[ν]ητος and Cognate Words in Athanasius," Journal of Theological Studies 34 (1933): 258-65. Only Origen, Methodius, and the author of the Adamantius ever distinguished them, and these did not do so clearly and consistently. See G.L. Prestige, God in Patristic Thought (London, 1956), pp. 51-2.
2. Prestige, "ἀγέν[ν]ητος and Cognate Words in Athanasius," p. 264.

> . . . from God alone do we define him genu-
> inely to be generated. For scripture teaches
> that the ungenerated and unbegun, the Father
> of Christ, is one . . . . We must not con-
> sider the Son to be co-unbegun and co-ungen-
> erated with the Father, for no one can properly
> be called Father or Son of one who is co-
> unbegun and co-ungenerated with him. But
> we acknowledge that the Father who alone is
> unbegun and ungenerated has generated incon-
> ceivably and incomprehensibly to all and
> that the Son has been generated before the
> ages and in no way to be ungenerated like
> the Father, but to have the Father who gen-
> erated him as his beginning, for "the head
> of Christ is God (1 Cor. 11:3)."

This statement yielded nothing at all to Athanasius:
God was conceived more primarily as ungenerated than
as Father, and the former term was used in contrast
with the Son, not only with generated things in
general. More importantly, the statement pointedly
rejected Athanasius' claim that the Son is in one
sense just as ungenerated as is the Father, and did
so in language reminiscent of that used in the early
Arian controversy. Who among the easterners, we may
ask, was responsible for these slaps at Athanasius?
The most likely answer is the new bishop of Antioch,
Leontius. As a Lucianist, he would have been particularly offended by Athanasius' view of the Son's ungeneratedness and by his misrepresentation of Asterius'
position. As the new bishop of the most honored see
represented at the Council of Antioch, 344, he was in
a superb position to act upon his feelings.[1]

---

1. If we are correct in our suggestion that
Leontius was responsible for the strong characterization of God as ungenerated in the Macrostich, this
would explain why Aetius, his student, made the ingeneracy of God the starting point of his thought, a
point to which we shall return later in this chapter.
The only problem with our suggestion regarding Leontius

Explanation number 3 of the Macrostich continued the anti-Athanasian emphasis on God as ungenerated, but it also was designed to state in a way that did not offend western sensibilities the eastern conviction that there are three separate hypostases in the God-head. Instead of "three hypostases," an expression suspect to the West, it substituted "three realities and three persons (τρία πράγματα καὶ τρία πρόσωπα)." The explanation concluded with a strong statement regarding the unity of God, a favorite axiom of the West: "We do not make three gods, since we achknowledge the self-perfect, ungenerated, unbegun, and invisible god to be one and only the God and Father (Jn. 20:17) of the only-begotten, who alone has being from himself and gives it to all others bountifully." Explanation number 4 then indicated that though the Father of Jesus Christ is the one and only ungenerated God, Christ is not an adopted man (the view of Paul of Samosata) but "God before the ages" and "God perfect and true in nature." With this point the Macrostich's direct defiance of Athanasius concluded.

The statement then turned to the second leading easterner vindicated by Sardica, Marcellus of Ancyra, and against him used his disciple Photinus of Sirmium. Photinus was a former Ancyran so Sabellian in his thought that Archibald Robertson could justly dub him "the scandal of Marcellus."[1] Explanation number 5 rejected the notion of Marcellus and Photinus (both of whom were named) that the pre-existent Word is not

---

and the Macrostich is that the document claimed that the ungenerate and unbegun Father "has generated inconceivably and incomprehensibly to all," a notion which runs counter to evidence from Philostorgius cited earlier which had Leontius hold to the conviction that God can be known and comprehended by the human mind (see above, pp. 72-3). Yet, perhaps Leontius, like Eusebius of Nicomedia, limited himself to claiming incomprehensibility only for the beginning of the Son's generation (see above, p. 72).

1. Robertson, p. xxxvi. For a sketch of his positions, see Kidd, 2:96-7.

a separately existing and real Son but the Father's
Word, who becomes Son only at the Incarnation. To
the contrary, the Macrostich affirmed, "Christ has
received no recent dignity, but we have believed him
to be perfect from the first, and like in all things
(ὅμοιον κατὰ πάντα) to the Father." With the expression "like in all things" to define the relationship
of Son to Father, the easterners introduced a formula
which foreshadowed the catchword "like in essence,"
the slogan of the later homoiousian party. But we
must also add that in using the expression, the
Macrostich was making a conciliatory bow in the
direction of Athanasius, for the Alexandrian bishop
used this formula (and related ones, such as "like
in essence" itself) in his <u>Orationes contra Arianos</u>
of A.D. 339 almost to the exclusion of the Nicene
catchword homoousion.[1] Explanations number 6 and 7
concluded the anti-Marcellan, anti-Sabellian remarks
of the Macrostich by claiming (1) that Father, Son,
and Holy Spirit cannot be used of the same reality
and person, and (2) that God's will and choice must
be preserved in the generation of the Son. This last
claim was, of course, also a favorite Arian theme and
may well have been "a covert attack on Athanasius,"
as B.J. Kidd has suggested.[2] But the easterners
quickly recovered and ended their treatise on a
conciliatory note, proclaiming both the Athanasian
doctrine of the Son's likeness to the Father and the
West's favorite doctrine, the unity of God:

> In saying that the Son is in himself and
> both lives and subsists in a manner like
> the Father, we do not separate him from
> the Father, conceiving of space and
> interval between their unity in the man-
> ner of bodies. For we believe that they
> are united with each other without mediation

---

1. See for instance, Athanasius, <u>Ar.</u> 1:40, 2:18,
compare 1:21; 1:52, 2:17, 2:27; 1:20-1, 3:66-7, compare
3:26.
2. Kidd, 2:98.

94

or distance and they exist inseparable, all
the Father embracing the Son, and all the
Son attached and adhering to the Father, and
alone resting on the Father's bosom continually. Believing then in an all-perfect Triad
. . . and calling the Father God and the Son
God, yet we confess in them, not two Gods,
but one dignity of divinity and one exact
harmony of dominion.

Considered as a whole the Macrostich was an attempt
to explain the East's anti-Athanasian and anti-Marcellan
stance while approximating as closely as possible the
West's view of the divinity of Christ and the unity of
God. Except for the modification of "like in all
things" into "like in essence"--which amounted merely
to a clarification justified by the "second" creed of
Antioch, 341[1]--the doctrine of the Macrostich was as
far as the East would go in the direction of Nicaea
until the Neo-Nicene Cappadocian Fathers decided that
they could live even with homoousion.

The West was not satisfied. At a Milanese synod
to which the Macrostich was presented in A.D. 345,
Photinus was declared a heretic, but that was all.
The Macrostich was ignored, and the eastern delegates
were asked both to sign the Nicene creed and to condemn the doctrine of three hypostases. Because this
was impossible, the easterners left the council in
anger.[2] Insult added to injury, Athanasius was received personally by Constantius; he then returned to
Alexandria in A.D. 346, Bishop Gregory of Alexandria
having died.[3] The eastern attempt at conciliation had
failed.

We have now rehearsed those developments of the
flurry of eastern theological activity in the early
A.D. 340s relevant to Neo-Arian history. We may,

---

1. The "second" creed had termed the Son the
"exact image" of the Father's "essence (οὐσία)."
See above, pp. 82-3.
2. See Lietzmann, 3:209 and Kidd, 2:98-9.
3. See Kidd, 2:99,101.

therefore, return to our discussion of Aetius' early biography. It was probably in early A.D. 346, after the Council of Milan had rejected the Macrostich, that Leontius decided to invite Aetius to become an Antiochene deacon.[1] Our sources for this episode and its

---

1. The date is made virtually certain by the chronology of Philostorgius, Book 3. Chapters 1-3 of this book dealt with events of A.D. 339/340 and were followed by a long digression on Theophilus the Ethiopian, later a fervent Neo-Arian devotee (chapters 4-11). After chapter 12, which treated Athanasius' experiences from A.D. 340 to A.D. 346, chapters 13 and 14 turned to Antioch at the time of Aetius' arrival from Alexandria--which, in the light of chapter 12, we may naturally put in A.D. 346, probably early in the year. This dating is supported by the fact that chapters 15-6 launched into a long digression on the early life of Aetius and ended with the narration in chapter 17 of Leontius' offer of the diaconate to Aetius after the former had become bishop (ἐπίσκοπος Ἀντιοχείας καταστάς). Since we know that Leontius assumed the episcopate in A.D. 344, the A.D. 346 date for the diaconate offer is seen to be eminently reasonable. We must mention, however, that our dating is approximately five years different from the traditional one first proposed by LeNain de Tillemont, Mémoires pour Servir a l'Histoire Ecclésiastique (Brussels, 1732), 6:407. Tillemont--who was followed by a myriad of authors (Venables, Hefele, Kidd, Downey, etc.)-- gave A.D. 350 as the date of Leontius' offer of the diaconate, on two grounds: (1) his belief that the Council of Sardica was held in A.D. 347 and that Leontius became bishop soon after in A.D. 348 and (2) the fact that the eastern emperor Constantius was in the West in A.D. 350, which was claimed to be the background of the threat of the Antiochene objectors to Aetius' deaconhood, that is, "to go to the West and make Leontius' intrigues manifest" (Theodoret, H.E. 2:19). But Tillemont's dating of the Council of Sardica is now universally agreed to be inaccurate (see Chadwick, "The Fall of Eustathius of Antioch,"

aftermath are two, the Neo-Arian Philostorgius and
the orthodox Theodoret. Philostorgius introduced
the episode by reporting that an Antiochene ascetic
named Flavian, supported by a large group of monks,
was the first to use the doxology, "Glory be to the
Father and to the Son and to the Holy Spirit." He
was obviously a zealous Nicene adherent (Philostorgius
later noted that he had supported Eustathius in A.D.
326), for the Neo-Arian historian pointed out that the
traditional doxologies in Antioch were either "Glory
be to the Father through the Son in the Holy Spirit"
or "Glory be to the Father in the Son and in the Holy
Spirit," both of which were more supportive of the
Arian position than the Nicene.[1] However, Philostorgius continued, though the Antiochene Arians and
Nicenes differed on doctrine, they communicated "in
prayers, hymns, deliberations, and in nearly all
other things except the mystic sacrifice." This
situation held until the arrival in Antioch of Aetius;
he stirred up differences by persuading "his party
(τὴν ὁμόδοξον συναγωγήν)" to break all bonds of
friendship and intimacy with those holding different
theological opinions.[2] Since this was the first
mention Philostorgius made of Aetius in his history,
he felt compelled to fill in some background and immediately embarked on a lengthy digression into Aetius'
early life.[3] The digression ended with the following
passage: "Leontius, having become bishop of Antioch,

---

p. 32). Moreover, the dating of Leontius' offer to
A.D. 350--after the death of Constans in February of
that year--competely ignored the chronological evidence
of Philostorgius, who did not report the death of
Constans until five chapters after he reported the
elevation of Leontius to the episcopate (see H.E. 3:17
and 3:22). As for Tillemont's remark that Constantius
was in the West in A.D. 350, we may point out that
the emperor involved may just as well have been Constans
as Constantius.

    1.   Philostorgius, H.E. 3:13.
    2.   Ibid., 3:14.
    3.   Ibid., 3:15-6.

selected his pupil for the diaconate and allowed him
to teach ecclesiastical doctrines (τὰ τῆς ἐκκλησίας
. . . δόγματα) in church. He shrank from the work of
the diaconate, but did undertake to teach, and having
remained what he thought was enough time to transmit
the divine learning, he went again to Alexandria, for
Athanasius was already there, being eloquent on behalf
of the homoousion, and it was necessary that someone
oppose him."[1] Clearly we are to understand that it was
after Aetius had been enrolled in the diaconate and had
become an official church teacher that he stirred up
those who were convinced by his teaching, "his party
(τὴν ὁμόδοξον συναγωγήν)," to separate themselves in
every way from Antiochene Nicenes like Flavian. Philostorgius then concluded his account with the following report: "Leontius deposed Flavian and Paulinus,
who later divided between themselves the see of Antioch,
inasmuch as they did not agree with him in their
opinions. These men were followers of Eustathius at
the time he was driven into exile."[2]

     If we turn now to the narrative of this episode
in Theodoret,[3] we find the general outline the same,
though a number of illuminating details have been
added, especially regarding the relationship between
the new bishop of Antioch, Leontius, and the two lay
ascetics, Flavian and Diodore. After having mentioned
the ascent to the Antiochene episcopate of Leontius
and a detail or two about his early life, Theodoret
reported that though the bishop was an Arian, he
always sought to conceal his theological convictions.
The example he gave concerned the fact that the clergy
and people of Antioch were divided on how to recite
the doxology. One group used the conjunction "and,"
whereas another group used "through" of the Son and
"in" of the Holy Spirit. A cautious man, Bishop
Leontius always recited the doxology in silence; all
anyone could ever hear him say was "world without
end." This could be interpreted as a sign that

---

1. Ibid., 3:17.
2. Ibid., 3:18.
3. Theodoret, H.E. 2:19.

Leontius desired harmony in the church if it were not for the fact that the bishop never ordained or encouraged Nicenes; on the other hand, he always gave complete liberty of expression to Arians and even admitted them to the priesthood. The example Theodoret gave was the following:

> At that time also Aetius, the teacher of Eunomius, who spread the blasphemy of Arius by his conceptions, was enrolled in the chorus of deacons. But Flavian and Diodore, who were embracing the ascetic way of life and were fighting openly on behalf of the apostolic doctrines, publicly exposed Leontius' schemes against piety. They said that a man raised in wicked pursuits and contriving to gain celebrity from impiety is to the outrage of the church deemed worthy of the name of the diaconate. And they threatened to withdraw from ecclesiastical communion and to go to the West and make Leontius' intrigues manifest. Afraid of this, Leontius made Aetius cease from his clerical ministry (τῆς λειτουργίας), but he deemed him worthy of other service (τῆς ἄλλης . . . θεραπείας).

Having surrendered to the threats of the lay ascetics Flavian and Diodore, Leontius tried to conciliate them further. Theodoret affirmed that these men were the first in Antioch to divide choirs into two groups so that they could sing the Psalms antiphonally, a practice they followed in celebrations at martyria. In order to soothe the ascetics and to keep the Antiochene church as unified as possible, Leontius did not forbid the practice; rather, he invited Flavian and Diodore to perform this form of worship in the city's churches, a request which the two men honored, though, Theodoret added, "they were perfectly well aware of his evil intent." Theodoret concluded his narrative by returning to his complaint that Leontius appointed only Arians and "unworthy" men to the clericate but passed by the Nicenes and

99

the "virtuous." Antioch was so cowed by the bishop
that "not even those who presented the teachings
(οἱ τὰς διδασκαλίας προσφέροντες)," presumably the
Antiochene catechetists, "had the courage to lay
bare the blasphemy of Leontius."

What is most striking about the narratives of
Philostorgius and Theodoret is that they followed the
same general sequence of events. Both began by reporting the dissension in the Antiochene church over
what form of the doxology ought to be used, both then
turned to the contention caused by Aetius' ordination,
and both ended by speaking about the relationship
between Leontius and Flavian subsequent to the ordination. We may assume this pattern was historical.
The differences between our two sources are directly
attributable to the religious commitments of Philostorgius and Theodoret--Neo-Arian and orthodox
respectively. Theodoret brought Leontius more center
stage than did Philostorgius because he wanted to
show his "heretical" inclinations. Philostorgius, on
the other hand, left the bishop in the wings, no doubt
because he wanted to report neither his hesitation to
express Arian convictions nor his conciliation of
Nicene leaders. Furthermore, Philostorgius argued
that Aetius gave up the diaconate of his own free
will, whereas Theodoret went into great detail to
show that the very opposite was the case, with
Flavian and Diodore leading the attack on him.
Philostorgius conveniently omitted Flavian and Diodore
from this episode, though he did mention Flavian in
the episode immediately following. And Philostorgius
stressed that Aetius, while not functioning as a
deacon, became very successful as a teacher of
ecclesiastical doctrine, a fact that Theodoret dismissed with the remark that Leontius "deemed him
worthy of other service." The next difference
between the two historians concerns the innovations
of Flavian and Diodore. Philostorgius pointed out
that it was Flavian who first introduced to the
Antiochene church the doxology "Glory be to the
Father and to the Son and to the Holy Spirit"; this
innovation led directly to contention with Aetius.
Theodoret, on the other hand, did not claim this

100

doxology was an innovation, omitted mentioning Flavian
in connection with it, and argued that Flavian (along
with Diodore) was the first to introduce to Antioch
not a new doxology but a new form of singing psalms--
an innovation that had nothing to do with doctrine.
Finally, Theodoret made a point of insisting that
Flavian and Diodore were not clerics during the
episcopate of Leontius; he made them out to be lay
ascetics. Philostorgius simply assumed that Flavian,
at least, was a cleric, for he reported that Leontius
deposed him (along with the Eustathian presbyter
Paulinus) after the episode concerning Aetius'
diaconate.

If we make due allowances for the biases and
omissions of our two historians, we are able to reconstruct with some assurance what transpired in
Antioch upon the arrival of Aetius. When Aetius
returned to his native city, Flavian, the leader of
the Nicene faction in the church, was seeking to
consolidate support by introducing a new doxology
which supported Nicene theology better than did
Antioch's traditional doxology. Others in the church,
especially those of more Arian proclivity, were un-
happy with the innovation. Although Bishop Leontius
was unwilling to enter the fray personally and so
simply kept silent during the recitation of the
doxology, he sought to counter the influence of
Flavian by enrolling in the diaconate his former
student and devoted Arian Aetius. Aetius immediately
began to encourage Antiochenes of more or less Arian
inclination to break off fellowship with Flavian's
adherents and, indeed, to oppose them actively.
(Philostorgius' claim that Arian and Nicene at Antioch
during this period did not attend the Eucharist together probably confused Nicenes like Flavian with the
Eustathian followers of Paulinus.[1]) Infuriated by
Aetius' activities, Flavian and his friend Diodore
protested Aetius' enrollment in the diaconate and
threatened Leontius that they would withdraw from
communion and travel to the West to make his intrigues

---

1. See Cavallera, p. 49 n. 2 and Baur, 1:49-50.

against them known. That the bishop was moved by
these threats, as Theodoret claimed, is quite believable, for Emperor Constans was strongly supporting
the western church and its Nicene allegiance during
this post-Sardica period; after the scandal caused by
Bishop Stephen of Antioch, Leontius surely would want
to avoid any further charges and accusations involving
the Antiochene episcopate. Therefore, we may trust
Theodoret's claim that the bishop "made Aetius cease
from his clerical ministry." Later he said that
Leontius "stripped him of the diaconate."[1] Philostorgius' claim that Aetius willingly "shrank from the
work of the diaconate" was surely a lame attempt on
the Neo-Arian historian's part to save face for the
founder of the movement to which he belonged. Having
acceded to Flavian's and Diodore's wishes, Leontius
sought to conciliate them further by inviting them to
perform within Antioch's churches the antiphonal
singing that they promoted among their adherents at
the martyria outside the walls. But while he was
willing to go this far, Leontius was unwilling to
abandon Aetius and, hence, appointed him to "other
service" than clerical service. Surely Philostorgius'
claim is to be believed, that Aetius "undertook to
teach" and "to transmit the divine learning." The
Arian was probably appointed to a catechetical teaching post; this would explain why the other Antiochene
catechetists, as Theodoret said, lacked "the courage
to lay bare the blasphemy of Leontius." However this
may have been, Leontius had worked a compromise which
satisfied both Flavian and Diodore on one side and
Aetius on the other. The bishop realized this was no
mean accomplishment; Sozomen reported that after Flavian and Diodore agreed to perform their antiphonal
singing in the churches, Leontius pointed to his white
head of hair and said, "When this snow melts, there
will be plenty of mud."[2]

---

1. Theodoret, H.E. 2:33. The fact that Socrates
(H.E. 2:37) noted that Bishop Eudoxius of Antioch later
tried to reinvest Aetius with the diaconate supports
Theodoret's view.
2. Sozomen, H.E. 3:20.

The calm in the Antiochene church did not last long. Philostorgius noted that after a time "Leontius deposed Flavian and Paulinus . . . because they did not agree with him in their opinion."[1] And he also implied that Aetius did not remain in his teaching post for more than a short time: "Having remained what he thought was enough time to transmit the divine learning, he went again to Alexandria"--in order to oppose Athanasius, who had returned there in A.D. 346.[2] Although the reasons for these developments were not further explained by the extant fragments of Philostorgius, it seems likely that a council held in Antioch, probably in A.D. 347 or 348, had more than a little to do with them.[3] Sozomen noted that in response to Athanasius' return to Alexandria, thirty bishops met in Antioch and "wrote a letter to all the bishops everywhere, in which they said that Athanasius had returned to his see against the canons of the church, that he had not justified himself in any council, and that he was only supported by some of his own faction; and they exhorted them not to hold communion with him, not to write to him, but to enter into communion with George, who had been ordained to succeed him."[4] Present at the council were a number of old opponents of Athanasius, including Narcissus of Neronias, Theodorus of Heraclea, Eugenius of Nicaea, Patrophilus of Scythopolis, and Menophantus of

---

1. Philostorgius, H.E. 3:18.
2. Ibid., 3:17.
3. See Sozomen, H.E. 4:8. The date of the council is reasonably certain, even though it is usually put after A.D. 350 (for example, by Gummerus, p. 34 n. 1). Sozomen tells us that Constans was still alive and that the council was a response to Athanasius' return to his see of Alexandria. Since Athanasius returned in A.D. 346, a date for the council in the next year or two is probably. This seems supported also by the narrative in Athanasius, H. Ar. 28-30.
4. Sozomen, H.E. 4:8 (trans. from NPNF 2:304, slightly altered).

Ephesus,[1] to whom we may surely add Leontius of
Antioch, George of Laodicea, and Acacius of Caesarea.[2]
The George ordained by the council to replace Athanasius was, like Bishop Gregory who had ruled Alexandria
from A.D. 339 to 346, a Cappadocian; he was the same
George who in A.D. 357 finally succeeded in taking
Athanasius' place in Alexandria. While the council of
A.D. 347/348 did not achieve the ouster of Athanasius,[3]
it must have created in the East in general and Antioch
in particular an atmosphere rather more hostile toward
supporters of Nicaea than the conciliatory atmosphere
of A.D. 344 created by the Macrostich. If we return
now to the two reports in Philostorgius with which we
began this paragraph, perhaps we can account for them.
The fact that Bishop Leontius deposed not only Flavian
but also a cleric named Paulinus for not agreeing with
him is an interesting piece of information, especially
since Philostorgius said of the two men that "they
were followers of Eustathius at the time he was driven
into exile."[4] Surely this Paulinus was the fervent
Nicene priest who led the Eustathian schism after
Eustathius' deposition in A.D. 326. Perhaps the
Council of Antioch produced so uncomfortable an atmosphere in the city for Flavian (nothing was said
about Diodore) that he decided to seek the support of
the schismatic Paulinus. Such a move, added to the
possibility that Flavian and Paulinus, like Apollinarius of Laodicea, may have openly spoken in favor of
Athanasius' return to Alexandria,[5] was all that
Leontius needed. Encouraged by the tone of the Antiochene council, the bishop decided that the time was
ripe to realize the goal which his student Aetius had
earlier sought to achieve, namely, a break in communion with such Nicenes as Flavian.[6] Leontius,

---

1. Ibid.
2. See Athanasius, H. Ar. 28.
3. Sozomen, H.E. 4:8.
4. Philostorgius, H.E. 3:18.
5. See Sozomen, H.E. 6:25.
6. Philostorgius' report of Flavian's and
Paulinus' deposition assumed, of course, the accuracy

furthermore, may not only have acted to depose Flavian and Paulinus but also have been the moving force behind Aetius' decision to return to Alexandria to oppose Athanasius (probably in A.D. 348). He perhaps reasoned that his radical student was a perfect choice to be a thorn in the bishop's side and to organize forces against him. If this suggestion is accurate, Leontius was not disappointed. We learn from Philostorgius that upon Aetius' arrival in Alexandria, the old Arian champions Secundus of Ptolemais and Serras of Paraetonius were so impressed that they tried to ordain him to the episcopate (of what city was not stated).[1] Aetius refused the offer, but on fascinating grounds. Philostorgius said that he declared that the two Arian bishops "did not exercise the priesthood purely, since they were in communion with those who professed the homoousion."[2] In other words, Aetius was seeking to effect in Egypt the same sort of break in communion between Arian and Nicene that he had promoted--and Leontius had finally achieved--in Antioch. Unfortunately, we do not know whether or not Secundus and Serras were persuaded.

Aetius was not only involved in ecclesiastical agitation in Egypt but also spent a good share of his time doing what he had done in Antioch--teaching theology; of course, he did not enjoy episcopal

---

of the Arian historian's presumption that Flavian, like Paulinus, was a cleric and not just a lay ascetic, as Theodoret claimed (H.E. 2:19). Theodoret does seem to us obsessive about his charge that Leontius never ordained Nicenes but only Arians. And he went very much out of his way to state that Flavian (and Diodore) was not a cleric. He probably was unable to believe that one who would later become a "Nicene" bishop of Antioch could have ever served in the ranks of the clergy under an "Arian" like Leontius. But such a phenomenon was not at all uncommon: for example, Apollinarius of Laodicea. See Sozomen, H.E. 6:25.

1. Philostorgius, H.E. 3:19.
2. Ibid.

sanction as he did in Antioch.[1] Whether he had many students or any appreciable effect on the Alexandrian theological climate is unclear; there is no evidence. Yet, we do know one thing about Aetius' teaching career in Alexandria: a student enrolled with him who would become his closest friend and Neo-Arianism's most important leader, save Aetius himself. This young man was Eunomius of Cappadocia. Perhaps influenced or taught by Asterius of Cappadocia or by the future bishop of Alexandria, George of Cappadocia,[2] Eunomius had heard of Aetius' teaching and had travelled to Antioch to study with him. When he arrived, Aetius was already in Alexandria. But Eunomius had an interview with his admirer, Bishop Serras, at the time visiting Antioch, and arranged an introduction. Continuing on to Egypt, the young Cappadocian finally met his hero. According to Philostorgius, "The two men formed an alliance, the one teaching, the other being trained in sacred studies (ὁ δὲ τοῖς ἱεροῖς μαθήμασι συνασκούμενος)."[3] The beginning of Eunomius' study with Aetius is to be dated to sometime within the period A.D. 348-350, seeing that Philostorgius' report of it preceded his narration of the death of Constans, which occurred in February, A.D. 350.

According to the traditional interpretation, the next episode in Aetius' life after his stay in Alexandria was a disputation in which he engaged Basil of Ancyra and Eustathius of Sebaste during the winter of A.D. 351/352, an affair which allegedly led to Aetius' being denounced to Gallus Caesar by the two clerics. This view, represented most notably by the eighteenth century scholar Louis Sebastian LeNain de Tillemont,[4] was based on two chapters of Philostorgius' history, namely, 3:16 and 3:27. The relevant sections read as follows:

Aetius, having engaged in a debate with Basil of Ancyra and Eustathius of Sebaste concerning

---

1. Ibid., 3:20.
2. See below, pp. 146-50.
3. Philostorgius, H.E. 3:20.
4. See Tillemont, 6:408.

the homoousion and having refuted them as
the most foolish of men . . . , became ir-
reconcilably hated by them (3:16).

Basil, Eustathius, and their adherents,
because of hatreds which developed against
Aetius, put together absurd accusations
and spurred Gallus on to believe them, so
that he, trusting the bishops and stirred
to anger, ordered that Aetius be sought out
and both of his legs broken. But since
Leontius, the bishop of Antioch, gave the
Caesar contradictory information, the con-
demnatory decree was lifted. Gallus came
into Aetius' presence not much later and
was judged a friend (3:27).

Tillemont's dating of the debate to the winter of
A.D. 351/352 was dependent both on the fact that
Gallus became Caesar of the East in March, A.D. 351
and on the supposition that Basil of Ancyra held
another debate, this time with Bishop Photinus of
Sirmium, about the same time.[1] There are serious
problems with this reconstruction. First of all,
there is the placement of the reports about the
debate in Philostorgius' narrative. Unless the Neo-
Arian historian had abandoned his usual rule of following chronological order, the debate would have to
be dated to the period before Aetius' elevation to
the diaconate, that is, before A.D. 346. This,
however, is impossible, since Philostorgius in H.E.
3:16 stated that at the time of the debate Eustathius
was bishop of Sebaste, a post he did not hold until
the A.D. 350s.[2] Second, the Basil/Photinus debate,
which Tillemont saw as prototypical to the one with
Aetius, may not have taken place, as Gwatkin has
pointed out, until considerably later than winter
A.D. 351/352.[3] Finally and most importantly, Johannes

_____

1. See Ibid. 6:408 and compare 6:353-4.
2. See Gummerus, p. 44 n. 3.
3. Gwatkin, p. 149 n. 6.

Schladebach argued persuasively in A.D. 1898[1] that
Philostorgius' account of the debate was an anachronistic doublet of a later debate involving precisely
the same three men. This debate was held, according
to Philostorgius, in Constantinople at the end of
A.D. 359. Schladebach suggested that Philostorgius
was motivated to the anachronism by a desire to explain
(a) the hatred which Basil and Eustathius came to have
for Aetius and (b) Gallus' initial antipathy toward
him. On the basis of these three points, I think we
may safely conclude that there is little likelihood
that a debate between Aetius and the two Asia Minor
prelates ever took place. Schladebach was certainly
correct when he wrote "dass der arianische Geschicht-
schreiber durch die Quellen ihre geleitet worden ist."[2]
Yet, however misled by his sources Philostorgius was,
perhaps there were grains of truth in his account. In
order to determine what these may have been, we must
consider a few other accounts which relate to the way
Aetius came to the attention of Gallus Caesar.

The first is that of Gregory of Nyssa, who
claimed as the origin of his information Bishops
Athanasius of Ancyra and George of Laodicea. Having
stated that Aetius did not at first set his hand "to
extraordinary doctrines (τῇ τῶν δογμάτων ἀτοπίᾳ)" but
only later offered such novelties "as a profession for
making a living (τέχνην βίου)," Gregory argued that
Aetius became interested in Arianism for the first
time after he had been successively a slave, a goldsmith, and a medical man. He continued:

> Arius, the fighter against God, having sown
> these evil seeds of tares, of which the fruit
> is the doctrine of the Anomoians, the schools
> of medicine at that time were echoing with
> uproars about this question. So, having
> engaged in study of the issue and having
> observed a syllogistic method of reasoning
> derived from Aristotelian schooling, Aetius

---

1. Schladebach, pp. 14-6.
2. Ibid., p. 15.

was famous for surpassing Arius, the father
of the heresy, in novelty of innovations.
Or rather, having perceived the consequences
of the things put forward by Arius, Aetius
seemed to be a sagacious person and a dis-
coverer of hidden things, since he declared
that that which is created and from nothing
is unlike (ἀνόμοιον) the one who created and
brought him forth from nothing. Now, when
he was tickling with these doctrines the
innovation-roving ears of those craving
these things, the Ethiopian Theophilus became aware of this vaintalking and, since
he was previously acquainted with Gallus,
Aetius crept into the palace through him.[1]

In addition to this report from Gregory of Nyssa, we
have some evidence in the ecclesiastical history of
Sozomen. Sozomen wrote:

Aetius was likewise held in high estimation
among the heterodox; he was dialectician,
apt in syllogism and proficient in disputation, and a diligent student of such forms,
but without art. He reasoned so boldly
concerning the nature of God that many
persons gave him the name of "Atheist".
It is said that he was originally a physician of Antioch in Syria, and that, as he
frequently attended meetings of the churches
and thought over the Sacred Scriptures, he
became acquainted with Gallus, who was then
Caesar, and who honored religion much and
cherished its professors. It seems likely
that, as Aetius obtained the esteem of
Caesar by means of these disputations, he
devoted himself the more assiduously to
these pursuits in order to progress in the
favor of the emperor.[2]

---

1. Gregory of Nyssa, C. Eun. (Jaeger, 1:37-8).
2. Sozomen, H.E. 3:15 (trans. from NPNF 2:295).

109

Finally, there is some pertinent evidence in the
synodical letter of a council held in Ancyra, A.D.
358.[1] The purpose of the gathering was to deal with
the growing threat of the Neo-Arian movement during
the preceding year. This council, the first self-
consciously homoiousian assembly, was called by Basil
of Ancyra; its synodical letter had as its first two
(and only distinguished[2]) signatures those of Basil
and Eustathius of Sebaste. The letter began[3] with a
prayer for ecclesiastical calm after the difficult
events of the previous six decades, enumerated as
follows: the persecutions at the beginning of the
century; the deposition of Marcellus [and his replacement by Basil of Ancyra] in A.D. 336; the definition
of the faith at Antioch, A.D. 341 and its redefinition
at Sardica [that is, Philippopolis], A.D. 343; the
explanations for the West provided by the Macrostich
of A.D. 344; and finally, the council against Photinus
held at Sirmium in A.D. 351. After all this, said
the letter of A.D. 358, "the devil" has not ceased
seeking to "effect apostasy . . . , contriving innovations against the ecclesiastical faith." The letter
continued, "We, hearing formerly that some were run-
ning about at Antioch and also were casting impious
sparks into the souls of the more simple in Alexandria
and, still further, in Lydia or in Asia, [we] were
hoping that the contrived heresy had died out and
the evil had disappeared because of the daring of the
impiety and their great shamelessness, since the
bishops in each place, our fellow-ministers, were
fighting against it."

Of all the evidence we have collected, the most
trustworthy is that from the synodical letter of
Ancyra 358, for surely Gummerus and Schladebach were
right in presuming that Basil was himself primarily
responsible for it.[4] We learn from this letter that

------

1. The letter is preserved by Epiphanius in
Haer. 73:2-11.
2. See Gummerus, p. 66.
3. Epiphanius, Haer. 73:2.
4. Gummerus, p. 66; Schladebach, pp. 21 and 65.

prior to the events of A.D. 357 which led to the Ancyran
council, Basil of Ancyra had already become concerned
about the Neo-Arianism of Aetius. He had been worried
about Neo-Arian activities in three geographical areas:
Antioch, Alexandria, and Lydia/Asia. Since previous
to 357 Aetius was in Alexandria as an active teacher
and agitator only during A.D. 348-351, we may assume
that Basil was closely watching his activities as
early as this period. And that Aetius was already in
the early A.D. 350s teaching his radical form of
Arianism (known later as Anomoianism) was reported by
Gregory of Nyssa, who, as we have seen, argued that
Aetius had formulated his peculiar brand of Arianism
sometime during the reign of Gallus Caesar, that is,
during the period A.D. 351-354. Therefore, it is very
possible that Philostorgius was right in his claim that
Basil of Ancyra (and perhaps also Eustathius) came to
"hate" Aetius and his theological position in the late
340s or early 350s, even if there never was a formal
meeting or debate between the opponents at this time.
Perhaps, then, we ought not to doubt Philostorgius'
claim that Basil and Eustathius were so upset over
Aetius' theology that they denounced him to Gallus
sometime during the early years of the caesar's reign
in the East (A.D. 351/352). At this time Aetius had
presumably returned to Antioch from his stint at
agitating and teaching in Alexandria. Moreover,
Philostorgius' further claim that Bishop Leontius of
Antioch came to Aetius' defense when he was accused
by Basil and Eustathius is also quite believable,
especially in light of their very close association in
the years after A.D. 346. So much, then, of Philostorgius' narrative may be accepted. Perfectly consonant
with this reconstruction are the details about the way
Aetius became a friend of Gallus Caesar added by
Gregory of Nyssa and the ecclesiastical historian
Sozomen. Given Aetius' career as a theological teacher
in Antioch ca. 346/347 and in Alexandria ca. 348-351,
we cannot doubt that Aetius attended church meetings,
studied scripture, and engaged in theological disputations after he returned to Antioch during the early
days of Gallus' reign. And since we know from Philostorgius that Constantius' protégé Theophilus the

111

Ethiopian was known to Gallus Caesar from the beginning of his reign (he was, in fact, the mediator of a treaty of mutual friendship contracted between Constantius and Gallus at the time of the latter's elevation to the purple[1]) and that Theophilus later became a leading Neo-Arian,[2] Gregory of Nyssa was probably right in his statement that Theophilus became entranced with Aetius' theology before Gallus did and was the individual who introduced the theologian to the caesar--perhaps even at a church meeting devoted to theological disputations, as Sozomen claimed.

We conclude, then, that though Aetius did not debate Basil of Ancyra and Eustathius of Sebaste in winter, A.D. 351/352, his activities in Egypt ca A.D. 350/351 were of great concern to the two men. This was because Aetius had begun to articulate a radically Arian theology which ignored the East's anti-Arian movement of the A.D. 340s. If Aetius had been alone in this activity, perhaps Basil and Eustathius would not have been so worried. But it was clear that Aetius' mentor, Bishop Leontius of Antioch, was not only giving moral support to his student but was supporting him ecclesiastically: he deposed the Antiochene anti-Arians Flavian and Paulinus. Furthermore, Arianism was spreading to Basil's and Eustathius' own territory of Asia Minor (that is, to the area of Lydia/Asia). So upset were the two Asia Minor clerics that when Aetius returned to Antioch during the early days of Gallus Caesar's reign, they denounced him to the new eastern ruler, hoping to nip the new Arian offensive in the bud. Unfortunately for them, not only did Bishop Leontius come to Aetius' defense but so did the powerful courtier Theophilus the Ethiopian, who had become bitten by Aetius' Arian bug. The outcome of Basil's and Eustathius' denunciation was exactly the opposite of what they hoped: because of Leontius' and

---

1. Philostorgius, H.E. 4:1.
2. Ibid., 4:8, 5:4, 7:6, 9:3. Philostorgius' belief that Theophilus was an Anomoian already in the A.D. 320s (2:6, compare 3:5) was, of course, anachronistic.

Theophilus' support for Aetius, Caesar Gallus himself
had become intrigued with the Antiochene Arian.

Once introduced to Aetius, Gallus became increasingly impressed with his intellectual abilities as a
theologian. He became so respectful of his capabili-
ties that he sent him repeatedly to meet with his
brother Julian, who at that time was covertly studying
pagan Neo-Platonism in the province of Asia, especially
with philosopher Maximus of Ephesus. Aetius' mission,
according to Philostorgius, was "to recall Julian from
his impiety."[1] Although Aetius, of course, did not
succeed with Julian, Gallus was obviously pleased with
his efforts, for he appointed him to the post of
"teacher of sacred studies."[2] This probably means
that Aetius became Gallus' personal teacher; yet, he
undoubtedly taught others also. Our Antiochene theologian and teacher, now in his early forties, had come
a long way since he was looked upon as a common artisan
by fellow-students when he was studying with Bishop
Paulinus. Now, in the same city of Antioch, he was an
intimate of the Caesar and doubtless more respected in
the court than any of those with whom he had as a youth
engaged in disputations. And he owed all of his success
to the church. For without the education provided him
by such clerics as Paulinus of Antioch, Athanasius of
Anazarbus, Antonius of Tarsus, and Leontius of Antioch,
and without the teaching opportunities given to him by
Bishop Leontius, Aetius would have never made his way
to court. The church allowed the young artisan to
attain the life of an intellectual and served as a
means of upward social mobility. One may also note,
however, that it probably did the former artisan no
harm in his efforts to establish himself with Gallus
that the caesar was himself not exactly of traditional
Greek upper-class stock (his Illyrian army family was
hardly illustrious and socially refined): Gallus did
not personally have the reputation of cultured taste--
to the contrary.

---

1. *Ibid.*, 3:27.
2. *Ibid.*

But with Gallus' career as caesar soon ending in execution at the hands of Constantius' supporters in A.D. 354,[1] Aetius' high position in imperial society also slipped away, though he escaped the extremes of punishment visited upon other members of Gallus' entourage.[2] We know nothing of his whereabouts or activities during the next two years. Perhaps he continued teaching in Antioch under the patronage of Leontius, at least for a portion of the time. Writing at the beginning of A.D. 358, George of Laodicea complained that Aetius' students were being raised to the clericate.[3] These students may have been taught by Aetius during the time he was Gallus' "teacher of sacred studies," that is, from ca. A.D. 352 to A.D. 354 or even while he taught in Antioch ca A.D. 346/347, but it is at least possible that the students about whom George complained were taught by Aetius after Gallus' demise. Among Aetius' students at this period (or during the earlier periods) of his teaching career in Antioch were probably a number of individuals who soon (by A.D. 358/359) became influential bishops in western Asia Minor, namely, Leontius, Theodosius, Euagrius, and Theodolus (in A.D. 358/359 bishops of Tripolis, Philadelphia, Mytilene, and Chaeretapa respectively). These men remained devoted to Aetius and to his theology for some time afterward. However this may be, Aetius does not re-emerge into our full view until the year A.D. 357, when we find him in Alexandria once again, this time, as Gregory of Nyssa wrote, "encouraged, boarded, and lodged" by Athanasius' replacement as bishop of Alexandria, the Cappadocian George.[4]

The eleven year period of Aetius' life we have just traced--from A.D. 346 to A.D. 356--was obviously most eventful and stimulating for him. As a teacher in the two leading intellectual centers of eastern

---

1. See Philostorgius, H.E. 4:1.
2. Gregory of Nyssa, C. Eun. (Jaeger, 1:38). See also Epiphanius, Haer. 76:1 and Theodoret, H.E. 2:23.
3. George of Laodicea apud Sozomen, H.E. 4:13.
4. Gregory of Nyssa, C. Eun. (Jaeger, 1:38).

Christianity--Antioch and Alexandria--and at the court
of Gallus Caesar, Aetius had achieved remarkable personal success. It is, therefore, to be regretted that
we do not have any writings penned by him during this
period. Contrariwise, one would also like to know
Basil's and Eustathius' theological thoughts at this
time. But just as the first edition of Aetius'
Syntagmation, his only extant treatise, was not published until A.D. 359, so the earliest document we
possess from the pens of his homoiousian opponents
was not published until Easter A.D. 358. Our situation, however, while difficult, is not completely
hopeless. To begin with, we recall that Philostorgius
claimed that the reason Aetius was in Alexandria from
ca. A.D. 348 to A.D. 351 was in order to oppose
Athanasius: "Aetius went again back to Alexandria,
where Athanasius was already in high repute and was so
courageously defending the doctrine of homoousion that
it was necessary to find someone to oppose him."[1] We
also recall that Gregory of Nyssa, relying on Bishops
Athanasius of Ancyra (Basil's successor in that see)
and George of Laodicea as his sources, reported that
in the next stage of Aetius' life, that is, during the
reign of Gallus Caesar (A.D. 351-354), Aetius was teaching that "that which is created from nothing is
unlike (ἀνόμοιον) the one who created and brought him
forth."[2] Assuming the accuracy of these reports, one
cannot help but wonder whether there was a direct
connection between Athanasius' championing of homoousion
and Aetius' teaching of anomoion. One's suspicions are
increased by two reports in a writing of Aetius'
opponent, the homoiousion supporter Basil of Ancyra.
In a memorandum published during the summer of A.D. 359
Basil (with George of Laodicea) suggested that Aetius
had been teaching not only unlikeness but unlikeness-
in-essence long before Basil and his supporters ever

---

1. Philostorgius, H.E. 3:17. The pro-Athanasian
phraseology of this quotation--for example, "so
courageously defending"--obviously came from Philostorgius' orthodox epitomizer Photius.
2. Gregory of Nyssa, C. Eun. (Jaeger, 1:37-8).

thought to use the term essence (οὐσία) in homoiousion,
which they were doing certainly as early as A.D. 357[1]
and probably earlier. Basil wrote that the Neo-Arians
were "the first to make mention of essence, saying
unlike-in-essence."[2] More important is a report in an
anti-Neo-Arian document penned in Lent, A.D. 358 by
Basil and Eustathius of Sebaste (who, as we have seen,
denounced Aetius to Gallus Caesar in A.D. 351/352). It
claimed that the Neo-Arian position of unlikeness-in-
essence was originally formulated in opposition to a
Sabellian identification of Father and Son, an identification believed by the East at large to be implied
in homoousion. Anathema #14 of the synodical letter
of the Council of Ancyra, 358 (at which Basil and
Eustathius were the leading bishops) contained the
following words: "If someone . . . should say, fearing lest the Son ever be thought to be the same as
the Father, that the Son is unlike-in-essence
(ἀνόμοιον . . . κατ'οὐσίαν) to the Father, let him be
anathema."[3] All this evidence suggests that Aetius
reacted to Athanasius' championing of homoousion ca.
A.D. 350 by forwarding in response the formula 'unlike-
in-essence'.

In order to test this conclusion, we must consider
carefully the document in which Athanasius publicly
unfurled the theological banner of homoousion ca. A.D.
350, his De Decretis.[4] We begin with some necessary
background. Since A.D. 339, when he wrote his Orationes Contra Arianos, Athanasius had been led to
change his theological strategy rather significantly.
Beginning at the Council of Sardica, A.D. 343, he had
come to recognize that the eastern church leaders were

_____

1. See the pronouncement of the Council of
Sirmium, 357, reproduced in Athanasius, Syn. 28.
2. Epiphanius, Haer. 73:22.
3. Ibid., 73:11.
4. For the date, see Eduard Schwartz, Nachrichten
der Kgl. Gesellschaft der Wissenschaften zu Göttingen,
1904, p. 401 and Opitz, Athanasius Werke, 2:1:2 n. on
lines 15f.

116

intent on supplanting, or at least supplementing, the
Nicene formulary with some other symbol. Therefore,
he had decided that the only proper response was to
back the Nicene creed, together with its homoousion,
wholeheartedly.[1] Doubtless his resolve to follow this
path was intensified by the Macrostich's theological
attack upon him in A.D. 344 and the Council of Antioch's
ecclesiastical attach upon him in A.D. 347/348. So
when he published his De Decretis ca. A.D. 350, he
revealed himself a fervent champion of the Nicene Creed;
gone was the almost total silence of the Orationes
regarding homoousion.

The immediate occasion of the De Decretis (formally
a letter) was discussions held between "advocates of
Arianism" and "Eusebians" on the one side and "those
who maintain the doctrines of the church" on the other
(#1). Since Acacius of Caesarea was named in #3, we
may presume that Athanasius' work was directed primarily against the ecclesiastical and theological circles
to which he belonged, that is, circles which included
Leontius of Antioch, George of Laodicea, Theodorus of
Heraclea, and Narcissus of Neronias.[2] While we do not
know further details about where the discussions took
place or who precisely was involved, Athanasius does
inform us (1) that the "Arians/Eusebians" accused the
Nicene creed of using non-scriptural terms, especially
"from the essence (ἐκ τῆς οὐσίας)" and "homoousion,"
and (2) that the supporters of the Nicene Creed had
written to him asking for an explanation of the
council's transactions (#1-2a). Athanasius' response
was designed to explain why the Nicaean Council came
to use the non-scriptural terms, to defend its theological orientation, and to refute Nicaea's opponents
in the process. He pointed out (#26-5) that when the
Eusebians finally perceived at Nicaea that Arianism
was rejected by the majority, they decided to subscribe
the Nicene Creed. Even Eusebius of Caesarea, who felt
the need to pen a letter to his church explaining his
actions (a copy of which Athanasius appended to his

---

1. Athanasius, Tom. 5.
2. See Athanasius, H. Ar. 28.

117

De Decretis), signed. Why then, Athanasius asked, did
Eusebius' successor in Caesarea, Acacius, feel free to
reject the creed? Granted that the Eusebians later
regretted their subscriptions, wavering with regard to
Nicaea was simply dishonorable. Athanasius then
explicated and refuted the Arian view of the Son (#6-
10). After quoting a collage of early Arian statements
which illustrated the full range of the Arian position,
he asked, "What in fact is a son and what does this
name signify?" Scripture, he answered, used the word
in two senses, an adoptive and a natural sense. Athanasius noted that the Arians accepted the adoptive meaning, which entailed God's bestowing sonship as a gift
for "bettering one's ways." But he did admit that the
Arians claimed that God in his foreknowledge bestowed
"the name and the glory of the name" upon the Monogenes
"at the time of his generation" (#6). It was not,
however, Arian adoptionism that elicited most of
Athanasius' venom. Rather, it was the fact that when
the Arians were pressed to be clear about the way in
which the Son differs from men, they said that he is
superior "because he only was brought into being by the
only God and all other things were created by God
through the Son"; thereby they made the Son a "servant
(ὑπουργός)" and "assistant (βοηθός)" to God (#7-9). To
the explication and refutation of this position Athanasius devoted the lion's share of his section on the
Arian view of the Son. He ended his discussion by
noting that the Arians also argued that the Son of God
is superior to all other things (1) "because he only
partakes of the Father while all other things partake
of the Son" and (2) because he "has come into being
first (πρῶτον γέγονεν)" (#9-10). Athanasius, on the
other hand, maintained that the Monogenes' sonship is
natural (#10-17). His defense of this view included
a strong statement of the doctrine of eternal generation and vigorous responses to accusations that Nicaea
taught (1) material generation and (2) a view contradicting the teaching of Prov. 8:22. Next, pointing
out that both Arianism and the Nicene Creed were,
strictly speaking, unscriptural in their language,
Athanasius developed the view (#18-24) that Nicaea's
"from the essence" and "homoousion" were scriptural

in intent. The Nicene Council, he said, tried to
exclude Arianism by saying that the Son was "like and
precisely similar to the Father in all things" but
found that this was insufficient, since the Eusebians
could explain their way out of it and still remain
Arian. Athanasius ended his sequence by arguing that
one faced an inevitable choice between homoousion (same
in essence) and heteroousion (difference in essence);
the former should not be feared, since it did have a
non-material denotation, popular theological opinion
notwithstanding (#23-24). After quoting from Theognos-
tus of Alexandria, Dionysius of Alexandria, Dionysius
of Rome, and Origen in support of the Nicene position
(#25-27), Athanasius concluded his tract with a lengthy
attack on the opponents of Nicaea's use of the unscriptural term ungenerated as their primary designation of
God (#28-32). Athanasius preferred the term Father.
In light of this analysis, the De Decretis may be
outlined as follows:

    (1)   The Eusebians and the Nicene Creed (#1-5),
    (2)   Arian and Athanasian views of the Son
          (#6-17),
    (3)   The formulas like-in-all-things, homoousion,
          and heterousion (#18-24),
    (4)   Third century Fathers whose positions
          supported Nicaea (#25-27),
    (5)   Against the term ungenerated (#28-32).

Apparently Athanasius' citation of Dionysius of
Alexandria in his De Decretis did not sit well with
some of Athanasius' opponents, for they protested that
Dionysius supported their view rather than Athanasius'.
This led the bishop to pen his De Sententia Dionysii
in defense of his judgment.

    Since the De Decretis was obviously intended to be
polemical, we are bound to ask ourselves against what
it was polemicizing. The answer seems to lie in the
tract's third and fifth sections. Clearly Athanasius
had the Macrostich of A.D. 344 primarily in mind when
he wrote these sections, for the Macrostich endorsed
"likeness in all things" and throughout described God
as ungenerated, the very two claims which sections
three and five rejected. Responding to the Macrostich,
Athanasius argued (1) that the formula of "likeness in

all things" had been considered and rejected at Nicaea
in favor of homoousion and (2) that God should be
termed Father rather than ungenerated. While Athanasius'
second argument was simply a reiteration of one he had
already made in his Orationes of ca. A.D. 339, his
first argument marked an advance, since the Orationes
actually endorsed the formula "likeness in all things."
The details of this advance are particularly interesting. With "likeness in all things" set aside as unable
to exclude Arianism, Athanasius addressed the supposed
anti-Arian circles which produced the Macrostich and
argued (#23-24) that homoousion was the only answer
"so that the Word of God not be mingled with the
essence of the Father as something foreign and unlike
(ξένον καὶ ἀνόμοιον)" and "so that the Word of God not
appear, in some way or wholly, to be different-in-
essence (ἑτεροούσιος)." "For unless he is shown to be
not from God but rather an instrument different-in-
nature and different-in-essence, surely the Council
[of Nicaea] was sound in its doctrine and correct in
its decree." According to Athanasius' position ca.
A.D. 350, a choice between homoousion and heteroousion
was necessary and inevitable.

If we return now to the conclusion suggested by
our evidence from Philostorgius, Gregory of Nyssa, and
Basil of Ancyra, it would seem reasonable to suggest
that Aetius read Athanasius' De Decretis and decided
boldly to emphasize the early Arian doctrine of
unlikeness-in-essence or heteroousion precisely because
Athanasius had rejected it. That this probably was
exactly how it happened is supported by a number of
interesting connections between Aetius' thought and the
arguments of the De Decretis. First of all, as is
evident from Aetius' Syntagmation of A.D. 359, the
Neo-Arian's fundamental justification for his doctrine
of unlikeness and for his opposition to homoousion was
that God is in essence ungenerated, whereas the Son is
in essence generated. To demonstrate this we quote
three of the Syntagmation's syllogisms.[1]

---

1. The translation is basically that of L.R.
Wickham, "The Syntagmation of Aetius the Anomoean,"

#4 If God remains endlessly in ungenerated nature and the generate (τὸ γέννημα) is endlessly generate, then the perverse doctrine of the 'homoousion' . . . will be demolished; incomparability in essence (τὸ ἐν οὐσίᾳ ἀσύγκριτον) is established when each nature abides unceasingly in the proper rank of its nature.

#5 If God is ungenerated in essence, what was generated was not generated by sundering of essence (οὐσίας διαστάσει), but he made it exist as a hypostasis by his power (ἐξουσίᾳ ὑπέστησεν αὐτό). For no reverent reasoning permits the same essence (τὴν αὐτὴν οὐσίαν) to be both generated and ungenerated.

#11 If Almighty God, being of ungenerated nature, does not know himself as of generated nature, but the Son, being of generated nature, knows himself to be what he is, how could the 'homoousion' not be a fallacy, when one knows himself to be ungenerated and the other generated?

Since the doctrines of the Son's unlikeness to God and of God's ingeneracy were explicitly and pointedly polemicized against in sections three and five of Athanasius' De Decretis, it is difficult to avoid the conclusion that Aetius formulated his teaching in response to Athanasius' arguments. But whereas Athanasius did not speak of a link between the two doctrines, Aetius established their logical connection. He began by making the characteristic Neo-Arian assumption that ingeneracy defines God's very essence and generacy the Son's very essence. This assumption seems

Journal of Theological Studies 19 (1968): 545-6, though I have modified it slightly in the interests of literal precision.

to have been based on two early Arian claims and a Middle Platonic view of language. The two early Arian claims are, first, that there is only one ungenerated being, God, and second, that God is comprehensible to the human mind. Although Arius denied the second assertion, it was maintained by Aetius' Lucianist teachers, Antonius and Leontius. The Middle Platonic view is that names used in normal parlance are, in general, revelatory of the essences of the things named. We shall consider this view at some length in our fourth chapter; suffice it to say here that it is crucial to Neo-Arian thought. Aetius reasoned that if God is comprehensible to men and ungeneratedness is the one characteristic differentiating him from all other things, ungeneratedness must be his name. And since names are revelatory of essences, God's essence must be ungenerated. The Son's essential generatedness, of course, is simply a logical deduction, as is the essential generatedness of all othe realities: if human minds can know God's essence, they inevitably can know the essences of all else. Thus, if God is not only ungenerated but essentially so, and the Son not only generated but essentially so, unlikeness in essence naturally follows. In exploiting what seemed to him to be the logical implications of God's ingeneracy, Aetius could congratulate himself on being the defender both of Arianism and of the eastern theological tradition represented by the Macrostich. We conclude, then, that there was a direct connection between Aetius' views and sections three and five of Athanasius' De Decretis. This probably was not the only connection, however, between Aetius' views and the De Decretis. It was most likely Aetius and his students who were the ones that objected to Athanasius' appeal to Dionysius of Alexandria in the fourth section of his tract and thereby caused Athanasius to write his De Sententia Dionysii in defense of his assessment. As far as we know, Aetius' teacher, Athanasius of Anazarbus, was the only early Arian to claim Dionysius as a supporter of the Arian position; Aetius undoubtedly learned this view from his mentor. This brings us to a final connection between Aetius' thought and the De Decretis. We remember that in section two of the De Decretis Athanasius devoted the lion's share of his refutation of the Arian view of the Son to the early Arian notion that the Son alone was created by God and then, in turn, created all other things as God's servant and assistant. Although Aetius' _Syntagmation_ did not mention this notion, undoubtedly because the _Syntagmation_ was concerned with the doctrine of God rather than the doctrine of the Son, it did appear prominently in the _Apologia_ of Eunomius, Aetius' one-time student and secretary. For instance, Eunomius wrote, "We attribute this much superiority to [the Son] as it is necessary for the creator to have over his own creations . . . so that he is the uniquely-generated God (θεὸς μονογενής) of all things which came into being after him and through him. For he only, having been generated and created by the power of the Ungenerated, has become the most perfect servant for all creating and willing of the Father."[1] That Aetius himself maintained this doctrine, despite its absence from the _Syntagmation_, is proven by the anti-Aetian synodical letter of the Council of Ancyra, 358 and Basil of Ancyra's anti-Neo-Arian memorandum of 359. Both took pains to reject the doctrine. We quote from the former: "Whether he [the Son] has come into being as the first because of necessity or whether he has been a servant for the creation of other things, in this way one will not make him external to the concept of created things."[2] Again, probably the reason why Aetius stressed precisely this view of the Son's superiority to other created things was because Athanasius polemicized against it at length in his _De Decretis_. In stressing this view perhaps Aetius saw himself as softening one of the more radical positions he had been taught as a youth, for we have seen that his Lucianist teacher Athanasius of Anazarbus was not very impressed with it. On the other hand, Paulinus, his first Arian mentor, probably was.[3]

---

1. Eunomius, _Apol._ 15, compare 12, 26, and 27.
2. Epiphanius, _Haer._ 73:4, compare 73:10; for Basil of Ancyra's memorandum of A.D. 359, see Epiphanius, _Haer._ 73:13.
3. See above, p. 70.

As much as Aetius may have been inclined to
support any early Arian position explicitly mentioned
by Athanasius, we cannot conclude that he was totally
without discrimination. For example, the notion of the
Son's participation in the Father, an early Arian
doctrine mentioned in the second section of the De
Decretis, not only did not occur in Aetius (or in
Eunomius) but was explicitly rejected by Syntagmation
32. Since, based on God's essential ingeneracy and
the Son's essential generacy, Aetius held to the Son's
unlikeness-in-essence to God, any meaningful doctrine
of participation would have to be rejected by him as
contradictory. Even more significantly, early Arian
adoptionism, which Athanasius also mentioned in the
second section of his De Decretis, found no place in
Aetius' thought or, for that matter, in Eunomius'.
Whereas adoptionist Christology and its accompanying
soteriology of reward for right ethical choice were at
the heart of Arius' thought, they are simply not to be
found in Neo-Arianism. In fact, Aetius took a position
diametrically opposed to Arius'. In his Thalia Arius
wrote, "Like all others, the Logos himself by nature
is changeable (τῇ μὲν φύσει . . . τρεπτὸς), but by his
own free will (τῷ δὲ ἰδίῳ αὐτεξουσίῳ), while he wishes,
he remains good."[1] Aetius, on the other hand, wrote in
his Syntagmation of A.D. 359, "If the generate [i.e.,
the Son] is by nature immutable because of the one who
generated it (ἄτρεπτον τὴν φύσιν . . . διὰ τὸν
γεννήσαντα), then the ungenerated essence is immutable,
not because of will (οὐ διὰ γνώμην) but because of its
essential rank."[2] Here the essential unchangeability
of the Son, an unchangeability willed by God, was used
to prove God's own essential--but unwilled--unchange-
ability! It is difficult to be certain why Aetius did
not develop Arius' adoptionism and soteriology, but
three points, I believe, are relevant. First of all,
he surely detected Arius' own inconsistency on the
issue of the Son's mutability. The only document of

1. Athanasius, Ar. 1:5 and Ep. Aeg. Lib. 12.
2. Syntagmation #15.

Arius directly quoted by a Neo-Arian[1] was one of two in which the Alexandrian presbyter did actually claim that the Son is unchangeable--and unchangeable not because of his own effort of will but because God willed him to be so: "We know one God, alone ungenerated . . . , unchangeable and immutable (ἄτρεπτον καὶ ἀναλλοίωτον) . . . who generated an uniquely-generated Son (γεννήσαντα υἱὸν μονογενῆ) before eternal times, through whom he made the ages and the universe, and generated him not in semblance but in truth, having made him to subsist by his own will as immutable and unchangeable, a perfect created thing but not as one of the created things (ὑποστήσαντα ἰδίῳ θελήματι ἄτρεπτον καὶ ἀναλλοίωτον κτίσμα τοῦ θεοῦ τέλειον, ἀλλ᾽οὐχ ὡς ἕν τῶν κτισμάτων) . . . ."[2] Of course, the phrase, "by his own will," is strictly speaking ambiguous; it can refer to the Son's will, but that is not the natural meaning of the Greek, for the antecedent of the controlling participle (ὑποστήσαντα) is God. Whether this was a bit of Arius' subtlety or not, Aetius followed the natural meaning of the profession of faith rather than the clear adoptionism of the Thalia. We have seen that Aetius had developed into a logically-minded dialectician; apparently he could not abide an inconsistency. But why did he choose to ignore Arius' frequent references to the Son's mutability in favor of two references to his immutability? This brings us to our second and third points. Although it is true that adoptionist Christology and its accompanying soteriology of reward for right ethical choice were prominent in Arius' Thalia and implied in Asterius the Sophist's Syntagmation, they are not to be found either in our extant fragments of Aetius' first teacher Paulinus or in those of his Lucianist mentors Athanasius, Antonius, and Leontius. This lack is, of course, not decisive, for the fragments are so few. On the other hand, one of early Arianism's

---

1. Eunomius quoted Arius' so-called "Profession of Faith" in a fragment usually printed as chapter 28 of his Apologia (PG 30:868B).

2. Athanasius, Syn. 16 and Epiphanius, Haer. 69:7 (Opitz, Urk. 6).

strongest supporters was Eusebius of Caesarea, and it
is well known, to quote J.N.D. Kelly once again, that
Eusebius' "overriding interest is cosmological rather
than soteriological."[1] He particularly expressed this
interest, as we have seen, in strongly endorsing
precisely the same document of Arius (his "profession
of faith") which the Neo-Arians later quoted and which
included Arius' attribution of unchangeability to the
Son.[2] It is quite possible that Eusebius' controlling
cosmological interest was shared by Paulinus and the
three Lucianists. After all, Paulinus was Eusebius'
friend, and Eusebius was the most influential bishop
in the Syrian/Palestinian area where the three Lucianists were clerics: it was he that the Syrian Arian
bishops preferred to fill Paulinus' see of Antioch in
A.D. 327. Perhaps it was simply a natural outgrowth
of Aetius' early Arian associations which led him to
ignore Arius' mutable Son and to focus--as he certainly
always did--on cosmology rather than soteriology.
Finally and perhaps most importantly, our next chapter
will make abundantly plain that Aetius became increasingly concerned in the A.D. 350s about Athanasius' preference for Father/Son language over ungenerated/generated
language to describe the relationship of God and the
Monogenes. To Aetius, such language was "bodily" and
necessarily involved God in "passion" and the Monogenes
in "incompleteness": fathers must undergo passion in
order to beget, and sons must "grow" to maturity.
Because Aetius was horrified by the notion of a passionate God, he logically had also to reject the notion
of a Monogenes who is essentially mutable.[3] It was no
doubt some combination of the three points we have
noted that led Aetius to abandon early Arian adoptionist
soteriology.[4]

---

1. Kelly, Doctrines, p. 225. Compare Berkhof,
passim.
2. See above, pp. 40-1.
3. See below, pp. 237-8.
4. One additional piece of information may be
relevant to Aetius' syllogistic argument that God's
unchangeability can be proven from the Son's

If we now recap what we have discovered about Aetius and the De Decretis of Athanasius, we have found that there is good evidence that Aetius consolidated his doctrine of God's ingeneracy in response to section 5 of Athanasius' treatise, his doctrine of heteroousion in response to section 3, and his doctrine of the Son's relationship to God and to other created things in response to section 2. Since these doctrines formed the heart of Neo-Arian theology, we conclude that the publication of Athanasius' De Decretis affected Aetius profoundly and stimulated him to formulate out of earlier Arian positions to which he had long subscribed the distinctive theological emphases for which Neo-Arianism became famous. Our review of Aetius' early life has shown that he was decidedly a dialectical disputant; the publication of the De Decretis provided him a marvelous opportunity for debate. And in light of Gregory of Nyssa's claim that Aetius was emphasizing the doctrine of unlikeness during the reign of Gallus Caesar, the Neo-Arian theological system was surely being taught very soon after the publication ca. A.D. 350 of the De Decretis. In fact, there is a good chance that the original

---

unchangeability. In his discussion of the (Pseudo) Clementina John Chapman observed that the Neo-Arian editor of the Recognitiones polemicized against an earlier Arian position which maintained that "men have unchangeable bodies, but that God changes as He pleases"; the Neo-Arian editor rejected both the earlier Arian's notion that God is changeable (and hence immortal) and his position that God has a body (Chapman, pp. 26-7). Chapman's observation is illuminating because Aetius' syllogism assumed the Son's unchangeability in an argument concerned with whether or not God is unchangeable. Apparently some early Arians made the same assumption as Aetius, though they drew the opposite conclusion. Aetius, of course, did not maintain that the Son's unchangeability concerned his body. Clearly much work needs to be done on the Neo-Arian dimensions of the (Pseudo) Clementina and their relevance to the movement's history.

versions of a number of the syllogisms contained in
Aetius' Syntagmation of A.D. 359, especially those we
have quoted or alluded to, were formulated in the early
A.D. 350s; the Syntagmation's translator and commentator,
L.R. Wickham, was most likely correct when he admitted
to the "impression that these [the syllogisms of the
Syntagmation] are arguments . . . which the author has
revised and used over a number of years and which he
has now strung together in a series."[1]

---

1. Wickham, p. 550. It is possible that syllogisms #4, 5, and 11 included in Aetius' Syntagmation
of 359 are not the only extant examples of Aetius'
thought in the period A.D. 356 and earlier. Five
fragments from a letter of Aetius to a (otherwise
unknown) tribune named Mazon (included in the Doctrina
Patrum and quoted by G. Bardy in "L'Héritage Littéraire
D'Aetius," Revue D'Histoire Ecclésiastique 24 (1928):
823-4) may also have originated in this period. The
first fragment read, "Athanasius the Egyptian, strug-
gling to prove that the Son is the same in essence as
the Father, ascribed two natures, two wills, and two
activities to him, mischievously ignorant that he
impiously proved him to be at odds with himself, for
every duality is at variance. All those who agree to
homoousion have contracted the same disease as he."
Now, Athanasius had set forth as early as his Orationes
of A.D. 339 a doctrine which virtually asserted two
natures in Christ, but, as we have seen, he did not
champion homoousion with any passion until A.D. 350.
Therefore, Aetius' letter to Mazon surely was written
after 350. How long after is impossible to determine
for sure, but it is quite possible that it was penned
before A.D. 356. The theological contents of the
fragments do not surprise us, except for the constantly
repeated duo θέλησις (or βούλησις)/ἐνεργεία, which were
probably interpolated by the editor (who was attacking
monothelites, see Bardy, "L'Héritage," pp. 825-6).
Aetius' denial of homoousion made his doctrine of
one nature nearly inevitable. The following points
were made in fragments #2-5 (for fragment #1, see
above):

The Aetian position we have just sketched, however, appears to have been not only a response to
Athanasius but also a stimulus to Basil of Ancyra and
Eustathius of Sebaste. As we have seen, their first
reaction to Aetius' teaching was practical rather than
theological: they denounced the Neo-Arian to Gallus
Caesar, hoping that the new ruler would move against
him. When this hope went unrealized, they began to

(#2)   Whereas God is creator by nature, the Son
       is only derivatively so, as Mt. 11:27
       ("For all things have been given to me
       from my Father") and Mt. 28:18 ("All
       authority in heaven and on earth has been
       given to me") implied. Thus, the Son is
       "pathetic" (παθητός).

(#3)   Since the Son is generated and produced, he
       cannot be the same in nature, will, or
       activity as the Father, who is "naturally"
       ungenerated and unproduced. This was vir-
       tually the same argument as the one we have
       already seen in Aetius' syllogism #4.
       However, Aetius' letter to Mazon used
       Jn. 5:19 ("Whatever I see the Father doing,
       similarly I do") and a paraphrase of
       Mk. 14:36 ("For not what I will, Father,
       but if you [will] anything") in support.

(#4)   Since the word became flesh, he became
       composite (σύνθετος) and, thus, "was by
       nature capable of composition." So he
       could not be the same as the Father,
       "who does not accept composition."

(#5)   Because scripture spoke of the Son as
       "single (μόνος)," "his nature" must be
       "one (μία)." "He would never become two
       natures in one, even when he became flesh,
       since he would clearly fail to be the
       single (μόνος) Son in his nature."

Finally, we may note at this point two Aetian fragments
quoted by Anastasius Sinaita (see Bardy, "L'Héritage,"
pp. 826-7 for the texts and a short critical discussion).
The first made about the same point as fragment #1 of

think about formulating an opposing theological position. Until this time the bête noire of the easterners
had been the Sabellian position of Marcellus and
Photinus, a theology they had at last decisively rejected at the Council of Sirmium during the winter of
A.D. 351/352. Now Basil and Eustathius felt they had
to do the same for the radical Arian position of
Aetius if they were to be true to the anti-Arian
stance of Antioch, 341, Philippopolis, 343, and Antioch,
344. Conscious that Athanasius had pointed out in
his De Decretis that the Macrostich's "like in all
things" was impotent as a weapon against Arianism and
had posed the only alternatives as either homoousion
or heteroousion,[1] Basil and Eustathius accepted
Athanasius' attitude toward "like in all things" but
rejected his alternatives as the only viable ones.
The Son, they argued, is neither the same-in-essence
(homoousion) as the Father nor different-in-essence
(heteroousion) but, rather, like-in-essence, that is,
homoiousion. In championing homoiousion, Basil and
Eustathius were, of course, merely reverting to a
theological formula which Athanasius himself had used
in his Orations of ca. A.D. 339.[2] Although Gummerus
rightly remarked that it is impossible to know for sure
when this new formula was first publicly reoffered as

Aetius' letter to Mazon: "The Son of Mary was certainly
not dual-willed, in order that the will of God not war
against the fleshly will, according to the laws of the
Manichaeans." The second fragment, however, attributed
a changeable nature to the Son (τρέπτη πάντως ἡ φύσις),
something Aetius and Eunomius consistently denied, as
we have already noted. I have trouble believing it is
authentic. So we may conclude that it is possible,
though not demonstrable, that the years A.D. 350-356
saw Aetius attacking not only Athanasius' doctrine of
homoousion but also his incipient doctrine of Christ's
two natures. Concern about Nicene or Neo-Nicene doctrines of Christ's two natures was rarely expressed
by the Neo-Arians.

1. Decr. 20 and 23-4.
2. See Athanasius, Ar. 1:20-1, 3:66, compare 3:26.

an alternative by Basil and Eustathius,[1] it could not
have been after _ca_. A.D. 356 nor before _ca_. A.D. 351.
We learn that it was not before _ca_. A.D. 351 from
Basil of Ancyra's and George of Laodicea's memorandum
of A.D. 359: it said to the Neo-Arians, "You were the
first to make mention of the term essence, saying
unlike in essence."[2] We learn that it was not first
used after _ca_. A.D. 356 from the pronouncement of the
so-called Council of Sirmium held in summer, A.D. 357,[3]
which condemned the use of homoousion _and_ homoiousion
because many churchmen were disturbed about them.[4]
Since we must allow some time for this disturbance to
become a problem, homoiousion must have been publicly
current at least by A.D. 356 and may have been so even
earlier. Furthermore, it is also quite possible that
during the first half of the A.D. 350s Basil and Eustathius
not only formulated their homoiousion slogan but also
began to back off the Macrostich's primary designation
of God as ungenerated. While the Council of Sirmium,
351 still employed this designation in six of its
twenty-seven anathemas,[5] the synodical letter of the
homoiousion Council of Ancyra held at Easter-time
A.D. 358 was decidedly wary of the term. Echoing
Athanasius' _De Decretis_ 31 and _Orations_ 1:34, the
synodical letter maintained, "For he [Jesus] did not
say, Baptizing them in the name . . . of the Ungenerated
and the Generated, but in the name of the Father, Son,
and Holy Spirit . . . ."[6] Instead of ungenerated as its

---

1. Gummerus, p. 84.
2. Epiphanius, _Haer_. 73:22.
3. For the date, see Gummerus, pp. 53-4.
4. See Athanasius, _Syn_. 28 for the text.
5. Anathemas numbers 4, 10, 15, 16, 20, and 26.
See the text in Athanasius, _Syn_. 27.
6. See Epiphanius, _Haer_. 73:3, but compare also
73:11, where in anathema number 17 the term ungenerated
was used, without criticism, of the Father. However,
by the time of the publication of Basil of Ancyra's and
George of Laodicea's memorandum of A.D. 359, the
homoiousians had thoroughly rejected the term ungenerated, as we shall see.

fundamental notion of God, the letter argued strenu-
ously, again following Athanasius, for Father. We
shall reserve a fuller discussion of the homoiousion
position for our next chapter. Suffice it to say here
that it seems quite clear that theological hostilities
between Aetius and the so-called Homoiousians were
under way by approximately the middle of the A.D. 350s.
They were soon to break out into full-scale war.

However significant was the increased theological
clarity of the early A.D. 350s brought by the unveiling
of homoousion, heteroousion, and homoiousion as theological banners, the most powerful bishops of the
eastern church--especially the Syrian/Palestinian
church--were less interested in theological advance
than in ecclesiastical politics. Such bishops as
Leontius of Antioch, George of Laodicea, Acacius of
Caesarea, Theodorus of Heraclea, and Narcissus of
Neronias were obsessed with removing Athanasius from
his Alexandrian see.[1] Already as early as the Council
of Antioch in A.D. 347/348 these prelates had been working hard to replace him with George of Cappadocia.
Upon the death of the western emperor Constans in early
A.D. 350 they stepped up their efforts, enlisting in
their project the former students of Arius and now
advisors to Constantius, Valens of Mursa and Ursacius
of Singidunum.[2] To the old ecclesiastical charges the
easterners had against Athanasius they added a new and
decisive one. Because the Alexandrian bishop had received an embassy from Constans' successor, the usurper
Magnentius, Athanasius' opponents were able to accuse
him of treason.[3] Emperor Constantius was turned
solidly against him. At councils held at Arles in
A.D. 353 and at Milan in A.D. 355 Constantius sought
and received the support of most of the western bishops
for his intention to depose the Alexandrian bishop.
Those who would not go along--for example, Paulinus of
Treves, Lucifer of Cagliari, Eusebius of Vercelli, and
Dionysius of Milan--were exiled. Later these were
joined by Hilary of Poitiers, who was banished to
Phrygia. Finally, on 8 February 356 Athanasius was

---

1. Athanasius, H. Ar. 28.
2. Ibid., 29.
3. Ibid., 30 and Apol. Const. 6-13.

forced to leave his see, and exactly a year later, to the month, George of Cappadocia entered the city of Alexandria as its new bishop.[1]

Only after Athanasius was out of the way did the Syrian/Palestinian bishops and their Danubean allies turn their collective attention wholeheartedly to theology. We know about this development from Athanasius' Ad Episcopos Aegypti et Libyae Epistola Encyclica, a letter which was circulated soon after Athanasius left Alexandria in February, A.D. 356. Claiming to be "falsely and unjustifiably accused of being Arians" and eminently "orthodox," Athanasius' opponents met in council and produced a statement of faith which they intended to send to the bishops of Egypt and Libya for subscription (#5). Unfortunately, Athanasius did not describe the exact nature of this creedal statement. But since he did identify, at least roughly, the council's participants and did characterize the creed in general, we may make an educated guess about its identity. After ridiculing his opponents for meeting "every year" (1) to "write about the faith" (clearly the reference was to the eastern councils of Antioch, 341, Philippopolis, 343, Antioch, 344, Antioch, 347/348 and Sirmium, 351) and (2) "to cancel by force the decrees of an uncorrupt, pure, and ecumenical council [that is, Nicaea]," Athanasius offered a list of his opponents (#6-7). The list was long and included the following: George of Laodicea, Leontius of Antioch, Theodorus of Heraclea, Acacius of Caesarea, Patrophilus of Scythopolis, Narcissus of Neronias, Demophilus of Berea, Eudoxius of Germanicia, Ursacius of Mursa, Ursacius of Singidunum, Germinius of Sirmium, Basil of Ancyra, Eustathius of Sebaste, Cecropius of Nicomedia, Auxentius of Milan, Epictetus of Civita Vecchia, and, finally, Athanasius' designated successor as bishop of Alexandria, the Cappadocian George. Perhaps not all of these men were actually present at the council about which Athanasius was concerned in the Ad Episcopos, for

---

1. Athanasius, H. Ar. 31-76. Compare Lietzmann, 3:211-6; Bardy, The Church in the Christian Roman Empire, pp. 168-73; 179-81, and Kidd, 2:120-32.

the Alexandrian exile seems simply to have listed all
the eastern bishops hostile to him, but probably most
were. The council's leaders were undoubtedly George
of Laodicea and Leontius of Antioch: they were listed
first in the Ad Episcopos and were also mentioned by
Athanasius in his Apologia De Fuga of autumn/winter
A.D. 357/358 as particularly opposed to him. Having
enumerated his opponents, Athanasius characterized the
creed promulgated at the council as written with
"phrases out of the scriptures" and in "the language
of the orthodox" (#8). If we consider that Athanasius'
list of opponents included the eastern leaders who
controlled the councils of Philippopolis, 343, Antioch,
344, and Sirmium, 351 and that the creed subscribed at
all these three councils was the scripturally-phrased,
anti-Arian "fourth" creed of Antioch, 341, we may with
some assurance presume that the council of A.D. 356
again issued the same definition.[1] The eastern bishops
obviously assumed that this anti-Arian creed would be
acceptable to the Egyptians and Libyans and could
serve as an instrument for achieving the theological
unity of the entire eastern half of the empire.

Things did not work out as the council's leaders
hoped. When Athanasius heard about the council, he
immediately penned his Ad Episcopos, exhorting the
Egyptian and Libyan bishops to "hold fast" to the
Nicene formula and stand like "the martyrs of old"
for the true faith (#8 and #21-23). The motivation
of the council in seeking the Egyptians' and Libyans'
subscriptions to their creed, he said, was (1) to put
forth Arianism without admiting the name and (2) to
cast a shade over the Council of Nicaea by replacing
its creed with a new one (#5). He warned that the use
of scriptural language was only a disguise for the
eastern bishops' true sentiments, which were revealed
by their continual failure to anathematize Arianism
forcefully (#9-11). It seems many of the Egyptians
and Libyans followed Athanasius and stood by homoousion.
Not only this, but Basil of Ancyra and Eustathius of
Sebaste, who apparently had gone along with the council

---

1. Compare Robertson, p. 222.

of A.D. 356, soon had second thoughts: they began to
promote their own formula of homoiousion, perhaps in
reaction to the Egyptian/Libyan reluctance. These two
developments are suggested by what transpired at the
Council of Sirmium, A.D. 357. In July or August of
357[1] a small number of western bishops who had been
present at the council of 356--that is, Valens,
Ursacius, and Germinius--gathered at Sirmium under the
aegis of Emperor Constantius and issued a Latin pronouncement, which in part read as follows: "Since
many persons are disturbed by questions concerning
substantia, called in Greek οὐσία--that is, to make it
understood more exactly, as to ὁμοούσιον or what is
called ὁμοιούσιον--there ought to be no mention made of
these at all. Nor ought any exposition to be made of
them for the reason that they are not contained in the
divine scriptures and that they are above man's understanding . . . ."[2] This quotation strongly suggests
to us that many of the Egyptians and Libyans responded
to the council of 356 by reasserting homoousion, and
Basil and Eustathius countered by promoting their substitute, homoiousion. The three Danubean bishops, on
the other hand, tried to bar homoousion and homoiousion
and stood firm with the scriptural language championed
by the council of A.D. 356; their position was soon
endorsed, under compulsion, by the exiled Ossius of
Cordova,[3] the president of both the Council of Nicaea
and the Council of Sardica. The Danubean position
would develop into the so-called 'homoian' stance
which finally became 'orthodox' at the Council of
Constantinople held in December of A.D. 359.

---

1. For the date, see Gummerus, pp. 53-4.
2. Hilary of Poitiers, Syn. 11; Athanasius,
Syn. 28.
3. See De Clercq, pp. 474-525. De Clercq's constant assumption that the Danubeans Valens, Ursacius,
and Germanius, who issued the pronouncement of A.D.
357, were Neo-Arians and that the pronouncement itself
was Neo-Arian was a mistake one continuously has to
correct when reading this otherwise fine account of
Ossius' signing of the 357 pronouncement.

136

At precisely the time Egypt was in turmoil over
homoousion and homoiousion and over the violent entrance of George of Cappadocia into Alexandria in
February, 357, we find Aetius once again in the Egyptian capital. Our sources for this visit are three:
Gregory of Nyssa, Epiphanius, and Theodoret. Gregory's
report was the fullest and read as follows: ". . .
when the great Athanasius had been moved by imperial
power from the church of Alexandria, and George of
Tarbasthena was tearing his people apart, Aetius was
an Alexandrian and had his full share of those encouraged, boarded, and lodged by the Cappadocian, for
he was not negligent in his flattery, so that George
(for he also was a Canaanite and, because of this, was
friendly to one of the same race and stock) both was
pleased with him, since he (George) had long been preoccupied with perverted doctrines, and was a windfall
for Aetius, putting his power at his disposal."[1]
Theodoret substantiated this report when he wrote,
"Aetius was he whom Leontius had formerly stripped of
the diaconate, fearing the charges of Flavian and
Diodore, and George, the treacherous bishop of Alexandria, had him as an associate both in his impious
words and his unholy deeds."[2] Finally, at the beginning and end of a long paragraph devoted mainly to a
rehearsal of the money-making enterprises of Bishop
George in Alexandria and to a report about how he was
murdered, Epiphanius wrote that "[the Anomoians] had
as their founder Aetius, a deacon who was promoted
because of his nonsense by George of Alexandria"; he
added that the Alexandrians killed George "on account
of no other reason but because of Aetius, who was
appointed by him a deacon."[3] After Leontius of Antioch
had released Aetius from the diaconate in A.D. 346,
Aetius had never again, as far as we know, been enrolled as a cleric until George reappointed him to this
ecclesiastical rank in A.D. 357. This reappointment
certainly supports Gregory of Nyssa's and Theodoret's

---

1. Gregory of Nyssa, C. Eun. (Jaeger, 1:38-9).
2. Theodoret, H.E. 2:23.
3. Epiphanius, Haer. 76:1.

claims about how close Aetius and George became. Our
sources, however, fail us at a crucial point; they do
not tell us why Aetius had once again decided to go to
Alexandria. Yet, judging from Aetius' activities when
he returned to Antioch toward the end of A.D. 357--that
is, his intense promotion of Neo-Arianism with Antioch's
new bishop, Eudoxius (Leontius apparently had died about
the middle of A.D. 357[1])--we may suggest that Aetius
had gone to Alexandria to convert George to his Neo-
Arian position. Indeed, perhaps Bishop Leontius himself was originally behind this strategy, thinking that
since the creed of the A.D. 356 council had succeeded
only in stirring up talk about homoousion and homoiousion, he might as well promote the theological position
to which he in his heart was committed--Arianism.
However, this may have been, for practical purposes we
are on safe ground in dating to Aetius' Alexandrian
visit of A.D. 357 the foundation of a Neo-Arian ecclesiastical party, for Bishop George of Alexandria
generally supported Aetius and his Neo-Arian associates
for years afterwards.

Particularly interesting about the budding Neo-
Arian party is the fact that its leaders had a great
deal in common with one another socially. It seems
that social bonds among them were every bit as important as were ideological or theological bonds. Take,
for instance, Aetius and George of Cappadocia. Both
began life near the bottom of society. Writing about
George in his oration on Athanasius, Gregory of Nazianzus said that he was "a monster from Cappadocia, born
on our farthest confines, of low birth and lower mind,
whose blood was not perfectly free, but mongrel, as we
know that of mules to be."[2] We would have to categor-
ize this as pure invective[3] were it not for a report
in Ammianus Marcellinus. It claimed that George was

---

1. See Gummerus, p. 54.
2. Gregory of Nazianzus, Or. 21:16 (trans. from
NPNF 7:273).
3. The view of Rosemary Radford Ruether, Gregory
of Nazianzus: Rhetor and Philosopher (Oxford, 1969),
p. 111.

born in a fuller's shop in Epiphania, a town in Cilicia."[1] While it is difficult, though perhaps not impossible, to explain the discrepancy between Gregory and Ammianus concerning the Roman province of George's origin,[2] the two sources agreed that he was of low birth.[3] It is not outside the realm of possibility that George <u>was</u> born of one slave parent and one free in a fuller's shop where his parents worked.

---

1. Ammianus Marcellinus, <u>Res Gestae</u> 22:11:4.
2. Two explanations may be given for the discrepancy. (1) Cappadocia and Cilicia were contiguous; since the location of Epiphania is not certain (see the <u>Classical Map of Asia Minor</u> by W. M. Calder and G. E. Bean, London, 1958), it is possible that the town was situated near the border of the two provinces. Gregory of Nazianzus (<u>Or</u>. 21:16) did say that George was born "on our farthest confines." (2) One of the ten geographical areas into which Cappadocia was divided during early Roman days was called Cilicia. Even though there is no such location as Epiphania known to us within Cappadocia Cilicia, that does not necessarily mean that such a place did not exist. Thus, there may have been a confusion between the province of Cilicia and the Cappadocian district of Cilicia in the "story" which Ammianus reported. On the other hand, Gregory of Nyssa, <u>C. Eun.</u> (Jaeger, 1:38) said that George was "of Tarbasthena." This does not help much, since we know nothing of this location, not even whether it was a village, town, city, or area (see Ruge, "Tarbasthena," in G. Wissowa, W. Kroll, and K. Mittelhaus, <u>Paulys Realencyclopädie der classischen Altertumswissenschaft</u> (Stuttgart, 1894ff), Vol. IV-A, col. 2292).
3. Gillard, p. 27, wrote of George, "There is no doubt, regardless of the circumstances of his birth, that he grew up to be a very well-educated decurion of some means." I have serious doubts whether George ever was a decurion. Gillard, basing himself on Marie-Madeleine Hauser-Meury, <u>Prosopographie zu den Schriften Gregors von Nazianze</u> (Bonn, 1960), p. 82 n. 151, argued that because Athanasius called him a ὑποδέκτης

But not only did Aetius and George have humble
origins in common. They also shared a common acquaint-
anceship with the imperial princes Julian and Gallus.
Whereas Aetius had intercourse with the brothers during
the reign of Gallus in the early A.D. 350s, George had
come to know them in the preceding decade, sometime
during the years A.D. 342 and 347. At this time Julian
and Gallus were living at Macellum,[1] a somewhat isolated imperial estate located near Mt. Argeus, not far
from Cappadocian Caesarea.[2] From two of Julian's
letters written in A.D. 362 we learn that the prince
had borrowed books from George's library to have them
copied;[3] this implies that they were rather intimate
acquaintances. Under what circumstances they came to
know each other is not clear, but perhaps relevant in
this connection is a passage in Gregory of Nazianzus.
Speaking of Julian's and Gallus' stay at Macellum,
Gregory wrote: "They had masters in all branches of
learning, their uncle and sovereign causing them to
be instructed in the complete and regular course of
education; they studied also, and still more exten-
sively, our own kind of philosophy . . . living in
intercourse with the most excellent of men . . . ."[4]
This passage contains two possible solutions to our
problem: George may have been either one of Julian's
secular or one of his clerical masters. If he had been
the former, one would think that Julian would have
mentioned the fact in his letters of A.D. 362, for he

---

and Gregory of Nazianzus called him a ὑποδόχευς,
terms used of active curials or decurions, George must
have been a decurion. I disagree; see my argument
below, pp. 142-4.

1. For the date, see A.F. Norman, Libanius:
Selected Works, Loeb Classical Library (Cambridge,
Massachusetts, 1969), Vol. 1, p. ix n. a.

2. Compare Sozomen, H.E. 5:2 and Julian, Ad
Ath. 271.

3. Julian, Epp. 23 and 38 (Wright's numbering,
Loeb Classical Library edition, which is hereafter
followed).

4. Gregory of Nazianzus, Or. 4:23.

was intensely proud of and interested in his Hellenic education. This leads us to suppose that George was one of Julian's clerical teachers, a conclusion supported by the fact that Julian indicated in both of his letters concerning George's library that it contained a great number of books written by Christians.[1] If this reconstruction is accurate, we might justifiably wonder whether George, a man of humble birth like Aetius, had received his education in the same way as Aetius had, that is, not from Hellenic schools but from Christian clerics, an avenue rather less guarded by upper-class social prejudice and tradition. In any case, we can with assurance conclude that the two men shared an intense devotion to education. If Aetius was particularly fascinated with logic and dialectic, George seems to have been interested in the full spectrum of ancient learning. Julian tells us that his library was "very large and complete," containing "philosophers of every school," books on rhetoric and "many historians, especially, among these, numerous books of all kinds by the Galileans."[2] It must have been an impressive collection to cause the then emperor Julian to demand its confiscation for his personal use after George's murder in A.D. 361.[3] How George was able to collect a library of such excellence and proportions that it would attract the attention of a Roman emperor is unknown to us, but we perhaps should remember that later tradition was unanimous in depicting George as an exceedingly resourceful and enterprising individual. As the report in Ammianus Marcellinus

---

1.   Julian, *Epp.* 23 and 38.
2.   *Ibid.* Despite--or rather because of--his clerical education, George may not have struck the more traditionally trained as very well-educated at all; Gregory of Nazianzus said that he was both "without *paideia*" and "without fluency in conversation" (Gregory of Nazianzus, *Or.* 21:16). Gregory was undoubtedly engaged in invective, but it may well have been justified invective.
3.   Julian, *Epp.* 23 and 38.

put it, " . . . he profited through the ruin of many people."[1]

Ammianus' comment brings us, finally, to a personal characteristic which Aetius and George had in common and which may well have served to attract them to each other, namely, an aggressive ambition. Like Aetius, George was determined to make his way in society. Soon after Julian and Gallus left Macellum in A.D. 347 George got himself chosen by the Synod of Antioch, A.D. 347/348, to be Athanasius' replacement as bishop of Alexandria. But Athanasius was not about to budge from his see.[2] Undeterred from his main ambition, George decided to wait until Athanasius was deposed; in the meanwhile he turned his attention to winning appointment to a non-ecclesiastical, and apparently lucrative, administrative position in Constantinople. If he would have to wait to administer the powerful see of Alexandria, he would try secular administration in the interim--to Athanasius and Gregory of Nazianzus, our sources for this phase of George's life, this meant making some money.[3] Judging from what is known about the administration of the later Roman Empire, they probably were right. George's official post in the capital city is difficult to identify positively. Athanasius said he served as a ὑποδέκτης of "store-houses," whereas Gregory of Nazianzus termed him more specifically a ὑποδοχεύς of "swine-flesh."[4] Even if we translate into the Latin equivalent, susceptor, no such officials are known to us from our sources for the administration of Constantinople--or for Rome, after which the New Rome's administration was patterned.[5] But perhaps we should not expect either Athanasius or Gregory of Nazianzus

---

1. Ammianus Marcellinus, Res Gestae 22:11:4.
2. Sozomen, H.E. 4:8.
3. Athanasius, H. Ar. 75; Gregory of Nazianzus, Or. 21:6.
4. Ibid.
5. Compare Jones, Chapter 18 (Rome and Constantinople) and Lammers, "Susceptor", in Wissowa-Kroll-Mittelhaus, Vol. IX-A, cols. 974-88.

142

to be experts in the technical terms used for admin-
istrators in the capital.[1] Both men were probably
more conversant with provincial municipal administration, where susceptores or ὑποδέκται were to be found.
They were curiales elected by city councils responsible
for collecting levies in kind set by the imperial
government--levies of meat, wine, and barley.[2] We may,
therefore, ask if there was an analogous official in
Constantinople, who may have gone by a different title
from susceptor or ὑποδέκτης but who had special responsibility for the swine collection. There is evidence
that there was, the tribunus fori suarii, a tribune of
the swine-market who had oversight of the complicated
process of supplying free pork to the capital.[3] It is

---

1. If Gregory of Nazianzus, Or. 21:6 was modelled
after Athanasius, H. Ar. 51 and 75, as seems to me
likely, it may be significant that Gregory changed
Athanasius' ὑποδέκτης to the related but less technical
ὑποδοχεύς. Gregory, who lived in Constantinople for a
few years, may have realized that Athanasius' word was
incorrect, though he did not recall the correct title.
2. Jones, pp. 456 and 727.
3. The evidence for the existence of the tribune
in Constantinople is indirect, primarily because our
sources for reconstructing the administration of Constantinople are scanty. But, as A.H.M. Jones pointed
out, "The administration of Constantinople seems to
have been deliberately copied from that of Rome, and,
so far as we can reconstruct it, followed its model
very closely" (Jones, p. 689). The tribunus fori
suarii certainly did exist in Rome (Ibid., pp. 690-1,
702-24), and by analogy most probably existed in
Constantinople; from Codex Theodosianus 8:7:22 of A.D.
426 we know that officials who ranked below the tribune
in Rome, the so-called suarii or hog collectors, also
existed in Constantinople. One minor problem remains.
Gregory of Nazianzus said that George was the "steward
of swine flesh, by means of which the military is fed."
The tribunus fori suarii was, it is true, originally
an officer of the urban cohorts who was detailed for
this special duty (Ibid., p. 691), but the pork was

likely that this was the post in which George served
while he waited for Athanasius to be ejected from
Alexandria and from which he sought to derive as much
personal gain as possible. Yet, Alexandria was still
the goal of George's ambition; soon he left Constantinople and travelled, in Gregory of Nazianzus' words,
"from country to country and city to city,"[1] presumably
seeking to consolidate support for his Alexandrian
ambition. He wound up finally at the Council of Milan
in A.D. 355, from where he was sent by Constantius
the next year to replace Athanasius.[2] His ambition
was not sated even in gaining the Alexandrian see, for
according to Epiphanius he sought to use his ecclesiastical power, as he did his secular power in Constantinople, for personal gain:

> . . . during his so-called episcopacy he dealt
> out much violence to the city and the people,
> expropriating ancestral estates from men . . . .
> He seized and carried off the nitre (sodium
> carbonate), and he contrived to control the
> marshes of papyrus and reed and the salt pools
> and to obtain them for himself, so that every
> shameful deed, right down to the smallest
> detail, was through much contrivance taken
> care of by him for the sake of his profit-
> oriented way of life; as, for instance, he
> contrived to make a certain number of caskets
> for the bodies of the departed, and without
> the things enjoined by him a body of the dead

---

available--free--for all who lived in the imperial
capitals, not just for the resident militia officialis.
(It is unclear whether the supply of the urban cohorts
was the responsibility of the tribune.) A simple
solution to this problem would be to speculate that
government bureaucrats were given priority in the dis-
tribution of the pork, and, therefore, it was particularly associated with them. But there is no
evidence for this.

1. Gregory of Nazianzus, Or. 21:16.
2. Athanasius, H. Ar. 51 and 75.

was not buried, especially of foreigners, not
because of hospitality but, as they said,
because of profit for his livelihood. For
if someone honored a body with funeral rites
by himself, he was in danger. And thus, some
gain was presented to him by each who was
burying a corpse . . . .[1]

George's experience in Constantinople had taught him
how to be an entrepreneur of the first order. It is
quite clear, then, that George, like Aetius, was a
self-made man; therefore, the two men were perhaps
attracted by each other's impressive success. With so
much in common from a social point of view, we can
easily understand why Aetius and George joined forces
in a new ecclesiastical party, the Anomoian party.
     Present with Aetius and George in Alexandria was
Aetius' one-time student Eunomius. Although none of
our primary sources explicitly mentions Eunomius'
presence, we are on solid grounds in assuming it, for
two reasons: first, during and after he had been
educated by Aetius in Alexandria during the late A.D.
340s, Eunomius was Aetius' secretary;[2] second, we know
for certain that when Aetius returned to Antioch after
his stay with George in Alexandria, Eunomius was with
him.[3] Eunomius seems always to have been Aetius' right
hand man: at his teacher's death he became the un-
disputed leader of the Anomoian movement, then called
Eunomianism. But at the present time, in A.D. 357, he
perhaps played another role. His Cappadocian nationality probably made him a valuable asset to Aetius
in the latter's campaign to win over Bishop George to
Neo-Arianism, for George also was a Cappadocian. In
fact, as we shall see directly, Eunomius may well have
known George before he travelled to Alexandria to study
with Aetius ca. A.D. 348-350 and, thus, could have been
doubly valuable. However that may be, in addition to
being of Cappadocian nationality like George, Eunomius

---

1. Epiphanius, Haer. 76:1.
2. Socrates, H.E. 2:35 and 4:7.
3. Philostorgius, H.E. 4:5.

had in common with both George and Aetius low-birth, an intense devotion to education, and a strong ambition to make his way in society. His grandfather, a man named Priscus, appears originally to have worked in a mill as a slave, but because we learn that his son, Eunomius' father, made his living as a farmer from his own small plot of land, we may conclude that the grandfather had been able to find a way to escape slavery.[1] Although Eunomius' father inherited a humble social condition from his ancestors, he also inherited from his father what Friedrich Loofs has termed a "Wissendrang," a "thirst for learning,"[2] for the father supplemented the family income during the winter by teaching children how to read and write.[3] Like Aetius and George before him, Eunomius found that education could be employed as a way to better his lot. His situation was comparable to Aetius' in that his family could not afford to send him to grammar and rhetorical school. Consequently, his parents, to quote Theodore of Mopsuestia, "introduced him into the profession of shorthand writers."[4] According to Gregory of Nyssa, Eunomius' shorthand abilities gained him employment as a secretary to a relative, for whose adolescent boys the young Cappadocian also performed the duty of paedogogue. Unfortunately, Gregory was less than detailed in his descriptions of the next

---

1. Gregory of Nyssa, C. Eun. (Jaeger, 1:33-4 and 39). Theodore of Mopsuestia claimed that Eunomius' ancestors were slaves of Basil of Caesarea's family and that his parents were freed by Basil's family (C. Eun.), text and translation in Vaggione, pp. 94* and 98*). Since Basil's own brother, Gregory, said nothing of this in his account of Eunomius' slave antecedents, Theodore was surely mistaken.

2. Friedrich Loofs, "Eunomius," in Realency-klopädie für protestantlische Theologie und Kirche, ed. by J.J. Herzog and Albert Hauck (Leipzig, 1896), 5:597.

3. Gregory of Nyssa, C. Eun. (Jaeger, 1:39).

4. C. Eun. (text and translation in Vaggione, pp. 94* and 98*).

episodes in Eunomius' life, those which preceded his joining Aetius in Alexandria sometime during the period A.D. 348-350. He wrote:

> . . . being a paedagogue for the boys of the
> man who was boarding him, after a short while
> he advanced to a desire for rhetoric. I pass
> by the things which occurred in the interim,
> both his life in his native land and the
> things in which he was discovered in Constan-
> tinople, and with whom he was discovered.
> And after this, busy "with the military cloak
> and the belt," as they say, when he saw that
> all was of little avail and nothing amassed
> from these exertions were sufficient for his
> desire, he abandoned the rest of the pursuits
> of his life and gave himself up solely to
> admiring Aetius . . . .[1]

At least one thing is clear from this passage, namely, Gregory believed that Eunomius worked in his native Cappadocia not only as a shorthand writer but as a paedagogue. This was contradicted, however, by our other source for Gregory's early life, Theodore of Mopsuestia. Theodore agreed that Eunomius worked as a shorthand writer in Cappadocia but maintained that he was a paedagogue in "a great house" in Constan-tinople, to which city he repaired after his parents' death.[2] Theodore's account was different in other respects also. Clearly referring to Eunomius' days in Cappadocia, Theodore wrote, "In accordance with the custom in force there, he used to go to the church, but got no profit from it, for he did not understand the custom of youth to practice perfection."[3] Gregory said nothing of Eunomius' religious activities in Cappadocia. Furthermore, whereas Theodore did not refer to Eunomius' less than honorable activities and

---

1. Gregory of Nyssa, C. Eun. (Jaeger, 1:39-40).
2. Theodore of Mopsuestia, C. Eun. (Vaggione, pp. 95* and 99*).
3. Ibid. (Vaggione, pp. 94*-5* and 98*-9*).

associations in Constantinople, which Gregory stressed, he did make two additional points not found in Gregory's account.[1] First, having noted that Eunomius developed a taste for grammar and rhetoric while a paedagogue, Theodore claimed that the young man was fired by his employer (for his charges' misconduct, not his own) and driven from Constantinople. Second, Theodore narrated that Eunomius wandered to Antioch, where he first studied with a sophist--tuition-free--and then, because his mentor soon began to demand payment, joined the Neo-Arians Eudoxius and Aetius. If we consider carefully our two sources, we see that they disagreed only on one point, that is, whether Eunomius worked as a paedagogue in Cappadocia. Otherwise, the differing information supplied was not mutually exclusive. Undoubtedly Theodore was right in his contention that Eunomius' paedagogical duties were performed in Constantinople. Gregory's account was internally less consistent. Although he claimed that Eunomius was a paedagogue in Cappadocia, he reserved the young man's development of a "desire for rhetoric" for his stay in Constantinople. And he gave no reason for this desire to develop there. Theodore's report that Eunomius "partook" of his Constantinopolitan charges' "education, and thereupon got a taste of grammatical and rhetorical learning"[2] is far more believable. Moreover, we can readily understand why Gregory would want to twist the facts. He probably knew as well as Theodore of Eunomius' church attendance in Cappadocia, but did not want to admit that the Cappadocian church to which he was so devoted had ever been Eunomius' church. In fact, both Gregory and his older brother Basil said precious little in their abundant writings about the Arian proclivities of the Cappadocian church in the period A.D. 323-362. These proclivities raise for us some interesting possibilities. Though there is no evidence in our meager sources, it is not outside the realm of possibility that a young Cappadocian like Eunomius, who had obvious intellectual gifts, would

---

1. _Ibid._ (Vaggione, pp. 95*-7* and 100*-2*).
2. _Ibid._ (Vaggione, pp. 95* and 99*).

have sought out the famous early Arian Asterius the Sophist. For during the early A.D. 340s not only was Eunomius resident in Cappadocia but so too was Asterius, as advisor to Bishop Dianius of Caesarea (whom the sophist accompanied to the Council of Antioch, 341).[1] Furthermore, even if Eunomius had never come into contact with Asterius, he might well have come into contact with George, the later Neo-Arian bishop of Alexandria. For George too was in Cappadocia during the early A.D. 340s; as we have seen, the cleric was an intimate acquaintance and perhaps teacher of the princes Julian and Gallus sometime during their Cappadocian stay of A.D. 342-347. Indeed, perhaps George is our key to two enigmatic comments made by Gregory of Nyssa in his rehearsal of Eunomius' early life. Gregory chose not to identify the persons in Constantinople whom he termed "those with whom Eunomius was discovered." And he did not explain Eunomius' preoccupation in the city "with the military cloak and belt." Relevant to these comments is the fact that George of Cappadocia, after having been chosen at Antioch, 347/348 to be Athanasius' replacement as bishop of Alexandria, spent the years directly following in a Constantinopolitan governmental post, serving as a _tribunus fori suarii_. Could it have been that when George came to Constantinople after the Antioch synod Eunomius made contact with him? Was it George and his friends "with whom Eunomius was discovered"? This possibility is supported by Gregory's remark that Eunomius was busy in Constantinople "with the military cloak and belt," which probably meant the _militia officialis_; after all, he was a qualified shorthand writer or _notarius_. If our speculations regarding Eunomius and George are at all well founded, it may have been from George that Eunomius learned about Aetius' teaching reputation. George had surely come to know about the Arian at the time of the Synod of Antioch, 347/348. In any case, one thing is certain: Eunomius, like Aetius and George, was devoted to education. Not only did he develop a taste for grammar

---

1. See above, p. 80.

and rhetoric while a paedagogue in Constantinople but
he indulged himself with sophistic study in Antioch,
as Theodore of Mopsuestia narrated. It does not surprise us, therefore, that when lack of finances precluded Eunomius from pursuing his rhetorical education
in Antioch, he followed up on Aetius' teaching reputation and went to study with the Arian theologian/
dialectician in Alexandria, as we noted when we dealt
with Aetius' early biography.[1] Having documented
Eunomius' low birth and devotion to education, it
remains for us, finally, to note that the manner in
which the young man sought to pull himself up by his
own bootstraps through education indicates that he was
an individual possessed of as strong interest in upward
social mobility as were Aetius and George. In fact,
the success of Aetius and George in rising from humble
and even servile beginnings to positions of some prom-
inence through education might well have attracted
Eunomius to them and have continually served as his
encouragement.

Now that they had won over George to Neo-Arianism
in A.D. 357, Aetius and Eunomius must have been most
distressed to learn of Bishop Leontius' death toward
the end of the year. Undoubtedly concerned that support for their position could quickly evaporate if the
new prelate of Antioch could not be won over to their
way of thinking, Aetius and his secretary immediately
returned to the Syrian capital. When they found as
Antioch's new bishop the former prelate of Germaniceia,
Eudoxius, their concern must have deepened. Although
the fifth century historians Sozomen and Theodoret
claimed that Eudoxius had been a supporter of Aetius
before he became bishop of Antioch,[2] the rest of our
evidence points in a different direction. During the
A.D. 340s Eudoxius had been in the mainstream of the
eastern theological movement which was seeking to
conciliate the West, a mainstream represented by the
councils of Antioch, 341, Philippopolis, 343, and
Antioch, 344 (at which he was present). Eudoxius was,

---

1. See above, p. 106.
2. Sozomen, H.E. 4:12; Theodoret, H.E. 2:23.

in fact, one of the eastern bishops given the responsibility of carrying the Macrostich Creed to the
western council of Milan in A.D. 345.[1] Then, if we
may believe Philostorgius, Eudoxius was somehow led by
the writings of Asterius the Sophist to sympathize
with the homoiousion position of Basil of Ancyra and
Eustathius of Sebaste,[2] presumably in the early A.D.
350s. His homoiousian sympathies, it is true, did not
last long, for he began to back away from the Homoiousians in A.D. 356, when he endorsed the scriptural creed
of that year's council of Antioch. Moreover, he
actively turned against the Homoiousians when, if
Gummerus was right, he participated in the Council of
Sirmium which outlawed the homoiousion.[3] Despite this,
Aetius and Eunomius had every reason to be suspicious
of him. After all, the Sirmium pronouncement of A.D.
357 had not only prohibited homoiousion and homoousion
but also the very term essence (οὐσία) itself, a term
fundamental to the Neo-Arian claim of heteroousion.
Faced with such a man as Leontius' successor, Aetius
and Eunomius began immediately upon their arrival in
Antioch to try to convert him. Their success was, at
first, limited. Though Eudoxius was prepared to
enlist Eunomius in the Antiochene diaconate, he was
hesitant about defining his theological position too
precisely. As Philostorgius phrased it, "Eudoxius
selected Eunomius for the diaconate, but Eunomius would
not accept the ministry until Eudoxius rose to a higher
degree of precision in his [theological] opinion."[4]
To the Neo-Arians' distress, the first council which
Eudoxius held in Antioch--in early A.D. 358--endorsed
the pronouncement of Sirmium, 357, and sent a letter to
the Danubean bishops (Valens, Ursacius, and Germanius)
thanking them for their efforts at Sirmium (the letter

---

1. See Friedrich Loofs, "Eudoxius," in Realencyklopädie für protestantische Theologie und
Kirche, 5:578.

2. Philostorgius, H.E. 4:4.

3. Gummerus, p. 55.

4. Philostorgius, H.E. 4:5.

151

particularly thanked them for their success in winning
the approval of the old Nicene champion Ossius of
Cordova for their pronouncement).[1] Surely Aetius and
Eunomius could not have helped being concerned that
Eudoxius had become so influenced by the "scriptural"
movement represented by Antioch, 356 and Sirmium,
357 that he was beyond conversion to their position.
On the other hand, there was at least a glimmer of
hope. If we may believe the historian Socrates,[2]
Eudoxius did agree to reinvest Aetius with the Antiochene diaconate he had lost under Leontius; presumably
the bishop brought up Aetius' case at the A.D. 358
Antiochene council. Although Eudoxius had good grounds
for his move, since Aetius was one of George's deacons
in Alexandria, the council would not go along; there
simply was too much opposition to Aetius in the Syrian/
Palestinian area.[3] Finally, as Easter, A.D. 358
approached, Aetius and Eunomius became more and more
successful with Eudoxius. We learn from George of
Laodicea that numerous students of Aetius were admitted
to the Antiochene clergy[4] and from the historian
Sozomen that many Antiochenes opposed to Aetius were
excommunicated.[5] Aetius himself was especially
honored.[6] As was the case with the Neo-Arians and
George of Alexandria, we may add, social factors perhaps played a significant role in the Neo-Arians'
"conversion" of Eudoxius. These factors were two.
First, Eudoxius had been at court in the West at the
time George was sent by Constantius to Alexandria,[7]
and, since both Eudoxius and George were from the
Cappadocian region,[8] they probably knew each other.

---

1. Sozomen, _H.E._ 4:12.
2. Socrates, _H.E._ 2:37.
3. _Ibid._
4. George of Laodicea _apud_ Sozomen, _H.E._ 4:13.
5. Sozomen, _H.E._ 4:13.
6. George of Laodicea _apud_ Sozomen, _H.E._ 4:13.
7. See Loofs, "Eudoxius," in _Realencyklopädie für protestantische Theologie und Kirche_, 5:578.
8. Eudoxius was from the greater Cappadocian town of Arabissus (Philostorgius, _H.E._ 4:4).

George's recommendation must have been a strong card
for Aetius to play to the new Antiochene bishop.
Second, not only was Aetius' patron, George, a Cappadocian countryman of Eudoxius but so was his secretary
and former student Eunomius. Such regional and personal connections certainly could not have hurt the Neo-
Arians' cause and conceivably could have helped a great
deal.[1] With Eudoxius' newly-acquired allegiance to the
Anomoian banner, Aetius and Eunomius had succeeded in
winning over the two most powerful sees of the Orient
to their budding ecclesiastical party, that is, Alexandria and Antioch. One wonders if it would have been
possible had George, Eudoxius, and Eunomius not shared
common Cappadocian origin and had Aetius, Eunomius,
and George not shared a common social class background.

Once consolidated, the Neo-Arian party immediately
stirred up stiff opposition, especially in Syria.
Eudoxius' honoring of Aetius, his elevation of Aetius'
students to the Antiochene clergy, and his excommunication of those who protested these developments caused
many of the protesters to leave Antioch and complain to
the neighboring bishops.[2] Their complaints fell on
receptive ears, for Eudoxius' translation from Germaniceia to Antioch was not widely supported by the
Syrian prelates, mainly because Eudoxius had more or
less simply appropriated the Antiochene see. Socrates
and Sozomen wrote[3] that when Eudoxius heard the news
of Leontius' death in A.D. 357, he was with Emperor
Constantius in the West. Representing to the emperor
that his see of Germaniceia needed attention and receiving his permission to return, Eudoxius travelled
not to Germaniceia but rather to Antioch, where he
installed himself as bishop with the claim that it was

---

1. Whether or not Eudoxius also shared a similar
social and educational past with Aetius and Eunomius
is impossible to determine; our sources fail to
provide us with pertinent information about such
matters.
2. See Sozomen, H.E. 4:13 (at the beginning) and
4:14 (at the end).
3. Sozomen, H.E. 4:12; Socrates, H.E. 2:37.

the emperor's will.[1] The bishops of Syria, especially the powerful prelates George of Laodicea and Mark of Arethusa, were not even consulted. When the Antiochene excommunicates complained to George both about the Neo-Arians' success with Eudoxius and about their own plights, George immediately took action. Knowing that Aetius' old opponent Basil of Ancyra had called a council to meet at Ancyra (in order to consecrate a church), he penned a letter to be delivered to the assembled bishops by the excommunicates.[2] He obviously intended to encourage the Homoiousians to enter the fray against Eudoxius and the Neo-Arians. The letter-- addressed to Macedonius of Constantinople, Basil of Ancyra, Cecropius of Nicomedia, and Eugenius of Nicea-- read as follows:

> The shipwreck of Aetius has laid hold of
> nearly the entire city of the Antiochenes.
> For Eudoxius, having laid hold of all the
> students of infamous Aetius, students whom
> you do not respect, has promoted them into
> the clergy, and he holds the heretic Aetius
> among those he specially honors. Now then,
> lay hold of this great city, lest the whole
> world also be swept away by its shipwreck.
> Gather together as many bishops you are able
> and demand subscription from other bishops
> so that Eudoxius will eject Aetius from the
> Antiochene church and will expel his students
> who have been appointed to the ranks of the
> clergy. For if he persists in invoking with
> Aetius dissimilarity (ἀνόμοιον) and in pre-
> ferring those who dare to say this to those
> who do not say it, the city of the Anti-
> ochenes, as I have already said, is lost
> to you.

George's letter was a most important document, not the least because it passed over the Syrian bishops'

---

1. Compare Sozomen, H.E. 4:14.
2. Ibid., 4:13.

canonical objections to Eudoxius' episcopacy and concentrated on urging the bishops of Asia Minor to theological combat. Its reception in Ancyra marked the beginning of a theological war between the Neo-Arians and the Homoiousians. It would not end until the two parties destroyed each other during the fall and winter of A.D. 359/360, thereby giving ultimate theological victory to the Danubean bishops and their preference for strict scriptural language in Christendom's creeds.

The Neo-Arians in Antioch were deeply concerned both about George's letter and the Ancyran council, for they quickly dispatched a zealous Aetian presbyter named Asphalius to the imperial court at Sirmium with the mission of eliciting from the emperor a letter of approval for Eudoxius' activities in Antioch.[1] Eudoxius recognized that with the Syrian and Asia Minor bishops against him, only imperial ratification of the legitimacy of his episcopacy could save the situation. Given his familiarity with the imperial court, he probably had high hopes. Asphalius nearly succeeded in his mission; he had the desired letter in hand when Constantius suddenly rescinded it.[2] The cause of the recision was a deputation from the Lenten Council of Ancyra, 358. The council had taken George of Laodicea's warning to heart and, under the leadership of Aetius' long-time enemies Basil of Ancyra and Eustathius of Sebaste, had produced a synodical letter--apparently the work primarily of Basil--which contained a blistering attack on Neo-Arian theology, as well as one of the first detailed statements of the homoiousian position. A fascinating and revealing document, the synodical letter demands close attention. It not only forms indispensible background for understanding Aetius' Syntagmation of A.D. 359 and Eunomius' Apologia of A.D. 359 but also is an excellent source for determining the kinds of claims the Neo-Arians were making in the years immediately preceding A.D. 358.

---

1. Ibid.
2. Ibid.

The letter--preserved in full for us in Epiphanius, _Haer_. 73:2-11--was divided into three parts: an historical introduction and solicitation of subscriptions (73:2), an exposition of homoiousian doctrine (73:3-9), and a series of nineteen anathemas (73:10-11). The historical introduction reveals to us that the council saw itself (1) as representative of the mainstream of the eastern church, claiming as its ancestors the great eastern councils held between Constantinople, 336 and Sirmium, 351, and (2) as supportive of Constantius' policy of theological unity for the empire. Strikingly, the scripturally-oriented Council of Antioch, 356, which undoubtedly also claimed to be the legitimate successor of the earlier eastern councils, was not mentioned, and the equally scripturally-oriented pronouncement of Sirmium, 357 was negatively alluded to. Though Ancyra, 358 was primarily against Neo-Arianism, it was also decidedly suspicious of the churchmen present at Antioch, 356 who remained satisfied with the "fourth" creed of Antioch, 341, and it totally opposed the Danubeans' outlawing of theological test-words compounded of οὐσία. The task which the council set for itself was to steer a middle course between the extremes of Neo-Arianism and Marcellan Sabellianism, but without limiting itself to vague scriptural language. This goal controlled both the anathemas, which alternately opposed the Neo-Arians and Marcellus, and the historical introduction. We learn from the introduction that the council's participants (primarily, of course, Basil and Eustathius) had been concerned during the years A.D. 336 to A.D. 351 with the theology of Marcellus and Photinus (whom the introduction mentioned by name) but, beginning with the late A.D. 340s, had become increasingly worried about the Arianism taught by Aetius. Especially in light of Aetius' success with George in Alexandria and Eudoxius in Antioch, Basil and Eustathius felt the need to balance the East's strong anti-Marcellan stance with an equally strong anti-Neo-Arian stance. So the introduction to the synodical letter represented the letter's contents as an attempt "to articulate precisely the faith in the holy Trinity of the Catholic Church" and requested subscriptions "in order that those daring to introduce the same impiety [that is, Neo-Arianism] . . . either will be shamed into being restored to right thinking or, continuing in their impiety , will be banished from the church." Interestingly, the Ancyran council was fully aware that its statement of the faith contained innovations, but it justified these by an appeal to the Holy Spirit: "we enjoin a policy of innovation only as the Spirit permits."

When we turn from the historical introduction to the synodical letter's exposition of homoiousian doctrine, we are met immediately with a most striking and pregnant passage:

> Our faith is in Father, Son, and Holy Spirit. For thus our Lord Jesus Christ taught his disciples, saying, "Go and teach all nations, baptizing them in the name of the Father and of the Son and of the Holy Spirit (Mt. 28:19)." Therefore, as those born again into this faith we ought to think piously the concepts which arise from the names (τὰς ἐκ τῶν ὀνομάτων ἐννοίας). For he did not say, "baptizing them in the name of the fleshless and the enfleshed or the immortal and the one who has received the trial of death or the ungenerated and the generated," but "in the name of the Father and the Son and the Holy Spirit," in order that, listening to the natural meanings of the names (ἵνα ὀνομάτων προσακούοντες ἀπὸ τῶν φυσικῶν), we may think that the Father is the cause (αἴτιον) of an essence like him, and, hearing the name of the Son, we may think that the Son is like the Father, of whom he is the son. (73:3)

Three dimensions of this passage demand explication: (1) its relationship to similar statements in Athanasius, (2) its revelations about Neo-Arian thought and practice in the period prior to the Ancyran council, and (3) its forthright raising of the issue of theological language, an issue destined to be debated for years by Neo-Arians and their opponents.

157

First, the passage's relationship to the work of
Athanasius. Quite obviously the bishops at Ancyra
were impressed with the Alexandrian's theology, for
their introductory theological statement was clearly
modelled on Athanasius' Orationes 1:34 and De Decretis
31, both of which attacked an emphasis on the
ungenerated/generated distinction as follows:

> 'Ungenerated' is a word of the Greeks who do
> not know the Son, but 'Father' has been known
> and graciously given by our Lord . . . .
> When he teaches us to pray, he does not say,
> "When you pray, say, 'God ungenerated',"
> but rather, "When you pray, say, 'Our Father,
> who art in heaven'." It was his will that
> the summary of our faith should have the
> same bearing, having commanded us to be bap-
> tized not into the name of ungenerated and
> generated, not into the name of the creator
> and the created, but into the name of the
> Father, the Son, and the Holy Spirit . . . .

In the Orationes Athanasius employed this argument
against the early Arians' use of the ungenerated/
generated distinction, whereas in the De Decretis he
repeated it as part of an attack on the distinction's
use in the Macrostich. The synodical letter of Ancyra
did not simply offer the argument a third time but
rather adapted and corrected it; the Ancyran bishops
were impressed with Athanasius, but not uncritically
so. Focusing on the baptismal formula, they excised
from their polemic the creator/created distinction
(which they then took up in the next paragraph of
their letter) and substituted polemics against distinctions between the fleshless and the enfleshed and
between the immortal and 'him who has received the
trial of death'.
  This brings us to the second dimension of the
synodical letter's opening theological statement,
namely, what it tells us about Neo-Arian thought and
practice prior to the Ancyran council. No doubt the
reason why the Ancyran bishops polemicized against
the fleshless/enfleshed distinction and the

immortal/mortal distinction was because they were being
employed by Aetius and the Neo-Arians. That they were
considered very important by the Neo-Arians is proven
by the following fragment from Eunomius' Apologia
Apologiae of A.D. 378: "If he [Basil of Caesarea] is
able to show that the God above all things, who is unapproachable light, having come in flesh or being able
to come, came under an authority, obeyed commands, was
governed by human laws, and bore the cross, let light
[God, the unapproachable light] be said to be equal to
light [the Son, the true light of the world]."[1] The
Neo-Arians were always exceedingly concerned to avoid
any suggestion that God had intimate contact with the
bodily world; Eunomius even went so far as to say the
Son "actively carried out the things which belong to
love of humanity" but God "remained inactive
(ἀνενέργητον) with respect to such grace."[2] Why were
the Neo-Arians stressing the distinction between the
fleshless and immortal God and the enfleshed and
mortal Lord in the middle and early A.D. 350s? Perhaps the most promising place to look for an answer
is in the sections of Athanasius' De Decretis which
first stimulated Aetius to stress the ungenerated/
generated distinction, a distinction which our passage
from the Ancyran letter also attacked. We are not
disappointed. In the sections where Athanasius argued
against ungenerated as theology's primary term for
God (that is, sections 28-32), he argued for the
primacy of the term Father; rejecting ungenerated/
generated language, Athanasius defended his preference
for Father/Son language. Most likely Aetius' formulation of a sharp distinction between the fleshless,
immortal God of Christianity and its enfleshed, dying
Lord was part of his reaction against Athanasius'
Father/Son language. We know the Neo-Arian feared
this language. Proof is in a passage of the Ancyran
letter itself, a passage which went so far as to
reveal Aetius' motives for being uneasy about the
language: "But if, fearing, because of the suspicion

---

1. Jaeger, 1:301, par. 29.
2. Ibid., 1:303, par. 36.

of passions which are found in bodily fathers, lest
the bodiless one who has begotten suffer some passion
or lest that which is begotten be imperfect, and being
wary about the things that happen to both the bodily
Father and the bodily Son, (if because of this) one
should take away the genuine concept of Father and Son,
he would say he is another sort of created thing and
will never say that the Son is a son (73:4)." So
then, Aetius seems to have been afraid that if God
should be construed as in any way the literal father
of one who bore flesh and endured bodily death on the
cross, one would be forced to admit that God, too,
was bodily and, hence, passionate. Consequently, he
posited a radical distinction between the Ungenerated's
fleshless and immortal mode of being and the Generated's
mode of being, which included incarnation and bodily
death. In other words, the Neo-Arians' fleshless/
enfleshed and immortal/mortal distinctions were probably
intended (1) to supplement and sharpen the major
distinction they made between the ungenerated God and
the generated Lord and (2) to turn the edge against
Athanasius' rather literally construed Father/Son
language. The only question that remains is whether
or not Neo-Arian clerics actually ever baptized
persons, to quote the Ancyran letter, "in the name of
the fleshless and the enfleshed or the immortal and
the one who has received the trial of death or the
ungenerated and the generated." Because these words
in the Ancyran letter were patterned after words
written in A.D. 339 and A.D. 350 by Athanasius, such
a possibility would seem remote. But, curiously, we
learn from Philostorgius that later on in Neo-Arian
history Aetius' student and successor Eunomius did
not baptize persons three times but only once, into
the death of the Lord, presumably following Rom. 6:3.[1]
Thus, it is not impossible that Neo-Arian clerics
already in the A.D. 350s were using a baptismal rite
which featured baptism into the enfleshed, dying,
generated Lord, and thereby were opposing Athanasius
not only in the realm of theological thought but also

---

1. Philostorgius, H.E. 10:4.

in that of liturgical practice. However this may have been, the bishops at Ancyra were ready to side with Athanasius and their own baptismal practice: they preferred Father/Son language to the language of the Neo-Arians.

This leads us to the third dimension we must explore of the Ancyran letter's opening theological passage. By the time of the Ancyran synod in A.D. 358 the Neo-Arians had caused the Homoiousians to take note of the problems raised by theological language. The Homoiousians wrote, "We ought to think piously the concepts which arise from the names [of the Trinity]," and, "listening to the natural meanings of the names, we think that the Father is the cause of an essence like him, and, hearing the name of the Son, we think that the Son is like the Father, of whom he is the son." The Ancyran bishops had obviously become self-consciously concerned about the nature of theological language; they were ready to raise and discuss the issue forthrightly. Though they were led by the Father/Son language of scripture and liturgy to maintain that the first two persons of the Trinity are homoiousioi or like-in-essence, just as human fathers and sons are like-in-essence, they were fully cognizant of the difficulties with this language which Aetius had pointed out. Therefore, they devoted virtually the rest of their synodical letter's body to facing up to these difficulties. In doing so, the Homoiousians began in A.D. 358 a discussion with the Neo-Arians about theological language which would go on for two years; then, after the Cappadocian Basil of Caesarea inherited the discussion in A.D. 360, it not only continued for another twenty years but developed into Christianity's first epistemological debate. Given the importance of the issue to Neo-Arian intellectual history, we must pay close attention to the Ancyran bishops' arguments. The bishops began as follows:

> Since the word Son has been taken from the
> bodily realm and since bodily fathers and
> sons are subject to passions and outflow-
> ings, the word Son does not correctly
> establish a concept for the existence of

161

a bodiless Son from a bodiless Father. On
account of this [scripture] has woven in
the concept of created thing taken from the
bodily realm. Since the created thing which
[God] makes is a Son, [scripture] has taken
from the creator and the created thing only
the passionlessness of the creator and the
fixity of the created thing ([which two
qualities] come from the creator who subsists
passionlessly and the created thing's
[subsisting] in just the way the creator
wills) and has correctly taught us from the
bodily father and son and the bodily
creator and created thing the perfect
concept (ἐννοία) of Father and Son.   (73:3)

This most fascinating passage sought a compromise
between the views of Athanasius and those of the Neo-
Arians. We have seen that in his _Orationes_ 1:34 and
De Decretis 31 the Alexandrian bishop spoke negatively
not only about the ungenerated/generated distinction
but also about the creator/created thing distinction.
The Ancyran bishops admitted that the latter is indeed
as scriptural as Father/Son. Most probably the Neo-
Arians were claiming this in the years prior to A.D.
358, as they claimed it in the years after.[1] But this
was not the only Neo-Arian claim that the passage from
the synodical letter granted; it also granted a
closely related one. We have seen above that the
Ancyran letter (73:4) revealed that in the years before
358 Aetius voiced concern about Father/Son language
not only "lest the bodiless one who has begotten
suffer some passion" but also "lest that which is
begotten be incomplete (ἀτελές)." Syllogism #9 of
Aetius' _Syntagmation_ of A.D. 359 explained this concern in detail: "If the generate was spermatically
within the ungenerated God, he, so to speak, reached
maturity after his generation, having received things
from outside of God. The Son, then, is complete not
as a result of the things he was generated with, but

---

1.   See, for example, Eunomius, _Apol._ 26.

as a result of the things which he received [from outside of God]." Here Aetius revealed that he was suspicious of theological Father/Son language because sperm does not reach maturity or completion until long after the time it leaves a father. The Ancyran Homoiousians admitted Aetius' point, arguing that theology must use the scriptural concept of creator/created thing to correct the scriptural concept of Father/Son. Just as the passions associated with bodily fathers must be excised from our understanding of the bodiless Father and must be corrected by the passionlessness connected with the concept of creation, so the incompleteness associated with bodily generation must be excised from our understanding and corrected. In the words of the synodical letter, God's Son "subsists in just the way the creator wills," with the "fixity of the created thing." Surely Aetius had claimed precisely this in the years prior to A.D. 358. That he claimed it after A.D. 358 is beyond dispute, for in syllogism #15 of his Syntagmation of A.D. 359 he wrote (as we have already noted in Chapter 2 of our work), "If the generate is immutable with respect to nature because of the one who generated it, then the ungenerated essence is immutable, not because of will but because of its essential rank." In other words, God willed the Son to be immutable or "fixed" in nature, as creators naturally do. While the Ancyran bishops were willing to grant so much of Aetius' objection to Father/Son language and his preference for creator/created thing language, they were unwilling to go any further. They argued that "the likeness in essence which causes us to think of a living Father" has to be preserved by theology; if it is not, the scriptural language of Father and Son would be rendered completely meaningless: "The names [that is, Father and Son] will be superfluous, since they introduce nothing from themselves, and, thus, God will be creator and in no way at all Father" (73:4). Consequently, the Son would be in no way different from other created things. None of the Neo-Arian ways of protecting the Son's superiority, said the bishops, made him anything more than a created thing, neither the view that "he is surpassing in greatness, as heaven compared with a

163

mountain or a hill," nor the position that "he has
come into being as the first because of necessity,"
nor the view that "he has been a servant for the
creation of other things":[1] "nothing will differentiate
'the one through whom are all things (1 Cor. 8:6)'
from the created things unless he is Son, since the
natural meaning [of Son] surpasses [the natural meaning
of created things]" (73:4). Hence, while the Ancyran
bishops respected the Neo-Arians' use of creator/
created thing language and admitted the legitimacy of
the Neo-Arian arguments against associating passion
with the Father and mutability with the Son, they were
unwilling to abandon what they considered to be the
essential meaning of Christian Father/Son language,
namely, likeness-in-essence.

Having defended themselves against the rational
objections of the Neo-Arians to their homoiousian
interpretation of Christian Father/Son language, the
Ancyran bishops turned in synodical letter 73:5 to
refuting some scriptural objections of the Neo-Arians.
They issued a warning that "no one should be sophistic
with the concept of the one properly Father and the
one properly Son" because of the many so-called sons
of God referred to by such scriptural passages as
Is. 1:2, Mal. 2:10, and Jn. 1:12-13, which call men
'sons of God', and as Job 38:28, which terms even
drops of dew 'begotten' by God. Aetius and the Neo-
Arians had presumably been arguing that God's
"fatherly" relationship with the Son is essentially
no different from his "fatherly" relationship with
men and drops of dew noted in scripture. Or, to use
the language of synodical letter 73:5, which probably
was the Neo-Arians' own, the Son is not a "true" son
but "only participates in the appellation of Son."
Clearly the Neo-Arians were arguing prior to A.D. 358,
as anathema #18 of the synodical letter phrased it,
that scripture indicates God to be "father" of the
Son only in "authority (ἐξουσία)," not in essence
(οὐσίᾳ). Now, one may doubt that the Neo-Arians

---

1. These views were repeated a second time in
anathema #1 of the synodical letter (73:10).

cited precisely the four scriptural passages noted by
the Ancyran bishops: the first three were used by
Athanasius in his Orationes 2:59 to the same purpose
as they were used by the synodical letter. The letter,
as Jaakko Gummerus has suggested,[1] was at this point
modelled on Athanasius' chapter. On the other hand,
the passages could very well have been employed by the
Neo-Arians, especially the one from Job, which was
quoted by an early Arian (by Eusebius of Nicomedia, in
his letter to Paulinus) but not by Athanasius. Moreover, as we saw in our last chapter, Aetius himself was
not at all reluctant to read Athanasius. The odds are
that the passages cited by the synodical letter were
so because Aetius and the Neo-Arians appealed to them.
How did the Homoiousians respond to the Neo-Arian
objections? Most ingeniously. Following a line of
argument first suggested by Athanasius in Orationes
Contra Arianos 1:23, they appealed to a scriptural
passage dear to the eastern Christian tradition, a
passage which occupied a prominent place in the "fourth"
creed of Antioch, 341 and which was repeated at Antioch,
344, Sirmium, 351, and Antioch, 356, namely, Eph. 3:14.
It said, "For this reason I bend my knees to the Father,
from whom every fatherhood (πᾶσα πατριά) in heaven and
on earth is named." The Homoiousians interpreted this
to mean that God "is named Father-in-the-heavens" and
that he is "the one from whom the fathers-on-earth in
essence have been named, (he) having his Son begotten
from him completely according to the likeness of his
own essence" (73:5). The Ancyran bishops have here
used scripture to trump Aetius and the Neo-Arians,
who objected to theological Father/Son language because such language uses terms naturally designed for
lower forms of bodily life and applies them to bodiless
divine beings for whom they are not appropriate.
Eph. 3:14 was used to prove the opposite is the case:
the language of fatherhood has its primary and natural
reference to deity and only a derivative and unnatural
reference to lower forms of life. Scripture turned
Aetius' argument on its head; if we desire to know the

---

1. Gummerus, p. 72 n. 3.

concept 'fatherhood', we must look to God, not to earthly beings. The Ancyran bishops added that when scripture referred to men and drops of dew as 'sons of God', it did so "by a misuse of language and by way of homonyms (καταχρηστικῶς καὶ ὁμωνύμως)" in no way "suiting the only-begotten" (73:5). Since the terms καταχρηστικῶς and ὁμωνύμως were favorites of the Neo-Arians, as we shall see, the synodical letter has simply turned them against their authors. Presumably the Neo-Arians had said that the terms father and son could be used of deity only "by a misuse of language and by way of homonyms."

Continuing the same theme in 73:6 that it introduced in 73:5, the synodical letter took up what was clearly a Neo-Arian charge that it is "irrational" and "non-syllogistic" to think of a father/son relationship without thinking of "passion or division or outflowing" (73:6). Having used Eph. 3:14 to excellent advantage in 73:5, the Ancyran bishops used the beginning of 1 Cor. to the same advantage in 73:6. They answered the Neo-Arian charge of irrationality by saying, if someone "should demand rational arguments, one should demand of him rational arguments how God is crucified and how the foolishness of the gospel proclamation, because of its non-syllogistic nature in the eyes of those of the world who seem to be wise, is wiser than men, whom the blessed Paul does not deem worthy of the Logos, since he made foolish by means of the non-syllogistic nature of power the wisdom of those able to argue syllogistically, for he has said, 'I have come proclaiming the mystery of God not in the wisdom of rationality, in order that the cross of Christ may not be emptied' "(73:6). So the first reaction of the bishops to Neo-Arian demands for syllogistic rationality was to downplay rationality in favor of Paul's notion of "mystery." The Neo-Arians had undoubtedly been playing up the rationality of their positions, surely by the use of syllogisms; as we shall see, Aetius' only extant treatise, his <u>Syntagmation</u> of A.D. 359, was simply a collection of syllogisms. For the Ancyran bishops, on the other hand, both the theology and the salvation of the Christian rest fundamentally on non-rational, non-syllogistic grounds: ". . .

having refuted all syllogistic wisdom as folly through non-syllogistic power, Paul admits faith alone for the salvation of those accepting the proclamation. Neither does he answer how the Father passionlessly begets the Son, in order that the mystery of the sonship from the Father of the Monogenes not be emptied . . . ." (73:6) After having said this, the bishops immediately offered at least a quasi-rational defense of their homoiousion doctrine. Developing an argument for a passionless begetting first offered by Athanasius in Orationes 1:28, the bishops proposed that since Wisdom subsists as the offspring of the wise God (according to Prov. 8:25) and since Wisdom is not a quality (ἕξις)[1] of God (who is wise in essence) but rather "an essence from the essence of the wise one," the Son--who is this Wisdom--is passionlessly begotten as like-in-essence to God.

At this point, with Prov. 8's concept of God's Wisdom introduced to counter Neo-Arianism's championing of the human wisdom rejected by Paul, the Ancyran bishops began an exegetical demonstration designed to show that both Paul and Prov. 8 supported the homoiousian understanding of Father/Son language (73:7). We remember that the fundamental suggestion of the synodical letter was that Christian thinkers must weave together both father/son and creator/created language in order to formulate an adequate theology. The concept of likeness-in-essence was to be taken from the father/son model and the concept of passionlessness from the creator/created model. The bishops said this was exactly what Prov. 8 recommended when it set back-to-back the following two sayings of God's Wisdom: "the Lord created (ἔκτισε) me the beginning of his ways for his works (Prov. 8:22)," and "before all things he begets (γεννᾷ) me (Prov. 8:25)." And in a passage which conveyed the exact same meaning as

---

1. The word ἕξις is an emendation of a corrupt text which was not accepted by the latest editor of the Ancyran letter, Karl Holl (Die Griechischen Christlichen Schriftsteller 37 (1933), p. 276), but it seems to me to make more sense than the text which Holl prints (compare Gummerus, p. 75).

Prov. 8:12-25, namely, Col. 1:15-16, Paul also combined
concepts from the two models when he spoke of the
"image of God" as "the <u>first-born</u> of all <u>creation</u>."
We may add in passing that the synodical letter particularly stressed the Pauline notion of the Son as
God's image and interpreted it in light of the "second"
creed of Antioch, 341, where the Son was confessed to
be the image not only of the Father's will, power, and
glory but also of his essence. Finally, in an attempt
to demonstrate that Paul was not the first early
Christian to maintain likeness-in-essence, the synodical letter appealed to the Gospel of John. Since
Jn. 1:1 said that in the beginning the "Word was with
God," the Word is obviously different from God; but
since it also says that "the Word was God," he is
just as obviously like God. So the bishops concluded,
"We have agreement in the mouth of two and three
witnesses for proof of likeness in essence of the Son
to the Father, for one says that the Son is the Wisdom
of the Wise One, and another that the only-begotten
God is the Word of God, and the third that the Son is
the Image of God, so that the Word and the Wisdom and
the Image of God is the Son who is like in all things
(as it has been said above) and also in essence to the
God and Father" (73:8).

Very conscious, however, that many eastern
Christians sympathized profoundly with the Neo-Arian
suspicion of the homoousion formula of Nicaea championed by both Marcellus of Ancyra and Athanasius of
Alexandria, the Ancyran bishops decided to conclude
the main body of their synodical letter by making it
crystal clear that their own homoiousion in no way
meant the same as homoousion. Citing Jn. 5:26 ("As
the Father has life in himself, so also he has given
life to the Son to have in himself") the bishops
argued that since God has "given" the life which he
has "in himself" to the Son for him to have "in himself," "it is clear that likeness is never able to be
the same thing as that to which it is like" (73:8).
Only likeness-in-essence captured the meaning of this
verse. The proof of this is the analogy of the incarnation: the Son of God "did not in all things become
the same as man" but only came "in the likeness of

sinful flesh (Rom. 8:3)," having not been begotten "by
sperm and intercourse" and "with the sin of flesh"
(73:8-9). Just as the Son of God is not in essence
the same as man but rather like man, so he is not in
essence the same as God but only like God. On this
note the main body of the Ancyran synodical letter
ended and the anathemas began.

As we have already noted, the anathemas alternately opposed the Neo-Arians and Marcellus. We may
say that the purpose of the anathemas in general was
to reject both the Marcellan extreme of same-in-essence
(ταὐτοούσιον or ὁμοούσιον[1]) and the Neo-Arian extreme
of different-in-essence (ἀνόμοιον κατ'οὐσίαν) in
favor of a golden mean, like-in-essence (ὁμοιούσιον).
This is illustrated particularly by anathemas #2-9
(73:10). Anathema #2 rejected those who said that
Wisdom and the wise God are the same, whereas #3
rejected those who said that they are essentially
different; anathema #4 cursed those who identified
the Word and God, while #5 cursed those who held that
they are in essence different; anathema #6 attacked
those who said that the image of the invisible God is
the same as the invisible God, whereas #7 attacked
those who maintained them to have essentially nothing
in common; and anathemas #8 and 9 rejected both
Marcellan and Neo-Arian exegeses of Jn. 5:26 and set
up as canonical an exegesis which saw the verse as
teaching "likeness of essence."

There was more in the anathemas than polemical
restatements of homoiousian theology that we have
already learned from the main body of the synodical
letter. A number of the anathemas described with
some precision Neo-Arian views which undoubtedly were
in circulation in the years prior to A.D. 358. The
anathemas are, thus, valuable sources for reconstructing the state of Neo-Arian thought in these years.
We learn from anathemas #1 (73:10) and 10 (73:11),
first of all, that the Neo-Arians not only were
teaching that father/son language is pseudonymous
when applied to deity and creator/created language

---

1. These two are identified in anathema #19 (73:11).

literal but were using this principle to interpret
Prov. 8:22 and 25. When Wisdom said "he created me,"
this was to be taken literally; when he said, "he
begets me," it was not. Second, we are told by
anathema #11 (73:11) that the Neo-Arians were quite
willing to adopt the Homoiousians' term likeness, but
they would "grant only likeness of activity," not
likeness in essence. Since this position was quoted
as being Neo-Arian in A.D. 359[1] and was argued at
length by Eunomius in his Apologia 24, we cannot doubt
the evidence of the synodical letter that it was
already being forwarded by the Neo-Arians in the years
prior to A.D. 358. The formulation of this position,
as we shall see, was of significant political importance to Neo-Arianism, for it allowed the movement to
subscribe the homoian formula of A.D. 359/360, which
was official orthodoxy henceforth until the Theodosian
settlement of A.D. 381. But since we have not yet
come across a full enough explication of the position
to make it entirely intelligible, we shall reserve
discussion of it to a later point in the present
chapter. The Neo-Arians themselves probably did not
develop their position fully until after the Ancyran
council of A.D. 358 proved to be exceedingly influential in eastern theological and political circles.
To return, then, to the synodical letter's anathemas,
we learn from anathemas #15 and 16 (73:11) that the
Neo-Arians argued for a pre-temporal "temporal"
priority of God to the Monogenes, just as did the
early Arians. Finally, there is anathema #14 (73:11).
The relevant portion read as follows: "If someone,
because the Father is never thought to be Son and the
Son is never thought to be Father, should say that the
Son is different from the Father . . . , since it
has been said that "the one witnessing concerning me
is another (Jn. 5:32)" and that "the one having sent
me, the Father, bears witness to me (Jn. 5:37)"
. . . , and should say, fearing lest the Son ever be
thought to be the same as the Father, that the Son is

_____

1. See Epiphanius, Haer. 73:21 (the memorandum
of Basil of Ancyra and George of Laodicea).

unlike-in-essence to the Father, let him be anathema."
This passage reveals to us that the Neo-Arians prior
to A.D. 358 appealed to Jn. 5:32 and 37 as scriptural
support for their doctrine of unlikeness-in-essence.
It also indicates, as we have seen in our previous
chapter, that the original enemies of Aetius and the
Neo-Arians were not the Homoiousians but rather those
who championed the Nicene formula of homoousion. The
Neo-Arian worry was lest the Son be construed as the
same as the Father.

Since for our purposes the synodical letter is
most important for what it tells us about Neo-Arian
thought in the years preceding A.D. 358, let us
summarize what we have learned.

(1) The Neo-Arians were strongly promoting their
formula of difference-in-essence (see
anathemas #2-9).

(2) The Neo-Arian difference-in-essence formula
was being justified on the basis of the
Macrostich's ungenerated/generated distinction (see 73:3).

(3) Aetius and the Neo-Arians were carrying on
a forceful campaign against Athanasius'
championing of Father/Son language in his
De Decretis of A.D. 350 (see 73:3-5):

   (a) Fearing the bodily connotations of the
language, the Neo-Arians were promoting
a sharp distinction between Christianity's fleshless, immortal God and its
enfleshed, dying Lord; and Neo-Arian
clerics may have begun to baptize
catechumens once into the death of the
Lord instead of three times into Father,
Son, and Holy Spirit.

   (b) Concerned that Father/Son language involves the Father in passion and the Son
in change, the Neo-Arians were promoting
creator/created language in its stead:
a creator creates without bodily passion, and a created thing is complete
and "fixed" from the time of its
creation, undergoing no process of
maturation.

171

(c) The Neo-Arians were interpreting scriptural Father/Son language by means of Is. 1:2, Mal. 2:10, Jn. 1:12-13, and Job 38:28, where men and drops of dew were designated "sons of God": just as these are not "true" sons of God, so the Son "only participates in the appellation of son." God is the Father of the Son, as he is of men and drops of dew, only "in authority," not "in essence." Father/Son terminology can be used of deity only "by a misuse of language and by way of homonyms."

(4) The Neo-Arians were arguing their position with syllogisms and were stressing the importance of rationality in theology (see 73:6).

(5) Although Neo-Arian theology was originally formulated as anti-Athanasian and anti-homoousion, the Neo-Arians had become increasingly conscious in the years before A.D. 358 of homoiousianism, as is evident from the Neo-Arians' admitting the accuracy of the term likeness when applied to the ungenerated/generated relationship--but only if it were interpreted as meaning likeness-in-activity and not likeness-in-essence (see anathema #11).

We must now return to historical narration.

Once the bishops at Ancyra had completed their synodical letter and thereby had complied with George of Laodicea's request for a theological statement against Neo-Arianism, they decided to send a deputation to the emperor. Its task was not only to inform Constantius about Eudoxius' activities in Antioch and his favoring of the Neo-Arian cause but also to request imperial support for homoiousianism. Chosen were Basil of Ancyra and Eustathius of Sebaste, who picked up on their way to court an additional member for the deputation, Bishop Eleusius of Cyzicus, and enlisted at court the presbyter of the imperial bedchamber,

172

Leontius.[1] As we have already mentioned, when they
arrived at their destination, they found the Aetian
presbyter Asphalius who had been sent by Eudoxius and
the Neo-Arians to gain imperial endorsement of their
takeover of Antioch. Since Asphalius had Constantius'
written endorsement in hand, the deputation had its
work cut out for it. It succeeded beautifully. Ap-
prised of the deputation's position, Constantius withdrew the letter he had given to Asphalius and issued
another to the Antiochene church--still extant in
Sozomen's Historia Ecclesiastica.[2] It shows that the
emperor had been completely won over by the deputation.

Constantius' letter revealed that the Ancyran
bishops had given up on George of Laodicea's hope that
Eudoxius could still be persuaded to separate himself
from the Neo-Arians, for the letter attacked not only
Neo-Arian theology but also--and especially--Eudoxius'
appropriation of the Antiochene see, as well as his
consequent advancement of Neo-Arians to the clergy.
Eudoxius was accused of unbridled ambition in leaving
behind Germaniceia for Antioch, and the Neo-Arians
were accused of being "vagabond quacks and sophists"
intent only on corrupting the people. In no way, said
the emperor, did he approve of Eudoxius' claims to the
Antiochene see nor his raising of Neo-Arians to the
clericate; any statements to the contrary were lies.
The imperial letter went on (1) to recommend to those
that had fled the Antiochene Church that they assent
to "the decree which the bishops who are wise in matters of divinity have suitably decreed for the better"
(undoubtedly the Ancyran synodical letter was the
decree in question[3]), (2) to confess the Ancyran
council's homoiousion position as the "faith of the
Fathers" and that of the emperor himself, and (3) to
urge that the Neo-Arians be excluded from both

---

1. Sozomen, H.E. 4:13.
2. Ibid., 4:14.
3. Gummerus' notion that the reference may be to
the decrees of the Council of Sirmium, A.D. 358, seems
to me far-fetched in light of the general thrust of
Constantius' letter. See Gummerus, p. 92.

ecclesiastical synods and ordinary church services
(συνόδων . . . καὶ συλλόγου κοινοῦ). This was a
calamity for the Neo-Arian party and an unexpected
personal setback for Eudoxius. Eudoxius had, after
all, spent the years A.D. 355-357 at court and must in
those years have become well known to Constantius.[1]
Only a very strong accusation can adequately explain
the emperor's change of heart and virulent attack upon
him. Philostorgius was probably right when he claimed
that Basil of Ancyra and Eustathius of Sebaste charged
that Aetius, his early devotee Theophilus the Ethiopian, and Eudoxius had participated in Gallus' A.D.
354 conspiracy against Constantius.[2] In other words,
Aetius, Eudoxius, and Theophilus were accused of
treason. Although this charge, in Eudoxius' case at
any rate, was probably pure slander, Constantius was
understandably moved. Hence the withdrawal of the
letter he had given to the Neo-Arian Asphalius and the
substitution of a strongly-worded one against the Neo-
Arians.

The Neo-Arian party's troubles were only beginning, for at a council held at Sirmium soon after
Constantius sent his letter to Antioch, Basil and
Eustathius consolidated the position of influence they
had established with the emperor. The occasion of the
council was an embassy of western bishops to the
emperor which asked for the return of Bishop Liberius
of Rome from exile in Berea. Firmly in control, the
Homoiousians put together a digest of theological
statements which Liberius was asked to sign. Its affirmations were taken from (1) a third-century Antiochene council against Paul of Samosata, (2) the
"second" creed of Antioch, 341, and (3) the anti-
Marcellan/Photinian Council of Sirmium, 351.[3] Since,
according to Sozomen,[4] Liberius was urged by both
Constantius and the Homoiousians "to confess that the

---

1. Compare Loofs, "Eudoxius," in Realencyklopädie
für protestantische Theologie und Kirche, 5:578.

2. Philostorgius, H.E. 4:8.
3. Sozomen, H.E. 4:15.
4. Ibid.

Son is not homoousion with the Father," the affirmations taken from the council against Paul were certainly those that condemned the use of homoousion.[1] With these the Danubean bishops Valens, Ursacius, and Germanius, who were present with the Homoiousians at Sirmium, 358, could readily agree. And the Danubeans were probably also not terribly disturbed by whatever statements the Homoiousians selected from the document of Sirmium, 351, since they, too, were hostile to Marcellus and Photinus and had at the 356 Council of Antioch themselves supported the creed of Sirmium, 351--which was the scriptural so-called "fourth" creed of Antioch, 341 endorsed by both Philippopolis, 343 and the Macrostich Council of Antioch, 344. Yet, when the Homoiousians took theological affirmations from the "second" creed of Antioch, 341, the Danubeans reacted strongly. The reason for this is not hard to see. The "second" Antiochene creed maintained that the Son is "the exact image (ἀπαράλλακτον ἐικόνα) of the divine, of the Father's essence (οὐσία), will (βουλή), power (δύναμις), and glory (δόξη)." Since this was explicitly homoiousian, the Danubeans protested that they saw no difference between homoousion, which Basil and his followers rejected, and homoiousion, which they accepted.[2] Presumably they wanted Liberius to stand by his previous adherence to the Sirmium pronouncement of 357, which rejected not only homoousion but also homoiousion. This profoundly disturbed the Homoiousians, not the least because Liberius' earlier adherence to the 357 pronouncement had caused their hated enemies, the Neo-Arians in Antioch, to circulate the interpretation that Liberius had thereby endorsed their position of dissimilarity in substance.[3] So they seem to have begun to nurse the suspicion--groundless, at least at this point--that the Danubeans were in league with the Neo-Arians; they decided to answer the Danubeans' objection in writing. As they had done at Ancyra a short time earlier, they roundly defended their

---

1. Compare Lietzmann, 3:224.
2. Hilary of Poitiers, Syn. 79.
3. Sozomen, H.E. 4:15.

homoiousian stance[1] and even added to the definitions
offered there the images that "the Father is the fountain of Wisdom and Life, and the Son is the radiance
of the eternal light, and the offspring (τὸ γέννημα)
from the fountain," using Jn. 14:6 and Prov. 8:12 in
support of their view.[2] Having defended homoiousion,
they distinguished it sharply from homoousion, which
they said was to be rejected on three grounds: (1)
it involved the materializing notion that there is a
prior substance which Father and Son divide between
themselves, (2) it was rejected by the anti-Paul of
Samosata council of Antioch during the third century,
and (3) it was unscriptural.[3] The letter was a
success. Liberius, concerned about the fact that he
was being made out to be a supporter of dissimilarity
by the Antiochene Neo-Arians, affixed his signature
to it.[4] And Emperor Constantius continued to favor the
Homoiousians. In fact, he went so far as to back up
his letter against Neo-Arianism by issuing orders for
the exile of Bishop Eudoxius of Antioch (to his
ancestral home in the greater Cappadocian province of
Armenia) and of the Neo-Arian Theophilus the Ethiopian
(to Heraclea in Pontus).[5] These decrees so disturbed
Aetius and Eunomius that Eunomius finally allowed himself to be raised to the Antiochene diaconate in order
that he could travel as an official ecclesiastical ambassador to convince Constantius to change his mind
and rescind the decrees. He was, however, intercepted
on the road to Sirmium by supporters of Basil and
Eustathius and exiled to Midaeus in Phrygia. Soon
after, Basil succeeded in forcing Aetius into Phrygian
exile (to the town of Pepuza) and in exiling no less
than seventy other Neo-Arians, presumably the majority
from Antioch. It was the summer of A.D. 358.[6]

---

1.   Hilary of Poitiers, Syn. 81.
2.   Athanasius, Syn. 41.
3.   Hilary of Poitiers, Syn. 81.
4.   Sozomen, H.E. 4:15.
5.   Philostorgius, H.E. 4:8.
6.   Ibid. Philostorgius' claim that Basil of
Ancyra maintained in the presence of the emperor "like

Within approximately a year, the Neo-Arian party had been formed with the support of the two most illustrious sees of the East, Alexandria and Antioch, and then had suffered virtual annihilation at the hands of Basil of Ancyra and his supporters. The councils of Ancyra and Sirmium, 358 and their aftermaths had been disasters for the party. The party's opponent Basil of Ancyra was now in an enviable position, for not only had he eliminated his Neo-Arian adversaries but also, when Constantius decided to hold a general council comparable to Nicaea to settle the question of the faith once and for all (Basil probably suggested the idea), the Ancyran bishop was the one entrusted with the task of determining the location.[1] He had become Constantius' right hand bishop. Enjoying imperial favor, Basil and his party, according to Philostorgius, "travelled everywhere, strengthening the homoiousion cause," winning over Bishop Macedonius of Constantinople and many other prelates.[2]

But the fate of Neo-Arianism as an ecclesiastical party had not yet been sealed, for Basil of Ancyra gradually lost his position of strength. After taking a poll of bishops' preferences for the new general council's location, Basil returned to court in May, A.D. 359 to make further preparations.[3] He found gathered at Sirmium the three Danubean bishops Pancratius of Pelusium, Mark of Arethusa, and Hypatianus of Heraclea, along with the Neo-Arian supporter George of Alexandria.[4] The purpose of the gathering was to hammer out a formulary which could claim the assent of major factions among the bishops who were to meet in the upcoming general council. The Neo-Arian party was at the outset not considered a legitimate ecclesiastical

---

in all things" and avoided the term οὐσία was a confusion of Sirmium, 358 with Sirmium, 359, where "like in all things" was subscribed by Basil.

   1.   Sozomen, H.E. 4:16.
   2.   Philostorgius, H.E. 4:9.
   3.   Sozomen, H.E. 4:16.
   4.   Epiphanius, Haer. 73:22 and 26ff; Hilary of Poitiers, Fr. 15; Socrates, H.E. 2:29; Sozomen, H.E. 4:16.

faction, since Emperor Constantius had clearly declared himself against it in his letter to the Antiochene church of spring, A.D. 358. Nor was the Nicene party which supported homoousion considered legitimate, since both Ossius of Cordova, the old Nicene Father, and Bishop Liberius of Rome were believed to have given up on homoousion. And Athanasius was no longer bishop of Alexandria. Therefore, the two factions which needed to be theologically reconciled were the Danubean proponents of the Sirmium pronouncement of 357 and the homoiousian faction led by Basil of Ancyra. The so-called Dated Creed, which resulted from the discussion, was quite ingenious. Its relevant portions were as follows:

> We believe in one only and true God, Father, almighty, creator and framer of all things;

> And in one only begotten Son of God, who has begotten impassibly from God before all ages and before all beginning and before all conceivable time and before all comprehensible essence, through whom the ages were fashioned and all things came into existence, begotten as only-begotten, the only one from the only Father, God from God, like the Father who begat him according to the scriptures (ὅμοιον τῷ γεννήσαντι αὐτὸν πατρὶ κατὰ τὰς γραφάς), whose generation no one knows, save only the Father who begat him . . . .

> But whereas the term 'ousia' has been adopted by the Fathers in simplicity and, being unknown by the people, is a stumbling block, because the scriptures do not contain it, it has seemed good to remove it, and it has seemed good that there should be no further mention of 'ousia' in regard to God, because the divine scriptures nowhere refer to the essence of the Father or the Son. But we say the Son is like the Father in all things (ὅμοιον δὲ λέγομεν τὸν υἱὸν τῷ πατρὶ κατὰ

πάντα), as the Holy Scriptures declare and teach.[1]

This document was a compromise. The homoiousian authors of the synodical letter of Ancyra, 358 were granted a number of their anti-Neo-Arian claims: God was described as both Father and creator, he was said to beget the Son without passion, and this begetting was said to have taken place before all time. The Danubeans, on the other hand, were granted the claim of their 357 pronouncement that the Son's generation is unknown to all but the Father and, more importantly, their barring of οὐσία as unscriptural. Because of the exclusion of οὐσία, the compromise was forced to protect the major affirmation of Ancyra, 358 by reoffering the 344 Macrostich's formula that the Son is "like" the Father "in all things." It seems the genius behind the Dated Creed was the Syrian Mark of Arethusa,[2] who was the first to sign.[3] The Danubean leader Valens was unsatisfied, presumably because he realized that "in all things" would naturally be interpreted to mean "in οὐσία" by the Homoiousians, even though the word itself was banned. Therefore, he sought in his subscription to write only "the Son is like the Father," which caused Emperor Constantius to force him to add "in all things" and caused Basil of Ancyra to become very suspicious. Basil became so suspicious that when it was his turn to subscribe the compromise creed, he affixed not only his signature but a full explanation of his theological position. He subscribed as follows:

> Basil, bishop of Ancyra: Thus I believe and join in approving what has been written above, confessing that the Son is like the Father in all things; and in __all__ things, not only in will but in hypostasis and in being (οὐ μόνον κατὰ τὴν βούλησιν, ἀλλὰ κατὰ ὑπόστασιν καὶ

---

1. The translation, with minor alterations, is that of J.N.D. Kelly, Creeds, pp. 289-90.
2. See Hilary of Poitiers, Fr. 15:3.
3. Epiphanius, Haer. 73:22.

κατὰ τὸ ετναι) as Son according to the
divine scriptures, Spirit from Spirit, Life
from Life, Light from Light, God from God,
true Son from true Father, Wisdom the Son
from the wise God and Father; and confessing that the Son is like the Father absolutely (καθάπαξ) in all things, as Son to
Father. And if someone says like [only] in
relation to something [that is, will], as
it has been written above, he is foreign
to the Catholic Church, since he does not
say according to the divine scriptures that
the Son is like the Father.[1]

Here was an ingenious defense of homoiousion which
fully respected the ban on οὐσία; Valeus' worst fears
were being realized. But for a history of Neo-Arianism
there is something even more interesting about Basil's
subscription, namely, his concern to state that the
likeness of the Son to the Father was not only "in
will." Although Valens and Ursacius were students of
Arius and might have at this point simply decided on
their own to emphasize this Arian doctrine in order to
counter the Homoiousians, another explanation seems
more likely. From anathema #11 of the 358 Ancyran
synodical letter we learned that the Homoiousians were
so disturbed by the Neo-Arians' claim that the Son was
like the Father "in activity" but not "in essence" that
they pointedly anathematized it. Since this position
was essentially the same as the position that Basil
was worried about in his subscription to the Dated
Creed, we are led to suspect that Valens and the Danubeans were encouraged to emphasize it by the Neo-
Arians--specifically, by the Neo-Arian supporter George
of Alexandria, who, as we have seen, was present at
the gathering that produced the dated compromise. Substantiation for this interpretation is provided by
Sozomen, who in his narration of the events of Sirmium,
359 noted for the first time that Valens and the

----

1. Ibid.

Danubeans "favored" the Neo-Arian heresy.[1] So we may
conclude that at Sirmium, 359 George of Alexandria had
made a crucial move. He had decided that since the
emperor, though clearly favoring Basil and the Homoiousians, was still open to the Danubeans and wanted them
conciliated, it was time to cultivate an alliance
between them and himself, the representative of the
exiled Neo-Arians Eudoxius, Aetius, and Eunomius. It
certainly did not hurt that Eudoxius' 358 Council of
Antioch had already made contact with the Danubeans in
order to thank them for issuing the pronouncement of
Sirmium, 357.

Encouraged by George's achievement, the Neo-Arians
immediately sought to accomplish two things. First,
they tried to rehabilitate themselves with the emperor,
and second, they endeavored to follow up the contacts
made with the Danubean bishops by George. Their rehabilitation was swiftly achieved. The old Arians Patrophilus of Scythopolis and Narcissus of Neronias,
having been won over to sympathy for the exiled Neo-
Arians, had only to inform Constantius of what Philostorgius called "the dramatic deeds" done by Basil of
Ancyra, and the emperor, "astonished and grieved,"
immediately recalled the over seventy exiled Neo-Arians
of Syria, including their leaders Eudoxius, Aetius,
and Eunomius.[2] The "dramatic deeds" were probably
those reported by Sozomen in connection with the deposition of Basil in early A.D. 360. At that time Basil
was charged with having given over, without trial,
clergy from Antioch, the Euphrates region, Cilicia,
Galatia and Asia "to the provincial rulers, to be
exiled and subjected to cruel punishments." He was
also charged with having written directions to Hermo-
genes, the prefect of Syria, stating who was to be
exiled and where they were to be sent. Finally, when
Emperor Constantius in 358 commanded Aetius to appear
before Bishop Cecropius of Nicodemia to answer accusations against himself, Basil was said to have inter-
vened with the one entrusted with delivering the

---

1. Sozomen, H.E. 4:15.
2. Philostorgius, H.E. 4:10.

181

emperor's edict, to Aetius' detriment. Although the embassy of Patrophilus and Narcissus was the immediate cause of the Neo-Arians' rehabilitation, it surely did not hurt that Constantius' Grand Chamberlain, the eunuch Eusebius, was a friend of Eudoxius and had come to sympathize with the Neo-Arians' position.[1] Eusebius was a powerful man; Ammianus Marcellinus said that Constantius had much influence with the eunuch![2]

As soon as Aetius and Eudoxius had returned from exile, they applied themselves to cultivating the relationship George of Alexandria had established with the Danubean bishops. The first problem at which the two groups worked together was whether to have one or two general councils (one for the East and one for the West) and where the council(s) should be held. The new allies apparently jelled, for they were rather successful in achieving their objectives on both counts. Perhaps no small reason for the immediate success of the new alliance was Acacius of Caesarea's decision to join.[3] The successor of the illustrious Eusebius in the see of Caesarea, Acacius was a man of great prestige and ecclesiastical experience, having been an important person at the synods of Antioch, 341, Philippopolis, 343, Milan, 355, and finally, Antioch, 358. This last synod, as we have already noted, was organized by Eudoxius and came to the decision to write to the Danubean bishops in approval of their Sirmium statement of 357,[4] an approval which foreshadowed the Danubean/Neo-Arian alliance.

With the acquisition of Acacius, the new alliance had become what may justly be termed 'grand'. It included from the East the most powerful prelates of Syria, Palestine, and Egypt and from the West the most influential bishops of the Danubean provinces. The

---

1. Sozomen, H.E. 4:16.
2. Ammianus Marcellinus, Res Gestae, 18:4:3.
3. See Sozomen, H.E. 4:16; Philostorgius, H.E. 4:12.
4. Compare Friedrich Loofs, "Acacius," in Realencyklopädie für protestantische Theologie und Kirche, 1:126.

Homoiousians--who were concentrated in Asia Minor--were literally caught in the middle. Even this middle region was not wholly theirs. From as early as the Lenten Council of Ancyra, 358, the Homoiousians had expressed concern about the theological views of certain unnamed bishops of Lydia and Asia.[1] These bishops could have been none other than the two Lydians Leontius of Tripolis and Theodosius of Philadelphia, and, in addition, Euagrius of Mytilene and Theodolus of Chaeretapa; all had become supporters of the grand alliance by the time of the Council of Seleucia in late A.D. 359[2] and were to develop into a hard core of the Neo-Arian party during the A.D. 360s. The formation of the alliance could not but have elated Aetius, Eunomius, and Eudoxius--especially Aetius, since he finally seemed on the verge of enjoying revenge on his old enemy and cause of his exile, Basil of Ancyra. The future of the Neo-Arians now looked brighter than it had before the party suffered the humiliation of mass exile.

Basil of Ancyra's future, on the other hand, was in serious jeopardy. So was that of George of Laodicea, for he had originally fired up the bishops at Ancyra against Aetius and Eudoxius and was now faced with their return and that of their supporters. Afraid that the new alliance would be successful at the upcoming general councils and concerned that the alliance had found a way to interpret the Dated Creed in accordance with Neo-Arian theology, Basil and George issued in the summer of A.D. 359 an apologetic and polemical memorandum.[3] The document was apologetic in that it defended the homoiousian understanding of the Dated Creed's Father/Son language and its formula, likeness-in-all-things; it was polemical in that it forcefully attacked Neo-Arianism. In their apologetic effort the bishops were particularly concerned to establish (1) that "the sense

---

1. Epiphanius, Haer. 73:2.
2. Ibid., 73:26; Athanasius, Syn. 12; Socrates, H.E. 2:40; Sulpicius Severus, Chron. 2:42; Sozomen, H.E. 4:22.
3. For the date, see Gummerus, p. 122.

of the term essence is conveyed everywhere in Old and New Testaments" even though "the term does not lie nakedly" anywhere[1] and (2) that the Dated Creed's formula, likeness-in-all-things, encompassed likeness-in-essence. What most concerns us, however, are the sections of the memorandum devoted to Neo-Arianism, for they tell us much about Neo-Arian thought in the period from the middle of A.D. 358 to the middle of A.D. 359, both indirectly, in their polemics, and directly, in their quotations from the Neo-Arians (presumably from Aetius). We must consider carefully this second extant homoiousian document--reproduced in full in Epiphanius, Haer. 73:12-22.

We begin by translating and commenting upon the section of the memorandum (73:21) which quoted at some length Neo-Arian statements. The statements were apparently forwarded in response to the Ancyran synodical letter of A.D. 358.

> In order that those innovating the heresy be known from their own statements, from the many things written by them as a subject for discussion, we have noted, for reasons of length, a few of these statements. From them Catholics, having learned the entire sense of the heresy, will decide--necessarily, we think--to anathematize those who have written them and to cast out from the Apostolic Faith both these people and the things that belong to them--and to anathematize both those who think and those who teach the same things as they do. For they write in precisely the following sentences:

> For I have earnestly desired to give to you in a few words most of the finest things said in respect of God. Those who assume that the Son preserves likeness-in-essence to the Father have gone outside of truth, since they condemn likeness-in-essence through the appellation ungenerated.

---

1. Epiphanius, Haer. 73:12.

And again they will say:

> And the Son, because of his generation,
> both is and is confessed to be inferior
> to the Ungenerated. Therefore, he does
> not preserve likeness-in-essence with the
> Ungenerated, but he preserves the will of
> God (ἀποσώζει . . . τὴν τοῦ θεοῦ βούλησιν),
> bearing it pure (ἀκραιφνῆ) in his own
> hypostasis. Therefore, he preserves like-
> ness, not in essence but in the relation
> of will (οὐ κατὰ τὴν οὐσίαν, ἀλλὰ κατὰ
> τὸν τῆς θελήσεως λόγον), wherefore God made
> him to exist as a hypostasis just as he
> willed (οἷον ἠθέλησεν ὑπεστήσατο).

And again:

> How do you yourself not confess along with
> me that the Son is not like the Father in
> essence?

And again:

> Since the Ungenerated Nature is endlessly
> greater than every power (ἐξουσίας), when-
> ever the Son is confessed to be without
> end, because he has his life not from his
> own nature but from the power (ἐκ τῆς . . .
> ἐξουσίας) of the Ungenerated, how are not
> the impious ones manifest who change the
> pious proclamation of difference-in-
> essence (ἑτεροούσιον) into likeness-of-
> essence?

And again:

> Therefore, the name 'Father' is not reve-
> latory of essence (οὐσίας), but of power
> (ἐξουσίας), which made the Son to exist
> as a hypostasis before the ages as God the
> Word (ὑποστησάσης τὸν υἱὸν πρὸ αἰώνων
> θεὸν λόγον), who endlessly possesses both

185

the essence and power given to him
(ἀτελευτήτως ἔχοντα τὴν αὐτῷ δωρηθεῖσαν
. . . οὐσίαν τε καὶ ἐξουσίαν), having
which he continues [to exist as a
hypostasis].

And again:

> If they wish that 'Father' be revelatory
> of essence (οὐσίας), but not of power
> (ἐξουσίας), let them address also the
> hypostasis of the Uniquely-Generated by
> the name Father.

The six Neo-Arian fragments quoted by Basil and
George were surely only a small proportion of the Neo-
Arian response to the Ancyran synodical letter, but
they probably were the main line of the Neo-Arian
attack. The first fragment was parallel to syllogism
#4 of Aetius' Syntagmation (A.D. 359), which read as
follows: "If God remains everlastingly in ungenerated
nature and the generate is everlastingly generate,
then the perverse doctrine of the homoousion will be
demolished; incomparability in essence is established
when each nature abides unceasingly in the proper rank
of its nature." Here the fact that God is ungenerated
and the Son generated was the basis for rejecting
homoousion. Similarly, the first Neo-Arian fragment
of Basil's and George's memorandum of A.D. 359 argued
that "those who assume that the Son preserves likeness-
in-essence to the Father have gone outside of truth,
since they condemn likeness-in-essence through the
appellation ungenerated." The unexpressed implication
of the fragment was the same as the expressed implication of God's ingeneracy in the syllogism, that is,
unlikeness-in-essence. But the fragment differed from
the syllogism by implying that the Homoiousians accepted
the premise of God's ingeneracy. How could the Neo-
Arians claim this, especially since the Ancyran letter
explicitly reminded its readers that Christians are
baptized into the names of Father and Son, not into the
names of ungenerated and generated? The answer, I
think, is two-fold. First, the introduction to the

186

synodical letter of 358 made the letter out to be a
theological descendant of the decisions and creeds of
a number of earlier eastern councils, including
Antioch, 344 and Sirmium, 351 (at which Basil of
Ancyra himself played an important role). Both the
explanations of the Macrostich (344) and the anathemas
of the Sirmium creed of 351 explicitly and often
described God as ungenerated. Second, although the
Ancyran letter said that Christians are baptized into
Father and Son and not into ungenerated and generated,
it did not engage in an all-out attack on God's ingeneracy. In fact, in anathema #17 (against Marcellus)
it actually identified God's essence as ungenerated.[1]
The Homoiousians in A.D. 358 were clearly bound by
eastern ecclesiastical tradition to describe God as
ungenerated, but for purposes of proving their position
of homoiousion they preferred to emphasize the biblical
term Father. They apparently had not yet fully realized
how pivotal a concept it was to the Neo-Arian position.
Neo-Arian fragment #1 of Basil's and George's memorandum made the situation perfectly clear, as did fragment #2. Fragment #2 pointed out that because the Son
is confessed to be generated, he necessarily must be
inferior to and, therefore, different from the Father,
certainly not like-in-essence. If in the spring of
A.D. 358 the Homoiousians did not perceive how central
the concepts of God's ingeneracy and the Son's generacy
were to the Neo-Arians, by the summer of A.D. 359
Basil of Ancyra and George of Laodicea perceived it
only too well. Hence, they argued in response that
ingeneracy and generacy are decidedly inferior concepts
to Father and Son, and they attacked the Neo-Arian use
of them at length. Their argument was introduced as
follows:

> Since we maintain . . . that the Son is a
> son and the Father is a father and not a
> son . . . , those allied with this heresy
> are anxious to elaborate two things: the
> one is no longer to say Father and Son but

---

1. Ibid., 73:11.

rather to say ungenerated and generated,
supposing through this sophism to introduce
the heresy into the church. For those who
are wise understand the things of God, that
the term Ungenerated is inferior to the name
of Father. Because he has not been generated,
he is thought to be the ungenerated, but the
term Ungenerated does not yet signify if he
is also Father; for the name Father is
superior to the name Ungenerated. In the
Ungenerated, we say, the power of the Father
is not manifested, but in the name Father
is manifested both that the Father is not
the Son, if at least he properly is thought
to be Father, and that he is the cause of
a Son like himself. This indeed is one thing
they elaborate. (73:14)

The essential homoiousian argument was that ungenerated/
generated terminology succeeded in differentiating God
and the Monogenes but did not succeed in any way in
communicating the intimate connection between them, a
connection to which both scripture and ecclesiastical
tradition witnessed. Father/Son language, on the other
hand, both differentiated them and indicated their
intimate connection. Having so argued near the beginning of their memorandum, Basil and George devoted two
long sections near the end of their document (73:19-20)
to a continuation of their polemic. They pointed out
that God was never designated as ungenerated in scripture and that the Son was only designated as generated
twice, in Ps. 110:3 and Prov. 8:22. Yet scripture was
full of Father/Son language. And again the bishops
used the baptism argument cited in the Ancyran synodical
letter of A.D. 358. Finally, they adduced two further
arguments. The first noted that the term generated
signifies that something has come into being but not
that the generated one is eternally Son. That is to
say, the memorandum explained, the term connects the
Son not with the Father but with other generated (that
is, created) things. The second argument pointed out
that the terms Father and Son have a natural reciprocal
relationship (σχέσις) which is not true of the terms

188

ungenerated and generated. When one says Father, one
necessarily implies that he is father of a son, and
vice-versa. When one says ungenerated, one does not
imply that it is the ungenerated of a generated--which
is to say, there is no necessary relationship between
God and the one scripture calls the Son.

The second fragment noted in the memorandum dealt
not only with the Neo-Arian doctrine of God's and the
Son's essential difference but also with the Neo-Arian
doctrine of their likeness. We learn from this fragment that the Neo-Arians responded to the 358 synodical
letter's recommendation of likeness-in-essence by
emphasizing the particular sense in which Neo-Arianism
considered God and the Son to be alike: "The Son does
not preserve likeness-in-essence with the Ungenerated,
but he preserves the will of God, bearing it pure in
his own hypostasis. Therefore, he preserves likeness,
not in essence but in the relation of will; wherefore
God made him to exist as a hypostasis just as he
willed." This doctrine of likeness, of course, was
nothing new for the Neo-Arians; because anathema #11
of the Ancyran letter cursed it, it must have been
publicly forwarded by the Neo-Arians even prior to
spring, A.D. 358. But given that three of the eleven
sections of the 359 memorandum were devoted to refuting
the position (73:13, 15 and 22), the Neo-Arians must
have promoted the doctrine vigorously in response to
the championing of likeness-in-essence by the synodical
letter. If we reflect upon the Neo-Arian doctrine, we
discover that it was a logical deduction from the
Neo-Arians' preference for creator/created theological
language over Father/Son language, or more precisely,
from their willingness to take literally only the former language. Creations are products of the wills of
creators, and thereby can legitimately be said to
reflect those wills or to be "like" them. Therefore,
since the Son is a creation of God, he must be "like"
God's will. But, as the fourth fragment quoted in
the memorandum made plain, one must be sure not to
confuse a being's "will" or "power ($\dot{\epsilon}\xi o \upsilon \sigma \acute{\iota} \alpha$)" with its
"nature ($\varphi \acute{\upsilon} \sigma \iota \varsigma$)." A being's nature is obviously
superior to its power, and its nature is even more
obviously superior to and different from the effects

189

of that power. Because the Son has his life not from
his own nature but from the power of the Ungenerated,
and because the Ungenerated Nature is endlessly great
than every power, the likeness of the Son cannot extend beyond God's power to his nature or essence.
Here then was the doctrine of likeness which the Neo-
Arians opposed to the Homoiousians'.

Before we leave the second Neo-Arian fragment,
however, we must note that in the year between the
Ancyran letter and Basil's and George's memorandum th
Neo-Arians had not at all changed their minds about
the Son's essential immutability. Continuing to fear
that the Homoiousians' way of interpreting theologica
Father/Son language logically made it necessary that
the Son be begotten as incomplete or imperfect, the
Neo-Arians insisted in fragment #1 of the memorandum
that the Son preserves God's will "<u>pure</u> in his own
hypostasis" or, to put the matter the other way
around, that "God made him to exist as a hypostasis
<u>just as he willed.</u>" The Neo-Arians would have nothin
to do with notions of change or development in the
Son's essence. Thus, while the Neo-Arians rejected
the essentialist concepts of their opponents (both
homoiousion and homoousion) in favor of voluntarist
concepts, we find in them no hint of early Arian
ethical voluntarism. They rejected essentialist concepts implied by begetting in favor of voluntarist
concepts implied by creation. The voluntarism of the
Neo-Arians was a creationist voluntarism of God, not
an early Arian ethical voluntarism of the Son.

Having explicated fragments #1, 2 and 4 of the
359 memorandum, we have now to treat fragments #5 and
6 (#3 is relatively insignificant). These fragments
are most striking, for they indicate that in response
to the Ancyran letter of A.D. 358 the Neo-Arians
decided to make a significant change in theological
tactics. Our evidence suggests that until the issuin
of the letter, the Neo-Arians' attitude toward theological Father/Son language was fundamentally critica
and negative. They feared it; they endeavored to
substitute for it creator/created language; they argu
that it was pseudonymous. In fragments #5 and 6, however, the Neo-Arians abandoned criticism and began

using the language in a positive fashion, weaving it into the fabric of their theological system. Apparently the Ancyran synodical letter had received widespread favorable response to its insistence that theological Father/Son language was eminently scriptural. So, assuming the legitimacy of the language, Neo-Arian fragment #5 argued that God's name of Father is not revelatory of his essence but rather of his power, the power by which he made the Son to exist as a hypostasis and gave the Son his eternal essence and power. Fragment #6 gave the rationale for this position. Addressing the Homoiousians, the fragment said that if the term Father is revelatory of essence, and God and the Monogenes are like-in-essence, then the Monogenes should also be termed Father--which is absurd. A Homoiousian had no choice but to conclude that the term Father designates God's will and not his essence. The Neo-Arian explanation for scriptural Father/Son language, then, was rather simple. The Neo-Arians had argued all along that the Son is unlike God in essence but like him in will. Now they added that the term Father refers to God's will, not to his essence. But since the Son preserves God's will "pure in his own hypostasis," and, for the Neo-Arians, hypostasis and essence are interchangeable, the Son's essence must be like the Father, that is, like God's will. The implication was evident: whereas the term Father denotes God's will, not his essence, the term Son denotes the Monogenes' essence, not his will (referred to as his 'power' in fragment #5). Precisely this same position would be argued in A.D. 360 by the Neo-Arian Eunomius (in his Apologia 21-24). After reiterating the Neo-Arian assumption that God's will is his activity (Apol. 23), Eunomius said, "The appellation Son reveals essence, but the appellation Father reveals the activity of the generating one" (Apol. 24). Thus, the term ungenerated refers to God's essence and the term Father to his will or activity, while the term Son refers to God the Word's essence and, since it denotes something that has come into being, is interchangeable with the term generated. In this way the Neo-Arians sought to clear themselves of the charge made in the Ancyran letter that they did not take

191

scriptural and traditional Father/Son terminology
seriously enough. Furthermore, by adding Father/Son
language to their more fundamental ungenerated/
generated language, the Neo-Arians now had a way of
indicating both the intimate connection between the
High God and God the Word (Father/Son) and the essential difference between them (Ingenerate/Generate).
But, as have seen, Basil and George either did not
grasp or refused to accept the Neo-Arians' interpretation of the Father/Son relationship, for they continued to maintain that the Neo-Arians were "anxious
. . . no longer to say Father and Son but rather to
say ungenerated and generated" (73:14). It is possible
that they did not fully grasp it, since the second
section of their memorandum attributed to the Neo-
Arians the view that the Son's will and activity are
like the Father's will and activity. This was simply
not the Neo-Arian position: 'Father' for them denoted
will and activity and, therefore, could not possess
them. The probability, however, is that the Homoiousian
chose to misrepresent the Neo-Arians, since, given their
new refinements, the Neo-Arians could now in good
conscience maintain that the Son in essence is like
the Father (that is, God's will) while at the same
time maintain that the Son in essence is unlike God
(that is, Ungenerated Essence). The Neo-Arians were
now maintaining the affirmation of the Dated Creed
that the Son is like the Father "in all things,"
for the Son preserves God's will--that is, the
Father--"pure in his own hypostasis." No wonder
Basil and George were so concerned to issue a defense
of their own homoiousian interpretation of the Dated
Creed! Through the rehabilitation of Eudoxius, Aetius,
and Eunomius, the Homoiousians had been outmaneuvered
ecclesiastically by the Neo-Arians, especially by
George of Alexandria; now they were worried that they
had also been outmaneuvered theologically.

We have now quoted and assessed all of the 359
memorandum's direct witness (and most of its indirect
witness) to the Neo-Arian views promoted between the
Ancyran council of spring 358 and the summer of 359.
We have also seen that because Basil and George
finally came to realize that the heart and core of

the Neo-Arian system was its use of the ungenerated/
generated distinction, they decided that they had to
break with the eastern theological tradition of the
Macrostich and Sirmium, 351 and to attack the dichotomy in favor of the Father/Son distinction. Whether
or not their attack was carried out in a manner completely fair to the new Neo-Arian explanation for
scriptural and traditional Father/Son terminology, it
is perfectly evident that Basil and George were being
led closer and closer to Athanasian positions, for
both Athanasius' Orationes of A.D. 339 and his De
Decretis of A.D. 350 contained comparable attacks on
the early Arians' use of the ungenerated/generated
dichotomy. The Athanasian attacks are surely to be
considered the prototypes of the memorandum's; the
attitude of respect for Athanasius' writings we
already noticed in the Ancyran synodical letter was
carried on also in the 359 memorandum.

This brings us to a most important point. The
sentence immediately preceding the memorandum's first
attack on the ungenerated/generated distinction argued
that in order to avoid Sabellianism, the Homoiousians
maintained that "in this is the exact recognition of
the persons (τῶν προσώπων), in the fact that the Father
is always a father, being fleshless and immortal, and
the Son is always a son and never a father; and being
said always to be because of the timelessness and incomprehensibility of his hypostasis, he assumed flesh
according to the will of the Father and submitted to
death on behalf of us" (73:14). It is interesting to
note that the Ancyran letter of 358 criticized the
Neo-Arians for emphasizing not only the ungenerated/
generated dichotomy but also the distinctions between
(1) the fleshless and the enfleshed and (2) the immortal and the one who has received the trial of death;
the 359 memorandum, on the other hand, used both of
these distinctions in a positive manner. Since they
easily could be recognized to bear an irreproachable
theological sense, Basil and George backed off
Ancyra's negative view of them in order to focus
attention on the memorandum's strong rejection of the
ungenerated/generated distinction. More importantly,
however, these two distinctions were used to establish

"the exact recognition of the persons." If we take
this statement, which occurred in the memorandum's
third section, in connection with the arguments of its
first and fifth sections (73:12 and 16), we may discern
Basil's and George's intent. Intensely conscious that
they were hemmed in on all sides by the new eastern
alliance, the Homoiousians realized that they needed
outside help. And the only viable outside ecclesiastical help was that of the western church. Therefore,
in addition to appropriating as much as they could of
the theological position taken by the West's favorite
easterner Athanasius, Basil and George tried to explain their own position in a way that would approxi-
mate as much as possible the theological position of
the West. In section one (73:12) they argued that
though the term οὐσία did not "lie nakedly" in scripture, its sense was conveyed everywhere; it was even
accepted by the eastern bishops who condemned Paul
of Samosata and his use of homoousion. Next, in
section three (73:14) the bishops sought to distinguish
between the "persons" of Father and Son. Finally, they
began section five (73:16) as follows: "Let the name
of hypostasis not disturb any. Because of this do the
easterners speak about hypostases, in order that they
may make known the peculiar properties of the persons
(τὰς ἰδιότητας τῶν προσώπων)." Nonetheless, the
easterners "confess that there is one divinity which
encompasses all things through the Son in the Holy
Spirit," and they confess "one divinity, one kingship,
and one rule." The intended implication was, it
seems, that the term οὐσία defended in section one of
the memorandum should be used to express the unity of
the divinity, while the term hypostasis should be used
to express each peculiar property of what the West
called the "three persons" of the Trinity;[1] Father,
Son, and Holy Spirit are similar in οὐσία but distin-
guishable in hypostasis.[2] This all seems to have been

---

1. Compare Gummerus, pp. 127-9.
2. That the Homoiousians were maintaining this
view was substantiated by the Neo-Arian Eunomius: in
his Apologia of December, A.D. 359 Eunomius assumed
that the Homoiousians argued this case.

194

a plea to the West to abandon three persons of the same essence (homoousion) and accept three persons of similar essence (homoiousion). Perhaps Basil and George hoped that Hilary of Poitiers, who had represented their position to the West so sympathetically in his De Synodis of early A.D. 359, would be stimulated to communicate the plea. Certainly they hoped Athanasius would be moved--which he was, as is evident from his De Synodis of late A.D. 359. Unfortunately, however, the Homoiousians' theology was expressed in a muddy fashion--primarily because of Basil's signing of the Dated Creed. The Dated Creed had committed Basil to supporting "like in all things" and to abstaining from the term οὐσία. As we learn from the fourth, sixth, and seventh sections of the memorandum (73:15, 17 and 18), it was very difficult for Basil and George to express themselves crisply and clearly with "in all things" substituted for οὐσία. They did the best they could.

Before we conclude our analysis of the memorandum we must consider one final passage, since it reveals to us the depth of the Homoiousians' fear of the new Danubean/Neo-Arian alliance. We learn how far Basil, in particular, had fallen since the spring of A.D. 358, when he had achieved the exile of the Neo-Arians from their positions of power. The bishops wrote as follows:

> . . . having already written that the Son
> is unlike the Father in essence, they [the
> Neo-Arians] thought that they could condemn
> the church through the written things which
> they chased from the venerable Bishop Ossius,
> in which unlike-in-essence is conveyed. But
> since those who went up from the East to
> Sirmium last year [Sirmium, 358] refuted the
> evil work of this heresy . . . , they en-
> deavored to take away from the ecclesiasti-
> cal teaching the term essence (οὐσία) in use
> by the Fathers [Sirmium, 359] . . . in order
> that also in this they might seem to strengthen
> their heresy. (73:14)

195

The reference to Ossius in this passage was to his so-
called "fall," namely, to his signing (under pressure)
of the Sirmium pronouncement of A.D. 357, which excluded οὐσία from theological discourse and banned both
homoousion and homoiousion.[1] Apparently the Neo-Arians
had circulated the same interpretation of Ossius' signing of this pronouncement as they had of Liberius',
namely, that a repudiation of homoousion and homoiousion
meant an endorsement of heteroousion. What is striking
about the memorandum's passage is that it accepted the
Neo-Arian interpretation of the 357 pronouncement and
thereby implied that the Danubeans were Neo-Arian in
theology as early as Sirmium, 357. The ecclesiastical
alliance which George of Alexandria had promoted for
the first time at Sirmium, 359 was represented by Basil
and George to have been a theological conspiracy of
two-years standing. Badly outmaneuvered in A.D. 359,
Basil and George could only account for their plight
by claiming that Neo-Arianism was the major theological
force not only at Sirmium, 359 but at Sirmium, 357 and
358 as well. By so implying, however, Basil discredited himself in the eyes of his own homoiousian party;
he had, after all, signed the Dated Creed. That Basil
was held to blame for the Dated Creed by other Homoiousians is evident from the fact that the leadership
of the party was taken over at the eastern Council of
Seleucia (autumn, A.D. 359) by George of Laodicea,
Sophronius of Pompeiopolis, and Eleusius of Cyzicus;
Basil did not even arrive until the proceedings were
well underway.[2] Furthermore, the theological position
finally defended at Seleucia by George, Sophronius,
and Eleusius was not the one signed by Basil at
Sirmium, 359 and explicated--as best it could be--in
the memorandum of 359. At Seleucia the Homoiousians
were forced to stand, as we shall see, on what they
termed the "faith of the Fathers," that is, the
"second" creed of the 341 Council of Antioch.[3] This
was, of course, interpreted in a homoiousian fashion:

---

1.   See De Clercq, pp. 474-525.
2.   Socrates, H.E. 2:29; Sozomen, H.E. 4:22.
3.   Socrates, H.E. 2:40; Sozomen, H.E. 4:22.

the creed's claim that the Son is the exact image of
the Father's essence was assumed to be the key to its
theological import.

To conclude our treatment of the homoiousian
memorandum, let us return to what the document reveals
to us about Neo-Arian thought in the year prior to its
writing and summarize our findings.

(1) As was the case throughout the early and
middle A.D. 350s, the Neo-Arians continued
to promote their formula of unlikeness-
in-essence and continued to justify the
formula by means of the ungenerated/
generated distinction, a distinction
whose importance to Neo-Arian thought
had finally been appreciated by the
Homoiousians.

(2) The Neo-Arians had begun to realize that
the Homoiousians were as much of a threat
to them as were Athanasius and homoousion.
Hence, they promoted an explanation of
the sense in which God and the Son are
'like' and added it to their explanation
of how they are 'unlike': they are unlike in essence, they are like in will.
The controlling voluntarism of the Neo-
Arian theological system was beginning
to become clear. However, though the
Neo-Arians were rejecting essentialist
concepts in favor of voluntarist ones,
they were promoting a creationist
voluntarism of God, not the early
Arian ethical voluntarism of the Son.

(3) The Neo-Arians had begun to ease their
criticism of theological Father/Son
language and, instead, had developed
a positive explanation for that language
which harmonized with their fundamental
beliefs. They argued that the term
Father designates God's will, not his
essence. Thus, Father and Son are
'like,' while God and the Son are
'unlike.'

197

During the period from the beginning of A.D. 357 to the summer of A.D. 359 Neo-Arian fortunes had ebbed and flowed more than once. By the end of the period, however, the Neo-Arians had formed and consolidated a rather definite ecclesiastical party and an even more definite theological platform. Furthermore, they had made an alliance with the politically astute Danubean bishops and the equally astute Acadius of Caesarea. Such developments could only have made them feel secure and confident as they looked forward to the general councils called by Constantius to meet at Rimini in Italy and at Seleucia in Asia Minor.

CHAPTER 4

THE COUNCIL OF SELEUCIA,
THE DE SYNODIS OF ATHANASIUS,
AND THE SYNTAGMATION OF AETIUS,
AUTUMN, A.D. 359

While the publication of Basil's and George's memorandum in the summer of A.D. 359 could only have been interpreted by the Neo-Arians as a sign that the alliance they had made with the Danubeans and Acacius of Caesarea had decisively turned the tide against the Homoiousians, they discovered in the next six months that the downfall of their hated theological enemies did not necessarily mean their own victory. The Danubeans and Acacius were their allies, but certainly not their converts; the Neo-Arians slowly learned that their allies had their own ecclesiastical objectives, which were of more concern to them than Neo-Arian fortunes. This began to emerge already at the Council of Seleucia, the eastern half of the twin councils summoned by Constantius to meet during the summer and fall of A.D. 359.

The council's first session took place on Monday, 27 September 359; between 150 and 160 bishops gathered under the watchful eye of an imperial questor Leonas. Since the Danubean bishops were westerners and, therefore, attended the council at Rimini, the cause of the alliance was defended at Seleucia by Eudoxius of Antioch, George of Alexandria, and, especially, Acacius of Caesarea and his ecclesiastical neighbor Uranius of Tyre. They were joined by the old Arian Patrophilus of Scythopolis; by such Neo-Arian prelates as the two Lydians Leontius of Tripolis and Theodosius of Philadelphia, by Evagrius of Mytilene and Theodolus of Chaeretapi (all from Asia Minor); and by a number of Egyptian bishops ordained by the now dead, staunch old Arian Secundus of Ptolemais, in particular, Bishops Stephen of Ptolemais, Serras of Paraetonius, Polydeuces of Libya, and Pancratius of Pelusium.[1] Because the

---

1. Athanasius, Syn. 12.

allies feared they were badly outnumbered,[1] their
strategy was to delay discussions on matters of theology and concentrate on discrediting their opponents.
So they brought charges against them for ecclesiastical
misconduct. Unfortunately, the chief candidates for
such accusations--namely, Basil of Ancyra, who was
responsible for the Neo-Arians' exile in A.D. 358, and
Macedonius of Constantinople, who was infamous for his
cruelty[2]--were not present. After a motion to suspend
proceedings until their arrival failed, the allies
levelled charges against Cyril of Jerusalem and Eustathius of Sebaste, moves which led to a long and spirit-
ed battle over procedure. Finally, they were forced
by the majority to deal with doctrinal questions.[3]
According to Socrates,[4] the allies argued against the
Nicene Creed and, according to Sozomen,[5] offered in
its stead the Dated Creed of Sirmium, 359, minus, it
seems, the words "in all things ($\varkappa \alpha \tau \grave{\alpha} \; \pi \acute{\alpha} \nu \tau \alpha$)."[6] The
Homoiousians responded by defending all the decisions
of Nicaea, with the sole exception of its decision to
use homoousion;[7] presumably they suggested that all
that was necessary was to substitute homoiousion.[8] It
hurt the alliance's cause that the leading Homoiousian
who had signed the Dated Creed, Basil of Ancyra, was
not present (surely by design, for he had badly com-
promised his party's position by agreeing at Sirmium
to bar the term $o\grave{\upsilon}\sigma\acute{\iota}\alpha$ from theological discourse).
It also did not help that Acacius of Caesarea had
written a letter to Macedonius of Constantinople
(apparently at a time after the Dated Creed was issued

----

1. See Gwatkin, pp. 194-6 for the numbers, though
they probably represented only the final outcome of the
council's deliberations.
2. Socrates, H.E. 2:38.
3. Ibid., 2:39; Sozomen, H.E. 4:22.
4. Socrates, H.E. 2:39. Compare Athanasius, Syn.
33.
5. Sozomen, H.E. 2:22.
6. See Gummerus, p. 141.
7. Athanasius, Syn. 41; Socrates, H.E. 2:39.
8. Compare Hilary of Poitiers, C. Const. 12.

in May, A.D. 359 but before Acacius had decided to
join the Danubean/Neo-Arian alliance) in which he
agreed that "the Son is in all things like the Father,
and of the same essence (τῆς αὐτῆς οὐσίας)."[1] But the
allies' cause at Seleucia was most damaged when, at
the mention of homoiousion and Father/Son language, the
Neo-Arians in full council opposed them with blistering polemic and irreverent interpretation. One of
those present at the council, Hilary of Poitiers,
tells us that the Neo-Arians denied (1) "that anything
is able to be like God's essence" and (2) "that generation from God is possible."[2] Christ is not something
generated from God's essence, they said, but rather
"is a creature"; his creation is to be considered his
"birth (nativitas)," "for he is from nothing, and,
consequently, is not a son, nor like God."[3] To back
up the polemic, a Neo-Arian read from a sermon delivered by Bishop Eudoxius of Antioch in which the bishop
argued, "God was what he is. Father he was not, because
he did not have a son: for if there was a son, it is
necessary that there also was a female, and conversation and dialogue, and a conjugal agreement, and
allurement (blandimentum), and, finally, a natural
organ (naturalis machinula) for generating."[4] Such
statements were taken as insults by the Homoiousians,
and the contention intensified.[5] Judging from the
fact that when the council met for its second full
session (on Wednesday, September 29, 359) Acacius of
Caesarea proposed to bar both homoiousion and the Neo-
Arian catchword anomoion (unlike), the first session
must have eventually degenerated into the hurling back
and forth of theological slogans. Finally the Homoiousian Silvanus of Tarsus, seeing the impossibility
of persuading the allies through theological discussion,
tried another tactic. He declared that it was the duty
of the council to leave aside new declarations of faith,

1. Sozomen, H.E. 4:22.
2. Hilary of Poitiers, C. Const. 12.
3. Ibid.
4. Ibid., 13.
5. Socrates, H.E. 2:39; Sozomen, H.E. 4:22.

such as the Dated Creed, which had led to the council's turmoil; it should confirm the "second" creed of Antioch, 341.[1] Since this creed was a revered eastern formula and included the claim that the Son is the "exact image of the Father's essence," it was the Homoiousians' best hope. By championing it, the Homoiousians could dismiss both the Dated Creed and all Neo-Arian claims as innovations. The Neo-Arians did not have close at hand a comparable creedal statement, endorsed by a recognized council, with which to counter. Distressed by Silvanus' move, Acacius of Caesarea reacted by leading the allies out of the meeting. After the Homoiousians had the "second" creed of Antioch, 341 read, presumably to refresh their memories so they could consider Silvanus' suggestion, they too left the meeting place. So ended the first day of the Seleucian council.

Because the council's first day had been so stormy, the imperial representative Leonas decided not to call a session for the second day, that is, Tuesday, September 28. Nonetheless, the Homoiousians decided to meet; they did so behind closed doors at the church of Seleucia, where they formally signed the "second" creed of Antioch, 341.[2] How many bishops were present at this meeting is not known, but there were enough to disturb the allies; the latter protested that "all such secret transactions were justly to be suspected, and had no validity whatever."[3] We cannot be totally certain, but we probably ought to date to Tuesday, September 28 the issuing of a document mentioned in Philostorgius' discussion of the council. The historian wrote that Eudoxius and Aetius, "confirming difference-in-essence in writing, sent their document everywhere."[4] The reason for our dating is that on the next day of the council, as we shall see, the Neo-Arians supported an ingeniously deceptive move by Acacius to bar from ecclesiastical usage not only

---

1. Ibid.
2. Socrates, H.E. 2:39.
3. Ibid., 2:40.
4. Philostorgius, H.E. 4:11.

homoousion and homoiousion but also the Neo-Arian
catchword anomoion. Aetius and Acacius seem to have
come to an agreement, for Aetius' Syntagmation, which
was published in late autumn A.D. 359, also refrained
from using both anomoion and heteroousion in its pre-
sentation of Neo-Arian theology. Eudoxius and Aetius
were certainly unnerved by the Homoiousians' signing
of the "second" creed of Antioch and, therefore, probably issued their Neo-Arian document as an attempt to
gain as much support as possible among the council's
participants and constituencies. Although the whole
document has not been preserved for us, there is
reason to suppose that Theodoret referred to it in his
ecclesiastical history and that not only Theodoret but
Basil of Caesarea and the Historia Acephala quoted
from it. We begin with Theodoret's reference.[1] Relating an episode which took place about three months
after the Council of Seleucia in the presence of
Emperor Constantius, Theodoret claimed that Eustathius
of Sebaste produced a Neo-Arian "exposition of faith"
which the Homoiousian bishop alleged was was written
by Eudoxius. He went on to say that Eudoxius repudi-
ated the authorship and affirmed it was penned by
Aetius, who admitted he wrote it. Obviously Eudoxius
was familiar enough with the document to attribute it
to Aetius; so it is plausible to suppose that the
exposition was the same one that Aetius and Eudoxius
circulated at Seleucia. If this is true, we are
fortunate, for Theodoret preserved a short but revealing fragment from the statement, and Basil of Caesarea
preserved a slightly fuller version of the same fragment. Basil's version read as follows:

> ". . . things unlike in nature are presented
> in unlike terms, and, conversely, things
> expressed in unlike terms are unlike in
> nature [Theodoret: unlike in essence]." In
> proof of this statement Aetius drags in the
> words of the Apostle, "There is one God and
> Father, from whom are all things, and one

---

1. Theodoret, H.E. 2:23.

Lord Jesus Christ, through whom are all
things." "Whatever, then," he goes on,
"is the relation of these terms to one
another, such will be the relation of the
natures indicated by them; but 'through
whom' is unlike 'from whom'; therefore, the
Son is unlike the [God and: Basil] Father."[1]

What is most interesting about this characteristically
Neo-Arian syllogism is that it was based on the affirmations of the same "second" creed of Antioch, 341 that
the Homoiousians had ratified on Tuesday, September 28!
Aetius and Eudoxius were claiming that the Antiochene
creed (especially its scriptural ingredient, 1 Cor.
8:6) supported their own anomoian position, not the
homoiousian. If we turn to the portions of Aetius'
and Eudoxius' encyclical quoted in the <u>Historia
Acephala</u>,[2] we see that the letter also claimed that
the creed's characteristic formula 'likeness
ἀπαραλλάκτως' described the Neo-Arian, not the homoiousian, position: Et in hoc possidet inuariabilem
apud patrem similitudinem, quod omnia uidet, quod
omnia potest, quod non mutatur bonitate. But the
Son's likeness to God does not mean that the Son is
properly God. Rather than God, he is "the Son of God,
the God of those after him." The letter made a clear
distinction between the Son's attributes and God's.
God is "ungenerated, beginningless, eternal, so that
he is not commanded, immutable, seeing all things,
infinite, incomparable, omnipotent, without foresight
knowing future things, without Lord," whereas the Son
"is commanded, is subject to command, is <u>ex nihilo</u>, has

---

1. Basil of Caesarea, <u>Spir.</u> 2.
2. To my knowledge, the first scholar to notice
that the <u>Expositio Patricii et Aetii</u> quoted in <u>Hist.
Aceph</u>. 14 was a selection of quotations (in Latin
translation) from the letter mentioned by Philostorgius,
<u>H.E.</u> 4:11 and Theodoret, <u>H.E.</u> 2:23 was R.P. Vaggione,
who discussed the matter at length in his 1976 Oxford
dissertation (Vaggione, pp. 103-14). I am delighted
to acknowledge my debt to his astuteness.

an end, is compared, the Father surpasses him . . . ,
is ignorant of the future." The encyclical, however,
not only claimed the "second" Antiochene creed for
Neo-Arianism and defended the movement's characteristic
subordinationism; it was also without quarter in its
direct polemic against the Homoiousians. Over and over
it rejected the notion that the Son is "ex natura
patris" and "similis natura." The letter reached its
polemical heights with the following words against
Homoiousianism:

> Si dixerimus 'deum' Dei filium, duos sine
> initio inducimus; imaginem dicimus dei. Qui
> dicit 'ex Deo' sabellizat: et qui dicit se
> ignorare dei natiuitatem manichizat. Et si
> quis dixerit sustantiam fili 'similem sub-
> stantiae' patris non nati blasphemat: sicut
> enim nix et simithium quantum ad albidinem
> similes, ad speciem autem non similes, sic
> et fili substantia alis est praeter patris
> substantia. Nix autem aliam habet albidinem.

According to Aetius and Eudoxius, Father and Son are
not like-in-essence but like-in-activity (ex opere, ex
operationibus).[1]

---

1. In two areas the theology of the encyclical
was out of tune with other statements of Neo-Arian
thought. First, as we have seen, between the Council
of Ancyra, 358 and the homoiousian memorandum of 359
the Neo-Arians had developed a clear distinction
between the referents of the terms Father and God.
That distinction was not maintained in the encyclical,
most likely because of the key role the term Father
played in the "second" creed of Antioch, 341: the
Neo-Arians' syllogistic response to the creed was
forced to use the creed's terms. Second, the encyclical seems to have claimed that no persons in the
supernatural hierarchy of being (angels, archangels,
cherubim, Holy Spirit, Monogenes, and God) "are able
to comprehend or understand" the nature of the beings
in the next higher rank. Both Aetius and Eunomius

If we are correct in our reconstruction of Neo-Arian activities on Tuesday, September 28, it is no wonder that the astute ecclesiastical politician Acacius determined that a compromise between the Homoiousians and the Neo-Arians (or what could pass for a compromise) was the only way to save the council from a hopeless row. He began working on one already on Tuesday,[1] and was far enough along by Wednesday to suggest to Leonas, who sympathized with him,[2] that a second full session of the council should be called. Eager for a resolution of the hostilities, Leonas complied, so on Wednesday the bishops once again gathered. This time Basil of Ancyra and Macedonius of Constantinople also were present, the former perhaps because his embarrassing signing of the Dated Creed had now been circumvented by the Homoiousians through their endorsement of the "second" creed of Antioch.[3] Angered by their sudden presence, Acacius demanded that the session should not proceed until deposed or accused bishops like Basil and Macadonius withdrew from the assembly. After some resistance, the Homoiousians agreed to this, and the session continued.[4] Apparently they felt themselves to be on very secure ground. Leonas announced that he wanted to read to them a document written on Tuesday by Acacius; it turned out to be a new creed, introduced by a shrewdly phrased preamble.[5] Reminding the council

---

held the very opposite, as we shall see. On the other hand, Vaggione has cited evidence which maintained that the Neo-Arians' episcopal patron Eudoxius held to this view (Vaggione, p. 107). Perhaps on this issue Aetius was molifying his patron. However, it is possible that the passage in the encyclical was ironic or part of a rhetorical argument. The Latin text is corrupt and this passage particularly without context.

1. Socrates, H.E. 2:40.
2. Sozomen, H.E. 4:22.
3. Compare Gummerus, pp. 141-2.
4. Socrates, H.E. 2:40; Sozomen, H.E. 4:22 (all translations are from NPNF 2:69).
5. The text is in Epiphanius, Haer. 73:25-6, Socrates, H.E. 2:40 and, in part, in Athanasius Syn. 29.

that the purpose of the Monday meeting was to preserve "the peace of the Church" and to determine doctrinal matters on the basis of scripture, as Emperor Constantius had ordered, the preamble went on to argue that the "tumult and disorder" of the session prevented this goal from being achieved. A description of Acacius' compromise followed:

> We do not repudiate the faith which was ratified at the consecration of the church at Antioch; for we give it our decided preference, because it received the concurrence of our Fathers who assembled there to consider some controverted points. Since, however, the terms homoousion and homoiousion have in time past troubled the minds of many, and still continue to disquiet them, and moreover, since a new term has recently been coined by some who assert the anomoion of the Son to the Father; we reject the first two, as expressions which are not found in the scriptures, but we utterly anathematize the last, as alienated from the church. We distinctly acknowledge the homoion of the Son to the Father, in accordance with what the Apostle has declared concerning him, "who is the image of the invisible God."

The terms of Acacius' proposed compromise having been outlined, the document ended with a creed. Although it is often said that the creed was simply the Dated Creed "revised for eastern acceptance,"[1] the differences were as many as the similarities. Yet, the basic theological position of both was the same--that is, they both were scriptural and vague on the crucial theological points at issue. The sections relevant to the Seleucian debate read as follows: "We confess and

---

1. Gwatkin, p. 178; Kidd, 2:170; Kelly, Creeds, p. 292, etc.

believe in one God the Father almighty, the maker of
heaven and earth, and of things visible and invisible.
We believe also in our Lord Jesus Christ, the Son of
God, who was begotten of him without passion before
all ages, God the Word, the only-begotten God from
God, the Light, the Life, the Truth, the Wisdom, the
Power, through whom all things were made which are in
the heavens and on the earth, whether visible or invisible."

The Acacian compromise and creed were evidently
intended to be as conciliatory as possible to the
Homoiousians. The "second" Antiochene creed which had
been ratified the day before was endorsed as the faith
of the Fathers, and Homoiousian objections to homoousion and, especially, to anomoion were registered and
accepted. Moreover, the Acacian creed used for the
Son a mixture of traditional terms found in both the
often-repeated "fourth" creed of Antioch, 341 and in
its "second" creed: whereas the Acacian creed spoke
of "God the Word, the only-begotten God from God, the
Light, the Life, the Truth, the Wisdom, the Power,
through whom all things were made which are in the
heavens and on the earth, whether invisible or visible,"
the "fourth" Antiochene creed had "Jesus Christ . . .
through whom all things were made which are in the
heavens and on the earth, visible and invisible, being
Word and Wisdom and Power and Life and true Light"[1] and
the "second" Antiochene creed had "the only-begotten
God, through whom are all things . . . , Living Word,
Living Wisdom, True Light . . . Truth."[2] All that was
required of Homoiousians was to refrain from using
the offensive term homoiousion and the unscriptural
phrase "exact image of the Father's essence." In place
of homoiousion, they should accept the less offensive
homoion (like), and in place of the unscriptural phrase
which regarded the Son as image of the Father's essence,
they should accept the emimently scriptural clause
"who is the image of the invisible God (Col. 1:15)."
Surely, argued Acacius, this was worth trading for a

---

1. Athanasius, _Syn_. 25.
2. _Ibid_., 23.

strong anathema against the anomoian catchword and for
the removal of the clause "from whom are all things"
as descriptive of God, a clause absolutely essential
to the Neo-Arians' syllogistic interpretation of the
"second" Antiochene creed.

At this point we must consider the inevitable
question: did Acacius' compromise and creed mean that
he had abandoned his Neo-Arian allies? After all,
"utterly to anathematize" his allies' formula of the
Son's unlikeness to the Father was to use rather strong
language of supposed friends. Judging from the fact
that Eudoxius, George of Alexandria, and such other
Neo-Arian devotees as the two Lydians Leontius of
Tripoli and Theodosius of Philadelphia signed the
document,[1] the answer is decidedly no. Acacius had
abandoned no one: the Neo-Arians had simply decided
to become very precise--and very deceptive--in their
theological terms. Hilary of Poitiers, for one, was
perplexed. He asked a Neo-Arian bishop how he could
sign such a document.[2] The bishop responded, "Christ
is not like God, but he is like the Father." When
Hilary admitted complete confusion, the bishop responded that the Son is unlike God but like the Father
because the Father willed to create a creature who
would will the same things as he. Therefore, the Son
is like the Father because he is a son of his will
(voluntatis) rather than of his divinity (divinitis),
"for he is unlike God because he is neither God nor
from God, that is, born from the Father's essence."
What lay behind this answer was the Neo-Arians' reservation of the term Father for God's will and their
denial of it to his essence, a usage we discussed in
connection with a Neo-Arian quotation in Basil's and
George's 359 memorandum. It is true that in the document the Neo-Arians circulated during the Seleucian
council they asserted that "the Son is unlike the God
and Father." But undoubtedly the reason the term
Father was used was because it occurred in the major
premise quoted from the "second" creed of Antioch, 341.

---

1. Epiphanius, _Haer_. 73:26.
2. Hilary of Poitiers, _C. Const_. 14.

The pressures of the moment had caused the Neo-Arians to be theologically imprecise in their response to the Homoiousians' championing of the "second" Antiochene creed. Now Acacius saw that their imprecision could be used to their advantage. A position which did not exactly represent Neo-Arian views could be anathematized, and the true Neo-Arian position would remain unscathed; so, even after signing the Acacian proposal, the Neo-Arians could be true to their basic view that the Son was like the Father (God's will) but different from God's essence. The term essence, of course, was not banned by Acacius' compromise, only its compounds, homoousion and homoiousion. And it was easy for the Neo-Arians to defend their view without using anomoion. Aetius would be able to write his entire Syntagmation of late autumn, 359 without ever using anomoion, or even heteroousion. His favorite substitute was "incomparability in essence (τὸ ἐν οὐσίᾳ ἀσύγκριτον)."

The success of Acacius' compromise was limited. In the end only 39 of the council's 150 to 160 bishops subscribed it: nearly half of the subscribers were from the Syrian/Palestinian region, another quarter from lower Egypt, and most of the rest from the province of Asia.[1] Among the signatories were the leaders of the alliance (George of Alexandria, Acacius of Caesarea, Uranius of Tyre, and Eudoxius of Antioch), an old Arian or two (most notably, Serras of Paraetonius in Libya), and a number of bishops from Asia Minor who would become in subsequent years stalwarts of the Neo-Arian movement (Leontius of Tripoli, Theodosius of Philadelphia, Phoebus of Polychalandus, and Evagrius of Mitylene). The compromise impressed the Homoiousians not at all. After it was read to the gathered bishops, the Homoiousians stubbornly refused even to consider it. Their position was expressed by Bishop Sophronius of Pompeiopolis, who said, "If we daily receive the opinions of individuals as an exposition of the faith, we shall fail in attaining precision in the truth."[2]

---

1.   Epiphanius, Haer. 73:26.
2.   Sozomen, H.E. 4:22. Compare Socrates, H.E. 2:20.

He obviously was referring to Acacius' exposition of
the faith following by only a day the one distributed
by Eudoxius and Aetius. At the beginning of the third
session of the council (held on Thursday, September 30)
Acacius responded to Sophronius' position by recalling
to the bishops that new formulations of the faith were
not at all to be forbidden, since the formula of Nicaea
itself had been often altered by easterners. The
Homoiousians remained unmoved. They decided, in fact,
to go on the attack, inquiring of the allies in what
way they thought the Son was like the Father. The
allies replied honestly, claiming that the likeness
was in will only, not in essence, at which point the
Homoiousians reminded Acacius of his earlier letter to
Macedonius, in which he endorsed "likeness in all
things." This angered Acacius; he not only retorted
that a person ought not to be held to his earlier
writings but apparently turned the accusation against
Basil, asking whether he wanted to be held to his subscription of the Dated Creed.[1] The situation was
hopeless. The imperial representative recognized it
by dissolving the council on Thursday and by refusing
to reconvene it the following day. Therefore, the
Homoiousian group met by themselves and expressed their
commitment by deposing the Palestinian bishops Acacius
and Uranius, the six leading Neo-Arian bishops (George
of Alexandria, Eudoxius of Antioch, Theodosius of
Philadelphia, Evagrius of Mytilene, Leontius of Tripolis, and Theodolus of Chaeretapi in Phrygia), and
Patrophilus of Scythopolis, who was responsible for
the Neo-Arians' rehabilitation with Constantius soon
after the meeting at Sirmium in May, 359. In addition,
nine other bishops were excommunicated.[2] These
actions had little meaning, for the Homoiousians had
no power to enforce their decisions; when they went so
far as to try to replace Eudoxius as bishop of Antioch

_____

1. Sozomen, H.E. 4:22; Socrates, H.E. 2:40.
2. Socrates, H.E. 2:40; Athanasius, Syn. 12. For
some reason not readily apparent, the names of Theodolus and Patrophilus did not appear on the subscription
list to Acacius' compromise and creed.

with a man named Anianus, the allies had had enough.
They apprehended Anianus and gave him over to the
imperial quaestor Leonas and the military commander of
Isauria Lauricus, who agreed to exile him.[1] On this
note of intense mutual hostility, the Council of
Seleucia ended.

No matter the hostility at Seleucia between the
Homoiousians and the representatives of the alliance,
the Neo-Arians could take consolation that the alliance
itself was still intact. The powerful bishops Acacius
of Caesarea, George of Alexandria, and Eudoxius of
Antioch continued firmly committed to defending Neo-
Arian fortunes. Yet, however encouraging this was, the
fact remained that the three primary ecclesiastical
patrons of the Neo-Arians had supported a pronouncement
and creed at Seleucia which in no sense was Neo-Arian
in theological content, even though it was susceptible
of a Neo-Arian interpretation. The inclusion of a
strong anathema of the term anomoion and of those who
used it indicated that the patrons realized full well
that compromises would have to be made. While Aetius
and Eunomius went along with the compromise offered
at Seleucia, they soon found that their patrons were
willing to make even more serious compromises. In
January of 360, for instance, they abandoned to exile
Aetius, the founder and symbol of Neo-Arianism, and
banned the terms essence and hypostasis from theological parlance. A Neo-Arian party without Aetius and
a Neo-Arian theology without the terms essence and hypostasis would be difficult to maintain. Eunomius
tried to live with these compromises, but in the end
he had to give up. The months immediately following
the Council of Seleucia witnessed the beginning of the
death-throes of the Neo-Arian ecclesiastical party.
They also witnessed the transformation of what we
have called the alliance--minus the Neo-Arians--into
a new theological and ecclesiastical party, the homoian
party. The new party adopted as its theological banner
a version of the Dated Creed which in essence differed
little from the Acacian compromise creed of Seleucia.

---

1.   Socrates, H.E. 2:40; Sozomen, H.E. 4:22.

In order to understand the decline of Neo-Arianism as an ecclesiastical party and the rise of homoianism, we must return to the Dated Creed of May, 359 and add to our narration of what had happened to it at Seleucia a brief account of its fortunes (1) at the Council of Rimini (held during the summer of 359) and (2) during the weeks after the Council of Seleucia.

The Dated Creed, which the Danubeans and George of Alexandria had hoped would be acceptable to a majority of the church's bishops, had proved to be less than a viable instrument for unity at Seleucia. Even the allies' representatives there abandoned it in favor, first, of Aetius' and Eudoxius' exposition and, then, of Acacius' compromise formula; given that only 39 bishops at Seleucia signed the Acacian formula, Hilary's estimate that 105 of the Seleucian bishops were firmly committed to the "second" Antiochene creed of 341[1] was probably not far wrong. The Dated Creed did not fare much better at the western Council of Rimini.[2] When it was offered by the Danubeans, the majority of the westerners responded by proposing an anathema against Arianism and by reaffirming their commitment to the formula of Nicaea. The Danubeans balked. Then, in the words of B.J. Kidd, the majority "decided (a) to approve the Nicene Creed and the use of the word 'essence'; and proceeded (b) to depose and excommunicate Ursacius, Valens, Germinius, and Gaius of Illyria as 'disturbers of the Church', and (c) to anathematize the errors of Arians, Sabellians, and Photinians. These decisions they communicated to Constantius in a letter, important for its insistence on 'No innovations'."[3] The results of the Council of Rimini were precisely parallel to the results of Seleucia, except that the majority at the former council endorsed homoousion rather than homoiousion. The Dated Creed and, indeed, the leaders of the alliance

---

1. Hilary of Poitiers, C. Const. 12.
2. See Gwatkin, pp. 174-5; Kidd, 2:166-7; Lietzmann, 3:227-8; and Bardy, The Church in the Christian Roman Empire, pp. 201-2.
3. Kidd, 2:167.

were decisively rejected by the majorities of both councils. The alliance's cause, however, was not yet lost. The councils at both Rimini and Seleucia had been directed by imperial command to send a delegation of ten representatives to court; there the ten from Rimini would confer with the ten from Seleucia--in the emperor's presence--and come up with a theological formula acceptable to all Christendom.[1] Therefore, both the Danubeans and their opponents, the Homoousians, and both the Seleucian representatives of the alliance and their enemies, the Homoiousians, sent delegations to court. Since the Council of Rimini was held much earlier than the Council of Seleucia, its two delegations arrived even before the Seleucian council had met. At court the Danubeans were in their element; they quickly used their skill to advantage. Constantius was preoccupied with preparations for a campaign against Persia and probably was encouraged by the Danubean bishops to concentrate on these duties rather than to concern himself with ecclesiastical affairs. He did just that, responding to a homoousian delegates' plea to be heard with a sharp note informing them to wait for him in Adrianople.[2] So they waited, week after week; meanwhile, their colleagues remained at Rimini, for the western council had not been dissolved. The Danubeans' strategy was to capitalize on the Homoousians' impatience and try to wear them down. Finally, on October 10, after the Seleucian council was over, the two delegations from Rimini were ordered by Constantius to meet at the town of Nike in Thrace.[3] The Danubeans falsely informed their opponents that the Council of Seleucia had unanimously rejected the term essence (οὐσία)[4] and, hence, their championing of the Nicene Creed and its homoousion was futile. Weary of the whole affair, the Homoousian delegation gave up; it signed a revision of the Dated Creed.[5] The

---

1. The imperial decree to this effect was preserved by Hilary of Poitiers, Fr. 7:1-2.
2. Athanasius, Syn. 55.
3. Socrates, H.E. 2:37; Sozomen, H.E. 4:19.
4. See Hilary of Poitiers, Fr. 11:4.
5. Text in Theodoret, H.E. 2:16.

214

Danubeans agreed to omit the original Dated Creed's
use of the title "eternal" for the emperor (for they
had denied it to the Son) and its date (for that had
offended many). Moreover, they assented to a ban on
use of the term hypostasis; it was the East's favorite
way of designating the persons of Father, Son, and
Holy Spirit, but was seen as tritheistic by the West.
In return, their opponents agreed to reject οὐσία--
hence also homoousion--and to adopt the formula that
the Son is "like the Father." The "in all things
(κατὰ πάντα)" of the original Dated Creed was omitted.
Thus, the crucial phrase of the October 10th creed was
the formula that the Son is "like the Father who generated him according to the scriptures (ὅμοιον τῷ
γεννήσαντι αὐτὸν πατρὶ κατὰ τὰς γραφάς)"--which was
identical to the central expressions of the Dated
Creed. To this we should compare the test-phrase of
the Acacian compromise of Wednesday, September 29,
namely, "We acknowledge the likeness (ὅμοιον) of the
Son to the Father, in accordance with what the Apostle
declared concerning him, 'who is the image of the
invisible God'." With "in all things" removed from
both confessions, the Danubeans and the Acacians were
on the road to success. Although the Danubeans had to
resort to deception, they were able with little difficulty to force their revised Dated Creed through the
full council at Rimini when they and their opposing
delegation returned there after October 10. For the
time being, the Neo-Arians surely thought that for
them also there was only clear sailing ahead: all
that remained was for the allies to pressure the long-
time Neo-Arian enemies, the Homoiousians, as the
Danubeans had pressured the Homoousians. This brings
us to the fateful month for the Neo-Arian cause,
December, 359. It was during this month that a theological showdown took place in Constantinople between
the Neo-Arians (led by Aetius and Eunomius) and the
Homoiousians (led by Basil of Ancyra and Eustathius of
Sebaste). However, we must defer examination of this
confrontation and its outcome (which was favorable to
neither of the two parties) to our next chapter. The
remainder of our present chapter will devote itself
to two theological documents published between the

215

meeting of the Council of Seleucia in the last week of
September, 359 and the Neo-Arian/Homoiousian showdown
in December--that is, Athanasius' De Synodis and
Aetius' Syntagmation.

We begin with Athanasius' De Synodis, a document
which was important in the history of Neo-Arianism
because, together with the events that transpired at
the Council of Seleucia, it formed the immediate background to Aetius' only completely extant writing, the
Syntagmation. In fact, a reasonable case can be made
that the Syntagmation was, in part, Aetius' conscious
response not only to the Seleucian council but also to
the publication of Athanasius' history of the twin
synods. The De Synodis can be dated with tolerable
certainty to the period between October 1, 359 and
October 10, 359, though two chapters (#30-31) were
inserted after the death of Constantius in A.D. 361.[1]
Therefore, it represented Athanasius' reaction to the
two councils during the time before the homousian
delegation from Rimini had given up its staunch resistance in favor of the Nicene Creed and had signed the
Danubeans' revised version of the Dated Creed at Nike.

The De Synodis was divided into three parts: the
first (#1-14) contained Athanasius' remarks about the
councils of Rimini and Seleucia, the second (#15-29,
32) his history of allegedly "Arian" opinions and
creeds from Arius' Thalia of the 320s to Acacius'
compromise creed of Seleucia, 359, and the third
(#33-55) the exiled bishop's attempt to confute the
alliance and conciliate Basil of Ancyra and the
Homoiousians. In Part I Athanasius affirmed that six
men, "who had always been of the Arian party" (#1),
were responsible for the twin-councils (from Pannonia:
Ursacius, Valens, and Germanius; from Syria: Acacius,
Eudoxius, and the old Arian Patrophilus of Scythopolis).
Because of the men's "obvious" Arianism, argued
Athanasius, there was no need for a new general council
in addition to the Nicene, for no new heresy had arisen
since then: Nicaea was sufficient to outlaw Arianism
(#5-6). The old bishop added an interesting comment:

---

1. See Robertson, p. 448; Kidd, 2:168.

'For even the notorious Aetius, who was surnamed
'atheist', vaunts not of the discovering of any mania
of his own, but under stress of weather has been
wrecked upon Arianism, himself and the persons whom
he has beguiled" (#6). Athanasius was conscious that
the alliance was to be feared and resisted especially
because of its Neo-Arian component. It was this component that made him positive that the intent of the
allies was to "annul the acts of Nicaea" (#7), for
Aetius' heteroousion was designed to be directly contradictory of Nicaea's homoousion. Substantiation for
this interpretation of Athanasius' mind is provided by
chapters 30-31 of the De Synodis, added after Constantius' death. After quoting the creed of Nike approved
in Constantinople during winter, A.D. 359/360, Athanasius wrote, "However, they did not stand even to this;
for coming down from Constantinople to Antioch, they
were dissatisfied that they had written at all that
the Son was "like the Father as the scriptures say";
and putting their ideas upon paper, they began reverting to their first doctrines, and said that "the Son
is altogether unlike the Father," and that the "Son
is in no manner like the Father," and so much did they
change, as to admit those who spoke the Arian doctrine
nakedly and to deliver to them the churches with license
to bring forth the words of blasphemy with impunity.
Because then of the extreme shamelessness of their
blasphemy they were called by all Anomoians . . ."
(#31).[1] Consequently, Athanasius applauded the summer
session of Rimini and the homoiousian group at Seleucia
for opposing the allies. And he criticized Eudoxius
of Antioch and Acacius of Caesarea (1) for abandoning
the faith of their ecclesiastical fathers, that is,
Eustathius of Antioch and Eusebius of Caesarea, both
of whom (with different kinds and degrees of commitment, of course) signed Nicaea's creed and its anathemas against Arianism and (2) for patronizing "the
Ariomanics", presumably the Neo-Arians (#13). This
led the exiled bishop to remark that the leaders of the

---

1. Trans. from NPNF 4:467. The underlining is
mine.

alliance not only had abandoned their fathers in the faith but also could not come to any agreement on a replacement exposition of the faith--witness all the different formulations of the councils held between Nicaea and the twin councils (#14). So ended the first part of the De Synodis; the second followed logically upon it. It reviewed eleven different, allegedly "Arian," documents, from Arius' Thalia to the Acacian creed of Seleucia, 359. Gwatkin accurately described the review when he wrote, "[Athanasius] is not . . . selecting documents like Hilary [in his De Synodis] to show the real drift of opinion in the East, but merely throwing them together as a satire on Arian vacillation, and commenting on them like an old dis-puter who knows the early history of the controversy much better than the later phases."[1] Athanasius even pinned complete responsibility for the councils of the A.D. 340s and early 350s on the allies; thus, by implication he absolved the Homoiousians, whom he highly praised in Part III. This was hardly a fair historical account.

For our purposes, Part III of the De Synodis is the most interesting of the document's three major divisions. The first thing we observe is that it was totally concerned with the eastern Council of Seleucia and not at all with Rimini. The reason: the homoousian delegates from Rimini had not yet caved in and signed the Dated Creed at Nike. On the other hand, at Seleucia no one was defending Nicaea's creed and its anathemas against Arianism, though Athanasius, as we shall see, now saw that the Homoiousians, led by Basil of Ancyra, were close enough to being Nicaea's defenders to be deserving of praise and encouragement. He did not begin with this encouragement, however, but with an attack upon the alliance's leaders at Seleucia: Acacius of Caesarea, Eudoxius of Antioch, and Patro-philus of Scythopolis (George of Alexandria--whom he predictably called "of Cappadocia" not "of Alexandria"-- he dismissed as an un-Christian monster not even worthy of attack). The three bishops' rejection of Nicaea's

---

1. Gwatkin, pp. 180-1.

218

"co-essential (homoousion)" and "of the essence," he
argued, revealed that when they confessed in the Acacian
creed of Seleucia that the Son was generated from Father
God, they meant that the Son was created by the Father;
otherwise, they would not have also rejected the Nicene
Creed and anathemas, which were designed to exclude
this view (#33-36). Their defense that the Nicene
terms were unscriptural Athanasius scorned as "an un-
blushing excuse"(#36). If they were against everything
unscriptural, why did they not speak against Arian unscriptural claims as well as against Nicaea's: for
instance, "out of nothing, the Son was not before his
generation," etc. (#36). And where in scripture, he
asked, did such terms as ungenerated, essence, and
three hypostases occur (#36)? Even more tellingly, how
could Acacius, who signed the "second" Antiochene creed,
with its claim that the Son is the "exact image of the
Father's essence," complain about the unscriptural
terms in the Nicene creed (#36)? Finally, Athanasius
turned to the Acacian compromise of Seleucia. He
asked Acacius and Eudoxius how they could say that they
did "not repudiate" the "second" Antiochene creed, yet
in the next breath rejected "the terms homoousion and
homoiousion as alien to the scriptures" and abolished
"the term essence (οὐσία) as not contained therein"
(#37). Here Athanasius has gotten a bit carried away,
for the Acacian compromise did reject homoousion and
homoiousion, but not essence (οὐσία). Athanasius'
development of his argument, which focused on the
Acacian compromise's rejection of homoiousion, was
better founded. It went as follows:

> For if, O Acacius and Eudoxius, you "do not
> repudiate the faith published at the Dedication,"
> and in it it is written that the Son is "exact
> image of God's essence," why is it you write
> in Isauria, "we reject homoiousion"? For if
> the Son is not like the Father according to
> essence, how is he "exact image of the es-
> sence"? But if you are dissatisfied with
> having written "exact image of the essence,"
> how is it that you "anathematize those who
> say that the Son is unlike (anomoion)"? For

> if he be not according to essence like, he is
> surely unlike: and the unlike cannot be an
> image . . . . By what artifice then do you
> call unlike like, and consider like to be
> unlike, and pretend to say that the Son is
> the Father's image?   (#38)[1]

Having exposed what he thought to be the logical contradictions of Acacius' compromise, Athanasius made it
crystal clear that he realized the alliance's leaders
were not at all serious about abiding by the "second"
Antiochene creed but were simply trying to conciliate
the Homoiousians, while not actually repudiating the
Neo-Arians. Athanasius continued:

> How is it that you expel the Arian Aetius as
> an heretic, though you say the same with him?
> For he is your companion, O Acacius, and he
> became Eudoxius' master in this so great ir-
> religion. This was the reason why Leontius
> the bishop made him deacon, that using the
> name of the diaconate as sheep's clothing,
> he might be able with impunity to pour forth
> the words of blasphemy. (#38)[2]

The answer to Athanasius' query was that Acacius and
Eudoxius were not expelling Aetius at all; Aetius had
simply agreed to a substitute expression for anomoion.
However that may be, Athanasius was quite right in his
view that Acacius and Eudoxius were still protecting
the Neo-Arian position of essential dissimilarity.
He also was right in claiming that, in the end, all
that mattered to the two bishops was "the patronage of
Constantius"(#39); in fact, he saw this much more
clearly than did Aetius, Eunomius, and the other truly
dedicated Neo-Arians.
  At this point Athanasius turned from addressing
the Seleucian leaders of the alliance to addressing
Basil of Ancyra and the Homoiousians. Because they

---

1.   Trans from NPNF 4:470 (slightly altered).
2.   Trans from NPNF 4:471 (slightly altered).

(1) accepted Nicaea's anathemas and its decisive phrase
"from the essence (ἐκ τῆς οὐσίας)" and (2) had reservations only about homoousion, Athanasius proclaimed
them to be neither "Ariomaniacs" nor "opponents of the
Fathers"; they were rather "brothers, who mean what we
mean, and dispute only about the word"(#41). While
their catchword homoiousion by itself did not exclude
a creator/creature relationship between God and the
Word, when they added "from the essence" to homoiousion,
the two together were equivalent to homousion (#41).
Having held out the right hand of peace to the Homoiousians, Athanasius then sought to answer their objections to homoousion, namely, (1) that it was materi-
alistic (#41-42) and (2) that it was condemned at the
Council of Antioch, A.D. 269 which had met to deal with
Paul of Samosata (#43-47). Athanasius' answer to the
Homoiousians' second objection is of particular
interest, for Aetius seems in his Syntagmation to
have been directly responding to a portion of it.
Athanasius argued that the rejection by one group
of church Fathers of a particular term accepted
by other groups did not justify barring its use.
Rather, one must "investigate their meaning" (#45),
and if one does, one quickly realizes that each
group "has a sufficient reason for its own language" (#45). The Council of Nicaea's use of homoousion to exclude Arianism was equally as justified as
the Council of Antioch's rejection of Paul of Samosata's use of it. Athanasius concluded by asking,
"Why do we not combine all our Fathers in religious
belief, those who depose the Samosatene as well as
those who proscribed the Arian heresy, instead of
making distinctions between them and refusing to
entertain a right opinion of them?" (#47) In order to
recommend this view to the two councils, the bishop
adapted the attitude toward the term ungenerated he
developed in his Orationes of A.D. 339 and his De
Decretis of A.D. 350; it was against this adaptation
that Aetius appears to have reacted in his Syntagmation. Athanasius began by admitting that although the
term ungenerated was unscriptural, it had many ecclesiastical authorities in its favor. The church ought to
listen to them even though they disagreed about the

221

proper way to employ the term. The basic disagreement, he pointed out, concerned whether or not the term can justifiably be used of the Son. On the one side was the second century bishop Ignatius of Antioch, who wrote that "there is one physician, fleshly and spiritual, generated and ungenerated (γενητὸς καὶ ἀγένητος), God in man, true life in death, both from Mary and from God" (#47). On the other side were (unnamed) ecclesiastical teachers who wrote, "There is one ungenerated (ἕν τὸ ἀγένητον), the Father, and one genuine Son from him, true generate (γέννημα ἀληθινόν), Word and Wisdom of the Father" (#47). Athanasius' attitude was to reconcile the two views. He wrote, "If . . . we are persuaded that the blessed Ignatius was right in writing that Christ was generate on account of the flesh (for he became flesh), yet ungenerated, because he is not in the number of things made and generated, but Son from Father; and if we are aware too that those who have said that the ungenerated is one, meaning the Father, did not mean to lay down that the Word was generated and made, but that the Father has no cause, but rather is himself Father of Wisdom, and in Wisdom has made all things that are generated; why do we not combine all our Fathers in religious belief . . . ?" (#47)[1] We shall discuss this sequence in depth when we consider Aetius' reaction; suffice it to say here that Athanasius obviously was less than just to the claims of the unnamed ecclesiastical teachers. There was more to their position than Athanasius cared to admit.

Athanasius concluded his treatise by trying to persuade the Homoiousians that the only way the Neo-Arian position could be successfully refuted was by opposing the Neo-Arian formula of heteroousion with Nicaea's homoousion. He began by posing the issue as follows:

If the Word be a created thing and foreign to the Father's essence, so that he is sep-arated from the Father by the difference of

---

1. Trans. from NPNF 4:475 (slightly altered).

nature, he cannot be homoousion with him, but
rather he is homogeneous by nature with the
created things, though he surpass them in
grace. On the other hand, if we confess that
he is not a created thing but the genuine
offspring of the Father's essence, it would
follow that he is inseparable from the Father,
being of the same nature, because he is begotten from him. And being such, good reason
he should be called homoousion. (#48)[1]

But Basil of Ancyra and his followers also confessed
that the Son is a genuine offspring of the Father's
essence and not a created thing; why was homoousion to
be preferred to homoiousion as a means of expressing
the relation of Father and Son? Athanasius answered
(#53) by arguing that the terms likeness (τὸ ὅμοιον)
and unlikeness (τὸ ἀνόμοιον) were to be used "not in
the case of essences but rather in the case of appearances and qualities (οὐκ ἐπὶ τῶν οὐσιῶν, ἀλλ᾽ἐπὶ
σχημάτων καὶ ποιοτήτων)"; in the case of essences one
should use the terms sameness (ταυτότης) or difference
(ἑτερότης). Thus:

Man is said to be like (ὅμοιος) man not in
essence but in appearance and character (οὐ
κατὰ τὴν οὐσίαν, ἀλλὰ κατὰ τὸ σχῆμα τὸν
χαρακτῆρα), for in essence men are of the
same nature (ὁμοφυεῖς). And again, man is
not said to be unlike (ἀνόμοιος) dog, but
to be of a different nature (ἑτεροφυής).
Accordingly, the former are the same in nature
and in essence (ὁμοφυὲς καὶ ὁμοούσιον), while
the latter are different in nature and in
essence (ἑτεροφυὲς καὶ ἑτεροούσιον). Therefore, when one says 'like in essence (ὅμοιον
κατ᾽οὐσίαν)', he means 'like by participation
ἐκ μετουσίας . . . ὅμοιον)'. For likeness is
a quality (ποιότης) which is added to essence.
And this would be proper to created things,

---

1. Trans. from NPNF 4:475 (slightly altered).

for they are made like God by participation
(ἐκ μετοχῆς).

This was an extraordinarily interesting statement for
Athanasius to make. We remember that in his <u>Orationes
Contra Arianos</u> of A.D. 339 the bishop had himself
termed Father and Son "like in essence";[1] now he was
not only preferring "same in essence" but arguing that
"like in essence" was linguistically improper. What
had caused this basic change in his thinking? We cannot doubt that it was Neo-Arianism's reservation of
"likeness" for God's quality or character of fatherhood
in relation to the Son. Athanasius understood perfectly Aetius' contention that the Son's likeness to
God does not extend beyond God's attributes to his
essence: for one thing to be "like" another necessarily implies they are essentially different. And he
understood perfectly that the Neo-Arians' willingness
to anathematize ἀνόμοιον or "unlikeness" at Seleucia
was a dialectical maneuver which did not affect their
fundamental position: they were simply being logically
precise and reserving the terms likeness and unlikeness
for "appearances, qualities, and characters" of
essences. By means of his statement in <u>De Synodis</u> 53
Athanasius was seeking to put the Homoiousians on
guard against Neo-Arian dialectical subtlety. Homoiousion not only did not exclude Neo-Arianism but
logically might be construed actually to imply it;
the confession of homoousion was the only effective
polemic against the essential difference of God and
the Son. The extent of Athanasius' fear of the Neo-
Arians' dialectical threat to the Homoiousians was
demonstrated by his devoting three entire sections of
his <u>De Synodis</u> to arguing that homoousion alone
logically refuted the position that God and the Son
are one in will but not in essence (#48-50). And he
added a section designed to prove that only homoousion
could protect the Christian's hope of deification: if,
as homoiousion implied, the Son is Son by participation,
then he could not deify the Christian, since he himself,

———————————

1. Athanasius, <u>Ar</u>. 1:20-1 and 3:66.

224

being alien to the Father's essence (ἀλλοτριοούσιος
. . . τοῦ πατρός), needs to be deified (#51). Athanasius was gently insistent that homoiousion was a
terminological muddle which in the end implied
difference-in-essence. Christians had to choose between homoousion and heteroousion, between Athanasius
and Aetius. Finally, the exiled Alexandrian prelate
tried to answer one last Homoiousian objection to
homoousion. It was a notion expressed by the Homoiousians at the 358 Council of Sirmium, namely, that
homoousion involved the materializing notion that there
is a prior essence pre-existing Father and Son which
they divide between themselves like "brothers" (#51).
Athanasius' answer was simple: scripture spoke of
parents having only one child; we must presume an only
child to be homoousion only with its parents.

Sometime between the publication of Athanasius'
De Synodis in the first week or so of October, 359
and Aetius' exile in December of the same year, the
Neo-Arian leader wrote the first edition of his Syntagmation, his only completely extant writing. This
dating is demanded by the following evidence. First,
there is an historical allusion Aetius made in his
document's introduction. He wrote:

> On the occasion of the persecution instituted
> against us by the 'temporists' [Aetius' term
> for his opponents[1]], some of the latter appro-
> priated, along with a good deal of other
> material, a little work, the product of par-
> ticular effort on my part, on the subject of
> the ungenerated God and the generated one.
> They ruined it with deliberate omissions,
> altered about the logical sequence of proof,
> and published it. Later on, it got to me at
> the hands of a conscientious person. I was
> obliged to clean the treatise up again like

---

1. The opponents were so-called "because . . .
they say the Son is generated from the Father and
being generated is, for the Arians, temporal" (Wickham,
p. 550).

> a father and send it off to you, heroes and
> heroines in the contest of true religion as
> you all are . . . .[1]

Because Aetius twiced underwent severe persecution at
the hands of his opponents--in A.D. 358, when Basil of
Ancyra effected his exile to Pepuza, and in December
359, when Constantius exiled him again after an investigation into his beliefs--Gummerus rightly dated the
original version of the treatise to A.D. 358 or afterward. A second piece of evidence, however, rules out
the exile to Pepuza as the persecution in question.
As we have observed previously, the Syntagmation never
used the term anomoion (unlike) in its defense of Neo-
Arian theology. The reason for this was the terms of
the Acacian compromise proposed on Wednesday, September 29, 359 at the Council of Seleucia. Since we have
found reason to believe Aetius and Eudoxius were still
using anomoion in the tract they distributed on Tuesday, September 28, the Syntagmation must date after
September 29th. The exile to Pepuza must be excluded,
and we conclude that the allusion to persecution in
the document's introduction was to Aetius' exile in
December, 359. So far, then, we have established that
the Syntagmation was written between September 28, 359
and Aetius' exile in December, 359. This conclusion
is substantiated by the fact that five of the document's thirty-seven syllogisms contain polemics
against the formula, the Son is "precisely similar in
essence (ἀπαράλλακτον εἰς οὐσίαν)" to God (#3, 22, 29,
33 and 35). Because this formula was the key theological claim of the "second" Antiochene creed of 341
championed at Seleucia, 359 by the Homoiousians, Aetius'
document was surely written after the Homoiousians
resolved at Seleucia to stand by this creed. On the
other hand, it must have been written before the
Homoiousians' notion of "precisely similar in essence"
was decisively rejected in December, 359 in favor of
simple "likeness according to the scriptures." Finally,
since much of the Syntagmation was intended to refute

---

1. Wickham's translation, slightly revised.

Athanasius' De Synodis, we must place the writing of Aetius' document after the De Synodis' publication during the first ten days of October, 359.

The Syntagmation falls naturally into four parts, which are preceded by an introduction. The introduction gave the historical occasion of the document, Aetius' purpose in writing, and a statement of the major theological problem addressed by the document (a statement usually numbered as syllogism #1). Part I turned immediately to polemic, rejecting first the homoiousian position and then the homoousian; throughout it sought to establish the Neo-Arian view of incomparability in essence (#2-11). What we may call the Neo-Arian theory of theological language was explicated in Part II (#12-18), while Part III dealt with the notions of privation (στέρησις), condition (ἕξις), and cause (αἴτιον) as possible categories to explain the concepts of ungeneratedness and generatedness (#19-30). Finally, Part IV returned to direct polemic against homoiousion and homoousion and concluded with a benediction (#31-37). Our procedure in analyzing the Syntagmation will be to translate and explicate each of the divisions of the tract in turn, seeking in our discussion to make plain both Aetius' fundamental theological claims and the positions against which he was polemizing.

Since we have already translated and discussed the sentences of the Syntagmation's introduction which dealt with the document's historical occasion, we begin with the introduction's statement of Aetius' purpose in writing and its formulation of the theological problem which the rest of the document treats.

. . . my little discourse is in accordance with the meaning of the Holy Scriptures (κατ' ἔννοιαν τῶν ἁγίων γραφῶν), through which you will be able to cut short the effrontery of any man who tries to gainsay you on the subject of the ungenerated God and the generated one, and especially the 'temporists' mentioned above. On grounds of clarity and ease in grasping the point of the proofs, I have set them out in the form of alternating

227

problems and solutions, taking as my starting
point the problems over the ungenerated God,
that is, if it is possible for the ungenerated
God to make (ποιῆσαι) the generated (τὸ
γεννητόν) ungenerated.[1]

In penning his <u>Syntagmation</u> Aetius intended to provide
his followers with an arsenal of weapons to use in
their battles against the "temporists," that is, the
Homoiousians and Homoousians. Given the consolidation
of the Homoiousian forces at Seleucia in late September, 359 and the publication of Athanasius' second
homoousion manifesto, the <u>De Synodis</u>, in early October,
Aetius realized that the next few months would be
crucial for the Neo-Arian cause. Long devoted to
dialectic and addicted to disputations, the Neo-Arian
leader was now in his element. He intended to insure
that his devotees were ready for the upcoming theological combat: a collection of terse and, as he put it,
"clear and easy to grasp" syllogisms would be the most
useful thing he could provide them. With these the
"effrontery" of the Homoiousians and Homoousians could
be "cut short." Because Aetius realized, as a dialectician of some experience, that the way a question for
disputation is posed is crucial to the success or
failure of the respective participants, he chose to
formulate all his syllogisms in terms of the concepts
ungeneratedness and generatedness; he obviously believed
his opponents' greatest vulnerability lay in the way
they dealt with them. He foreshadowed what he would
argue to be the hopeless logical tangle of his opponents' position when he said that the topic of the
<u>Syntagmation</u> was the "problem over the ungenerated
God, that is, if it is possible for the ungenerated
God to make the generated ungenerated." Moreover, in
presenting the Neo-Arian case in terms of these concepts, Aetius was pointing out to his adherents that
the essential theological issue facing Christendom had
not changed since the early A.D. 320s, when Arius and
Eusebius of Caesarea objected to Alexander of

---

1. Wickham's translation.

Alexandria's teaching that there is more than one ungenerated being. Aetius' position was thereby put
forward as representing not only the claims of logic
but also the claims of a long tradition. The tradition, indeed, was claimed to extend past the early
Arians to scripture itself, for the Syntagmation
represented itself as conveying "the meaning of
scripture." We must hasten to point out that Aetius
was nowhere very inclined to appeal to scripture in
his syllogisms: scriptural passages were sometimes
obliquely alluded to but never quoted. But Aetius'
concern to present the "meaning" of scripture rather
than its letter should not be taken too quickly to
imply that he was not much interested in the authority
of scripture. He had spent many years studying exegesis
under Athanasius of Anazarbus, Antonius of Tarsus, and
Leontius of Antioch. A more likely explanation for
the Neo-Arian's procedure is that he realized positions
based on scriptural exegesis could not as easily be
defended as those based on syllogistic inferences from
commonly admitted premises. He wanted his followers
not only to be right in their theological combats but
to win; like Tertullian, he realized that theological
victories could not be assured by appeals to scripture.[1]
To see how Aetius went about recommending to his adherents that they proceed, we turn to Part I of the
Syntagmation, which contained ten syllogisms.[2]

The Syntagmation: Part I

> #2. If the ungenerated God is superior to
>   every cause, he must, because of that,
>   be superior to generation (γένεσις).
>   If he is superior to every cause, it

----

1. Compare Tertullian, Praesc. 19.
2. All translations of the Syntagmation's syllogisms are my own, unless otherwise indicated. I have,
however, studied Wickham's translation carefully and
often have not been able to improve on his wording.
I gratefully acknowledge my debt to his work.

is clear that he also is superior to
generation, for he neither received
existence (τὸ εἶναι) from another nature
nor did he himself supply existence to
himself.

#3. If he himself did not supply existence
to himself (not because of his feebleness
of nature, but because he transcends every
cause), how could anyone allow that the
nature made to exist as a hypostasis is
precisely similar in essence (τὸ ἀπαράλλακτον εἰς οὐσίαν) to the nature which
has made it to exist as a hypostasis,
when such a hypostasis as the latter
does not admit of generation?

#4. If God remains endlessly (ἀτελευτήτως)
in ungenerated essence and the generate
(τὸ γέννημα) is endlessly generate, then
the perverse doctrine of homoousion and
homoiousion will be destroyed. And incomparability in essence (τὸ ἐν οὐσίᾳ
ἀσύγκριτον) is established when each of
the two natures remains unceasingly in
its proper rank of nature (ἐν τῷ ἰδίῳ
τῆς φύσεως ἀξιώματι).

#5. If God is ungenerated with respect to
essence, what was generated was not
generated by a partition (διαστάσει)
of essence, but he has made it to exist
as a hypostasis by his power (ἐξουσίᾳ).
For no pious reasoning permits the same
essence (τὴν αὐτὴν οὐσίαν) to be generated and ungenerated.

#6. If the ungenerated has been generated,
what prevents the generated from having
become ungenerated? For every nature
shuns what is improper to it for what
is proper to it.

#7. If God is not entirely ungenerated, nothing hinders him from having generated essentially (γεγεννηκέναι οὐσιωδῶς). But if he is entirely ungenerated, he was not partitioned (διέστη) essentially in generation, but he made the generate (γέννημα) to exist as a hypostasis by his power (ἐξουσίᾳ).

#8. If the ungenerated God is entirely generative (γεννητικὸς), what was generated was not generated essentially, since his entire essence is able to generate but not to be generated. If the essence of God, having been transformed (μετασχηματισθεῖσα), is said to be generate (γέννημα), his essence is not unchangeable (ἀμετάβλητος), since the change effected the formation (εἰδοποίησιν) of the Son. If the essence of God be unchangeable and superior to generation, relationship with the Son (τὸ κατὰ τὸν υἱὸν) will be confessed to be a mere mode of address (ψιλῆς προσηγορίας).

#9. If the generate (τὸ γέννημα) was spermatically (σπερματικῶς) within the ungenerated God, he, so to speak, reached maturity (ἠνδρώθη) after his generation, having received [things] from outside [of God] (ἔξωθεν προσλαβὸν). The Son, then, is complete (τέλειος) not as a result of the things he was generated with (οὐκ ἐξ ὧν ἐγεννήθη), but as a result of the things which he received. No, this cannot be so--for things which receive [completion] by inheritance (συγγενικῶς), since they are constituted of those inherited things, have the nature of admitting the title 'complete' (τὸ τοῦ τελείου ὄνομα) in a different sense (διαφόρως).

231

#10. If the generate was complete (τέλειον)
within the ungenerated, it is generate
as a result of the things which were
within the ungenerated and not as a result
of the things from which the ungenerated
generated it. This is false, for it is
not possible that a generated nature be
within an ungenerated essence. For the
same thing is not able both to be and
not to be. For a generate thing is not
able to be ungenerated, and being ungenerated could not have been a generate
thing, since to say that God consists
of unlike parts presents to him the
height of blasphemy and hybris (τοῦ
ἀνομοιομεροῦς ἐπὶ θεοῦ βλασφημίας
τύπον καὶ ὕβριν ἐπέχοντος).

#11. If God Almighty, being of ungenerated
nature, does not know himself as of
generated nature, but the Son, being
of generated nature, knows himself to
be that which he is (ὅπερ ἐστί), how
could homoousion not be false, since
one knows himself to be ungenerated and
the other knows himself to be generated.

Nearly all eastern parties to the theological controversies of the A.D. 340s and 350s had admitted that
God could be described as ungenerated. This was true
of the Homoiousians as late as their synodical letter
of spring, A.D. 358. Although Athanasius had voiced
strong reservations in his Orationes of 339 and his
De Decretis of 350 about using the term as one's main
theological characterization of God, preferring the
more scriptural 'Father', even he had second thoughts
by the time he wrote his De Synodis of 359. In this
last work Athanasius admitted that the term had a long
history in orthodox Christian tradition, beginning as
early as with the second century author Ignatius of
Antioch. Therefore, Aetius decided that there was no
reason to abandon use of the term as the keystone of
his theological position, despite Basil of Ancyra's 359

accusation (in his memorandum) that he was using the
ungenerated/generated distinction as a "sophism to
introduce the heresy [the Neo-Arian heresy] into the
church." Aetius no doubt hoped that many homoiousian
sympathizers would be more influenced by Athanasius'
De Synodis than by his earlier Orationes and De
Decretis or by the memorandum of a discredited signa-
tory to the Dated Creed of Sirmium, 359 (a hope supported by the minor role Basil had played at Seleucia
in the fall of A.D. 359). But conscious that the term
required some defense, Aetius began his Syntagmation's
series of syllogisms with a proof of God's ungeneratedness. Assuming that all Christians would agree that
God is uncaused, Aetius suggested that if God is
superior to every cause, he not only "did not receive
existence from another nature" but also "did not
supply existence to himself." He is completely superior
to cause, not having been caused to exist by another nor
having caused himself to exist. And if he was in no
way caused to exist, he must not have come into existence, that is, have been generated. So he must be
"superior to generation" or ungenerated. Presumably
Aetius was recommending that his adherents should
begin disputations with this proof. If they could
bring their opponents to assent to it, then, Aetius
believed, both the homoiousian and the homoousian
causes would logically have to be abandoned. He turned first to the Homoiousians, who at Seleucia had
decided to stand by the commitment of the "second"
Antiochene creed to the Son's "precise similarity of
essence (οὐσίας . . . ἀπαράλλακτον εἰκόνα)" to God.
Reiterating that God did not supply existence to himself but did supply existence to the Uniquely-Generated,
reiterating, that is, that God is ungenerated and the
result of his causation is generated, Aetius concluded
that no reasonable person could allow an ungenerated
being and a generated being to be "precisely similar
in essence (τὸ ἀπαράλλακτον εἰς οὐσίαν)." Having
mustered a first wave of syllogistic attack upon
homoiousion in syllogism #3, Aetius mustered a second
wave in syllogism #4, while expanding his argument to
include both a stab at homoousion and a defense of his
own view. Making the assumption that ungeneratedness

233

and generatedness relate to essence, Aetius argued
that if God remains endlessly in ungenerated essence
and the generate one (τὸ γέννημα)--that is, the Son--
remains endlessly generate, then at no time could the
two be anything but different in essence, or as Aetius
now preferred to phrase it, incomparable in essence.
It also stands to reason that God and the Son must be
"endlessly" of ungenerated and generated essence
respectively; if they are not, at some time the ungenerated will become generated and vice-versa--which
are logical impossibilities. Thus, the two natures
have differing natural and eternal hierarchial ranks
(ἀξιώματα). We note in passing that syllogism #4
referred to the homoousian and homoiousian positions
not as two but simply as one "perverse doctrine (ἡ τοῦ
ὁμοουσίου καὶ ὁμοιουσίου κακοδοξία)"; Aetius apparently saw little essential difference between them.

Despite this, the Neo-Arian was rather more concerned at the beginning of the Syntagmation with the
homoousion formulation than with the homoiousian:
not only did he include an attack upon it in syllogism
#4 but he devoted his next three syllogisms to its
refutation.[1] Aetius seems to have been persuaded that
Athanasius, his early opponent in the late A.D. 340s
and early 350s, was an exceedingly dangerous adversary.
He may well have thought that the exiled bishop's
De Synodis would be successful in convincing the
Homoiousians that the essential choice facing Christendom was between the Neo-Arian heteroousion and his own
homoousion. The series of syllogisms, in fact, could
possibly have been developed in the early A.D. 350s
and simply have been inserted into this place in the
Syntagmation as a battery of tested objections to
homoousion which Neo-Arian devotees would find useful.

Because the term homoousion originally referred
to material reality,[2] as did its constituent part
οὐσία, Aetius--like Arius before him--spoke throughout
his attack upon it (syllogisms #5-7) in language

---

1. So, too, was the last syllogism of Part I,
syllogism #11, directed against it.
2. See Prestige, God in Patristic Thought, p. 197.

consistent with this primary signification. Surely he
was conscious that the Homoiousians at Sirmium, 358
also accepted this signification. Continuing the
assumption that the terms ungenerated and generated
describe essence, he recommended to his devotees in
syllogism #5 that they should point out to homoousian
disputants that to claim the Son was generated as
homoousion from God's essence means a partition took
place, a partition after the model of normal material
partition. Given such a partition, one of the parts
must be ungenerated and the other generated, while at
the same time both must be the same-in-essence or
homoousion. This is absurd, said Aetius; no Christian
intellectual could possibly agree to the logical
fallacy of maintaining the same essence (τὴν αὐτὴν
οὐσίαν) to be self-contradictorily both ungenerated
and generated. Aetius suggested that the concept of
essential partition should be abandoned in favor of
the concept of creation; this was the thrust of his
view that God made the "Son" to exist as a hypostasis
by his power. He implied that failure to abandon the
concept of essential partition would result in a compound God, a result offensive to the piety of every
sophisticated Christian who was committed--as sophisticated Christians traditionally were--to God's unity
or simplicity.[1] Syllogism #6 added that to allow the
logic which yields the monstrosity of a compound God
both ungenerated and generated forces one to allow an
even more horrendous possibility, that generated
beings may become ungenerated--a conclusion not only
logically but religiously shocking to Christians.
For if the Homoousians granted that the ungenerated
can become generated, it follows necessarily that
generated things can become ungenerated; if the
absolute and ultimate God can become a creature, then
creatures can become the absolute and ultimate God.
The thrust of syllogism #6 was that the same religious
class lines which prevent creatures from upward
mobility into the preserve of God prevent God from
debasing his essence by downward mobility into the

---

1. Compare syllogism #11.

class of creatures. In other words, by providing his disciples with syllogisms #5 and 6, Aetius was suggesting that they object to homoousion on both logical and religious grounds.

We have seen from our discussion of syllogisms #5 and 6 that Aetius based at least part of his argument against homoousion on the expectation that his opponents would agree to the axiom of God's essential unity or simplicity. Certainly syllogisms #7 and 8a depended on this axiom. If God is admitted to be essentially compound, argued #7, then part of God's essence could remain ungenerated, while the other part would be able to become generated--or, as syllogism #8b put it, "be transformed" into that which is generated. But since God is admitted not to be compound, if he is ungenerated, he must be entirely ungenerated (#7). On the other hand, the Christian tradition was unanimous in believing that he in some way caused the Son to exist as a separate entity. With partition ruled out, the only alternative left, reiterated Aetius, is that God's essence created the Son, that "he made the generate to exist as a hypostasis by his power" (#7). Moreover, given God's simplicity, the entire essence of God must have been involved in the creation of the Son and, in that sense, to have been "entirely generative (γεννητικὸς)" (#8a). The implication was that God's essence could have been generated in no sense whatsoever. Homoousion of the entirely generative one with the generated one is impossible. We see how crucial the assumption of God's unity or simplicity was to Aetius' arguments; this will become apparent once again when we consider syllogism #10.

So far the Syntagmation has sought to prove that God is ungenerated and, using the ungenerated/generated distinction, to show that of the three formulas being promoted in Christian theological circles--namely, homoousion, homoiousion, and heteroousion--only the last was logically defensible. Nothing has yet been said of Athanasius' preference for Father/Son language over ungenerated/generated language, a preference lately endorsed during the summer of A.D. 359 by the Homoiousians, specifically by Basil of Ancyra

nd George of Laodicea. As we saw in our previous
chapter, Aetius had devoted much thought to Father/Son
language throughout the A.D. 350s. In syllogisms
#8b, 9, and 10 Aetius dealt with it thoroughly. How-
ever, we find none of the positive employment of this
terminology we found in the Neo-Arian fragments quoted
in Basil's and George's memorandum of a few months
earlier. In syllogisms #8b-10 Aetius gave no quarter
in his attack upon the language. Undoubtedly the
reason for the Syntagmation's extremely critical view
is to be found in the document's purpose: the tract
was an arsenal of weapons to be used in theological
disputations with Homoousians and Homoiousians; it
was the means by which their "effrontery" could be
"cut short." Syllogisms #8b-10 were intended to aid
in the "cutting," not in positive theological con-
struction.

Aetius argued in syllogism #8b that if theological
Father/Son language is taken to imply an essential
relationship between God and the Son in any way comparable to the relationship between organic fathers and
sons, God would have to be construed as changeable.
Since Homoousians and Homoiousians must argue, according to Aetius, that at least part of God's essence was
"transformed" from ungeneratedness into the generate
Son, then God cannot be unchangeable for them. Because
sophisticated Christians traditionally had maintained
God's unchangeability, Aetius recommended to his adherents that they exploit this flaw in their opponents'
thought. They should insist that God's unchangeability
makes it necessary that the relationship of the Son to
God be a relationship of created to creator, not a
relationship like that of organic son to organic father.
Or to use Aetius' words, God's fatherly relationship
with the Son is a "mere mode of address." Now that he
has introduced the model of organic father/son rela-
tionships used by his opponents, Aetius examined the
model in syllogism #9. If God the Father is a father
akin to normal organic fathers, the Son was originally
spiritual semen within the Father's essence; the semen
was ejaculated and then achieved completion outside of
the Father's essence, presumably within and from his
"mother." This means that the Son was not complete by

237

inheritance (συγγενιϰῶς) from God but rather achieved
maturity as a Son because of what he received from
elsewhere. The logic of this situation forces one to
admit to a lack in God: he was unable to constitute
the Son as complete by inheritance from him--an
unacceptable consequence for early Christian minds.
One may add that it involves the seed of the immutable
God's essence in the necessity of having to change and
develop. But what if God is not conceived after the
model of a normal organic father but rather after the
model of an abnormal organic father, that is, after
the model of an hermaphrodite? Surprisingly, this
seems to have been the possibility explored in Syntagmation, syllogism #10. Of course, to conceive of God
as an "hermaphrodite" is not totally bizarre, for
Gen. 1:27 may be, and has been, interpreted to imply
this; the Genesis passage was so interpreted, in fact,
by the fourth century author of the (Pseudo) Clementine
Grundschrift and was explicitly rejected by the Neo-
Arian editor of the Recognitiones.[1] But if the generate
is construed to achieve completion within the ungenerated, like a fetus come to term within God's herma-
phroditic womb, one finds oneself in the logically
impossible situation of having to conclude that God's
ungenerated essence carries within itself its contradictory, that is, generated essence. Aetius added that
such a conclusion not only is logically impossible
("for the same thing is not able both to be and not to
be") but is religiously unacceptable to Christians,
who assumed God's simplicity ("to say that God consists
of unlike parts presents to him the height of blasphemy
and hybris").

Having demolished organically-modelled Father/Son
language to his satisfaction in syllogisms #8-10,
Aetius returned in syllogism #11 to an attack on
homoousion, an attack which had occupied him previously
in syllogisms #4-7. Never did he address the peculiar-
ly Homoiousian defense of theological Father/Son
language (with its appeal to Eph. 3:14) forwarded in
the Ancyran synodical letter ot A.D. 358. These two

---

1. See Chapman, p. 25.

238

facts lead us to conclude that Aetius was aiming his attack upon theological Father/Son language at Athanasius' interpretation of it. Thus, despite Aetius' thrusts at the Homoiousians in syllogisms #3 and 4, Part I of the Neo-Arian's Syntagmation was concerned primarily with Athanasian positions. The indomitable Alexandrian was Aetius' bête noire; the Neo-Arian wanted to prepare his disciples to cope with his homoousian theology should it turn out to be a serious force in upcoming theological debates.

If we turn now to syllogism #11, which concluded the Syntagmation's first part, we find that for the first time in the entire document Aetius appealed, though rather obliquely, to scripture. The language of 'knowing' (using οἶδα and γιγνώσκω) was undoubtedly intended to be scriptural, reflecting the usage of Jn. 7:29 and, especially, 17:3[1] (compare also Jn. 10:15 and 17:25 and Mt. 11:27). But the appeal hardly affected the syllogism's content, for, as Basil of Ancyra pointed out in his memorandum of summer A.D. 359, the Son was literally designated as generated only twice in scripture (Prov. 8:22 and Ps. 110:3), and God was never literally designated as ungenerated.[2] What we really have in syllogism #11 is a logical argument with scriptural overtones. As L.R. Wickham so nicely phrased it, the syllogism "depends upon the general impossibility of knowing falsehoods: if A knows that he is ungenerate and B knows that he is generate, they cannot share a common essence."[3]

----

1. Jn. 17:3 was particularly important as background to this syllogism because the verse was the only scriptural passage to be quoted by Aetius in the entire Syntagmation (in syllogism #37).
2. Epiphanius, Haer. 73:19.
3. Wickham, p. 557. Wickham also provided a reconstruction of scriptural texts which he believed to be the exegetical foundation of Aetius' argument (Ibid.). The passages were all ones which Eunomius used in his writings. It is, therefore, better to consider them in their proper historical context.

Aetius probably wanted to end his sequence against homoousion with an authoritative syllogism. One which invoked scriptural authority through linguistic affinities with scriptural passages was perfect, especially since Aetius probably intended sarcasm when, in a syllogism which alluded particularly to Jn. 17:3 and its talk of "knowing the only true (ἀληθινὸν) God," he spoke of the homoousion as false (ψεῦδος).

Now that we have explicated the basic strategy Aetius recommended to his disciples to use in disputations with Homoiousians and Homoousians, it will be enlightening if we interrupt our syllogism by syllogism explication and delve in more detail into the wider intellectual/historical significance of the suggested strategy. In light of the fact that most of the Syntagmation's first part was directed against Athanasian positions, we cannot avoid the conclusion that the full significance of Aetius' strategy in Part I can only be grasped if it is seen as a response to Athanasius' recently published De Synodis, a document in which the homoousion was presented as the only true Christian position. Assuming this, we first examine De Synodis 47. In this section Athanasius admitted that there were two traditional Christian ways of employing the term ungenerated. It surely seems a reasonable hypothesis that Aetius' formulation of the "problem" with which all the Syntagmation's syllogisms dealt (see syllogism #1) and his formulation of proof that God is ungenerated (see syllogism #2) were in response to this section of Athanasius' treatise. The exiled Alexandrian, we remember, asserted in De Synodis 47 that one traditional Christian use of ungenerated was represented by Bishop Ignatius of Antioch, who said that the Son is both ungenerated and generated whereas a second was represented by (unnamed) ecclesiastical "teachers" who said that only the Father is ungenerated, the Son being "true generate (γέννημα ἀληθινόν)." Athanasius firmly asserted that there is no contradiction between the two usages. He said that Christ was called generated or created (γενητός) by Ignatius not because he was created by God like other creatures but only because he assumed the created or generated flesh of Mary. His divine self is ungenerate

240

(ἀγένητος). According to Athanasius, the teachers were
dealing with a different problem. Of course, they said
that only the Father is ungenerated, but they did not
mean by this that the Son is created or generated.
This was shown (1) by the fact that they called the
Son "true γέννημα," which Athanasius understood to
mean true offspring and not true generate, and (2) by
the fact that they termed the Son "Word and Wisdom of
the Father." When these teachers said that only the
Father is ungenerated, they meant he alone is uncaused.
When they added the Son is "true offspring" and "Word
and Wisdom of the Father," while they did imply that
he is caused, they did not imply that he is created,
for, Athanasius assumed, as "true offspring" the Son
was begotten homoousion from the Father's essence and
as "Word and Wisdom of the Father" he himself was the
creator of "all things" and, thus, could not be created.
That these unnamed teachers did not choose to use the
term ungenerated of the Son but reserved it for the
Father was to be explained by the simple fact that
they operated with a different definition of ungenerated than did people like Ignatius. They defined the
term as meaning "that which is, but neither is generated nor has any cause at all (τὸ ὂν μέν, μήτε δὲ
γεννηθὲν μήτε ὅλως ἔχον τὸν αἴτιον)," whereas Ignatius
meant by it simply "uncreated (ἄκτιστον)." The differing definitions explained why Ignatius was willing
to attribute ungeneratedness to the Son and why the
teachers were unwilling. Athanasius was sure that
adherents of each of the two usages "would not blame"
one another; they would realize their respective in-
tentions were different. Therefore, Christians ought
to respect both traditional usages and, indeed, "combine" or harmonize them": in one sense the Son is
ungenerated, in another he is not. When Aetius read
this sequence in the De Synodis, he apparently was
horrified. He could not grasp how Athanasius could
suggest that the Son is ungenerated in any sense. Nor
could he grasp how there could be more than one
acceptable definition of the word ungenerated. Thus,
he (1) formulated the "problem" of the Syntagmation
as "whether it is possible for the ungenerated God to
make the generated ungenerated" (syllogism #1), which

241

seemed to be implied by Athanasius' harmonization, and (2) decided to open his treatise with a proof of God as ungenerated which operated with precisely the same definition of ungenerated used by the unnamed teachers. Aetius even went so far as to make sure that the ὅλως in the definition cited by Athanasius was taken absolutely literally. That is, if the ungenerated has no cause "at all (ὅλως)," this means that he is not even cause to himself. Although Athanasius was willing to accept all the theological affirmations of the Christian tradition and to explain away seeming contradictions, Aetius was not. For him, contradictory usages demanded a choice. In order to put the attitudes of Athanasius and Aetius into some perspective, however, we must inquire more closely--and at some length--into the two early Christian trends of thought regarding the ungenerated and also consider the term's intellectual/ historical derivation.

Athanasius was always at pains to point out, not only in the De Synodis but also in the Orationes Contra Arianos and the De Decretis, that the term ungenerated was originally not Christian at all: it never occurred in scripture. The term was Greek. Athanasius was right; the term went back, in fact, to the very beginnings of Greek philosophy. It was used by Parmenides of Elea to describe 'that which is' (τὸ ὄν) as over against what later became termed 'that which is generated' (τὸ γιγνόμενον): "Very much, since it is ungenerated and indestructible (ὡς ἀγένητον ἐὸν καὶ ἀνώλεθρον), is it whole, unique, unmoveable, and ungenerated (ἀγένητον)."[1] After Parmenides the term was picked up by Plato and given an important role in his discussion of the soul both in the Phaedrus 24 (245c) and in the cosmology of the Timaeus (50-52).[2] Arguing in the Phaedrus that the soul is that which moves itself and is the source and beginning of motion for all other things, Plato noted that the soul as beginning or first

---

1. Parmenides of Elea apud Clement of Alexandria, Strom. 5:14:112, 2.
2. All translations of Plato are basically those of the Loeb Classical Library edition.

principle is ungenerated: "For it is necessary that
everything generated be generated from a first principle, but the first principle not be generated from
anything." Furthermore, like Parmenides, Plato
argued that this first principle is not only ungenerated but also indestructible, for "otherwise the entire
heaven and all generation must fall in ruin and stop."
Finally, self-motion was set forward as the "essence
and very meaning of the soul." In the Timaeus, Plato
used ungenerated in a somewhat more cosmological
context. In Timaeus 50c-d he distinguished among
three kinds of things (γένη): 'that which is
generated' (τὸ γιγνόμενον), that 'in which' it is
generated (τὸ ἐν ᾧ γίγνεται), and that 'from where'
that which is generated, being copied, is produced
(τὸ ὅθεν ἀφομοιούμενον φύεται τὸ γιγνόμενον). The
generated was likened to an offspring of Mother
Receptacle and Father Source. But Plato quickly
pointed out that while the generated is a copy of the
"forms" which are its "father," it is in no way
"essentially similar (ὅμοιον) to those forms," else
it would be a poor copy. A little later in the Timaeus
(51d) Plato argued for two different kinds (γένη) of
knowing, corresponding to the objective realities of
'that which is' (as we may designate the totality of
the "forms") and 'that which is generated'. These
are, respectively, "reason (νοῦς)" and "true opinion
(δόξα ἀληθής)." Like their objective correspondents,
they are also "unlike" (ἀνομοίως ἔχετον). Finally, in
Timaeus 52a Plato described 'that which is' and 'that
which is generated': "It being so, one must confess
that self-identical form (τὸ κατὰ ταὐτὰ εἶδος ἔχον) is
one thing, ungenerated and indestructible (ἀγέννητον
καὶ ἀνώλεθρον), neither receiving into itself anything
from anywhere nor itself entering into anything, invisible and altogether imperceptible--that which reason
(νόησις) has been allotted to contemplate; and a second
thing with the same name is like the first (τὸ δ'
ὁμώνυμον ὅμοιόν τε ἐκείνῳ δεύτερον), perceptible,
generated (γεννητὸν), always carried about, both generated (γιγνόμενον) in a certain place and again
perishing from there, apprehensible by opinion along
with sensation." So, for Plato, 'that which is', like

243

the soul of the Phaedrus, is ungenerated and indestructible, while 'that which is generated' is a second
kind of thing which, though a copy of 'that which is'
and, therefore, "like" it in one sense, is essentially
not like it. The first is ungenerated, the second
generated. One is struck by how much this sounds like
Aetius' position. After Plato we find Aristotle
analyzing the term ungenerated at some length in his
De Caelo 281bff (to which analysis, as we shall see,
Athanasius appealed), and we find the expression
cropping up in both Stoicism and Epicureanism.[1] But
as far as early Christianity was concerned, it was
primarily from the Platonic, specifically the Middle
Platonic, tradition that the term entered Christianity,
as Jean Daniélou has pointed out.[2]

It is not justified for us to concern ourselves
overmuch with the relative absence of the term from
the scattered and mostly fragmentary remains of the
leading Middle Platonists,[3] for its constant employment
by such second and third century Christians as Justin
Martyr, Athenagoras, and Clement of Alexandria (who
were otherwise heavily influenced by Middle Platonism)
suggests that it was a common designation of 'that
which is' (God) in Middle Platonic circles. Its widespread use is also supported by the fact that the term
was standard in second century philosophical doxographies, "that is, collections of the opinions of

---

1. Jules Lebreton, "ΑΓΕΝΝΗΤΟΣ dans la tradition
philosophique et dans la littérature chrétienne du IIe
siècle," Recherches de Science Religieuse 16 (1926):439.

2. Jean Daniélou, Gospel Message and Hellenistic
Culture, Vol. 2 of A History of Early Christian Doctrine
before the Council of Nicaea, trans. and ed. by John
Austin Baker (London, 1973), pp. 330-1.

3. It did not, for instance, occupy a central
place in the best preserved of the leading Middle Platonists, Albinus. He used it primarily in a passage
which simply reported Plato's doctrine of the soul set
forth in Phaedrus 24. See Albinus, Intr. 5:5, but
compare Intr. 12:1, where it was used of God, and 10:8,
where by implication it was used of God, etc.

philosophers, more or less superficial manuals containing summaries and sometimes quotations."[1] It occurred in handbooks employed both by the Christian apologist Athenagoras and by his contemporary Theophilus of Antioch. Athenagoras (Legatio 6:2) wrote:

> Since it is impossible to show without mentioning names that we [Christians] are not alone in insisting on the oneness of God, we have turned to the Opinions [The Doxographies]--so then, Plato says: "It is a hard task to find the Maker and Father of this universe, and having found him it is impossible to declare him to all." Here he understands the ungenerated and everlasting God to be one. If he acknowledges other gods such as sun, moon, and stars, he recognizes that they are generated . . . . Now if Plato is no atheist when he understands the creator of all things to be the one ungenerated God, neither are we atheists . . . .[2]

Similarly, Theophilus (Ad Autolycum 2:4) reported, "Plato and his sect confess that God is ungenerated, and the Father and Maker of the universe." Since both doxographies were reporting on Plato, Timaeus 28 and since Plato never once used the term ungenerated in this passage (though he used nearly every conceivable alternative), we can hardly doubt that the term was standard in second century Middle Platonic usage. But before we turn directly to a consideration of early Christian literature, it will repay us to consider in some detail the employment of the term ungenerated in two of the more pious of the non-Christian Platonists of the early Roman Empire, the somewhat popular, pagan Middle Platonist Plutarch and the Jewish Platonist Philo. That the Timaeus was one

---

1. William R. Schoedel, Athenagoras: Legatio and De Resurrectione (Oxford, 1972), p. 12 n. 3.
2. The translation is basically that provided by Schoedel, pp. 13-4.

of the Middle Platonists' favorite works of the master
is well-known. And that the passage in which Plato
distinguished between a higher ungenerated level of
reality ("the Father") and a lower generated level
(the "Offspring")--namely, Timaeus 50c-52a--was
particularly popular is borne out by an extended discussion in Plutarch's De Iside et Osiride. Here Isis
was identified as the Receptacle, Osiris as 'that which
is', and Horus as 'that which is generated' (372d-374b).
In this passage, however, while the god Osiris or 'that
which is' was described as "everlasting," "indestructible," "intelligible," and "superior to destruction
and change," he was not termed ungenerated. But in a
striking sequence in another of Plutarch's religious
works, De E apud Delphos 392a-e, God was so designated.
Plutarch began by pointing out (1) that we must address
God as "you are" (since the "assertion of being" is
appropriate only for him) and (2) that all mortal
nature is always at some stage "between generation and
destruction" (thus setting forth the Timaeus' distinction between 'that which is' and 'that which is
generated'). Then he asked, "what truly is being
(τί οὖν ὄντως ὄν ἐστι)?" He answered, "It is that
which is everlasting, ungenerated, and indestructible,
to which no period of time brings change." Here
ungenerated was added to the terms everlasting and
indestructible used in the De Iside et Osiride. All
are basic designations for 'that which is' or, as
Plutarch expressedly said, "God (ὁ θεὸς)." Indeed,
Plutarch went on to stress (De E apud Delphos 393a-c)
not only that God is ungenerated and indestructible
(using such substitute expressions as οὐ γεγονὸς
οὐδ'ἐσόμενον and οὐδ'ἀρξάμενον οὐδὲ παυσόμενον) but
that he is also "one":

> For the Deity is not many . . . but it is
> necessary that 'that which is' be one, just
> as it is necessary that 'the one' be.
> Difference, because of its distinction
> from 'that which is', withdraws into the
> generation of that which is not . . . . But
> 'the one' is simple and pure.

Here then, in a deeply pious, pagan Middle Platonist
we have the ungenerated and indestructible God described as both one and superior to all generation and
change--precisely the same way Athenagoras' doxography
described him. When we turn to the Jewish Platonist
Philo, we find the exact same situation. In fact, the
duo 'ungenerated and indestructible', which we found
first in the pre-Socratic Parmenides, has become in
Philo a common formula to describe God. For example,
in Quis rerum div. heres. 14 God was contrasted to
mortals and termed "the ungenerated and indestructible";
and the Passover was said to be the Passover of "the
ungenerated and indestructible" in De sacrificiis
Abelis et Caini 63. Moreover, just as Plutarch described God as "everlasting, ungenerated, and indestructible"
in De E apud Delphos 392e, so Philo in De Iosepho 265
contrasted him with an earthly "generated father" and
termed him "the ungenerated, the indestructible, the
eternal father."[1] The evidence we have cited from
Plutarch and Philo leaves little room for doubting
Daniélou's assertion that it was from Middle Platonic
circles--aided by the doxographies--that the term
ungenerated (and, we may add, its correlative, the
generated) entered early Christianity.

Before we leave Philo, however, two further passages which bear directly on the traditional Christian
use of ungenerated must be cited. Both concern Philo's
doctrine of the Logos, specifically the Logos' relation
to ungeneratedness and generatedness. This doctrine
was destined greatly to influence early Christianity,
for Philo was for all practical purposes considered
more a Christian than a Jew. In Leg. Alleg. 3:207-8
Philo[2] wrote:

> . . . men who say that they swear by God
> should be considered actually impious; for
> naturally no-one swears by him, seeing that
> he is unable to possess knowledge regarding

---

1. Compare also Philo, De Opificio Mundi 9 and 12.
2. All translations from Philo are basically those
found in the Loeb Classical Library edition.

247

his nature. No, we may be content if we are
able to swear by his name, which means . . .
the interpreting Logos . . . . Moses too,
let us observe, filled with wonder at the
transcendence of the ungenerated says, "and
thou shalt swear by his Name" (Deut. 6:13),
not "by Him," for it is enough for the
generated being that he should be accredited
and have witness borne to him by the divine
word . . . .

This passage, we may suggest, was prototypical of one
of the two early Christian trends of thought regarding
the ungenerated which Athanasius identified. Claiming
that God's ungenerated nature is transcendent and incomprehensible, it clearly implied, as Jules Lebreton
has noted, that "the Logos himself is not ungenerated."[1]
Prototypical of Athanasius' second traditional Christian
usage, on the other hand, was Quis rerum div. heres.
205-6, the relevant portion of which read as follows:

To his Logos, his chief messenger, highest
in age and honor, the Father of all has
given the special prerogative to stand on
the border and separate that which is generated from the creator. This same Logos
both pleads with the incorruptible as suppliant
for afflicted mortality and acts as ambassador
of the ruler to the subject. He glories in
this prerogative and proudly describes it in
these words,"and I stood between the Lord and
you" (Deut. 5:5), that is, neither ungenerated
like God nor generated like you, but midway
between the two extremes, a surety to both
sides.

Since Philo's Logos is here said "to stand on the
border" between the Father and 'that which is generated'
(the latter expression, because it is contrasted with
"the creator," obviously meant for Philo 'that which is

---

1. Lebreton, p. 437.

created') and to be "neither ungenerated like God nor generated like you," he is either (1) neither ungenerated nor generated or (2) in some sense both ungenerated and generated. Undoubtedly Philo meant to imply the latter, for his passage was surely influenced by Plato's description of the World-Soul in _Timaeus_ 34c-35b. Plato wrote:

> . . . God composed her [the World-Soul] of
> the materials and in the fashion which I
> shall now describe. Midway between the es-
> sence which is indivisible and remains always
> the same and that which is is generated and
> divisible in bodies, he blended a third form
> of essence composed of the two. And again,
> concerning the nature of sameness and the
> nature of difference, he also in the same
> way made a compound midway between the in-
> divisible one and the one divisible into
> bodies. And he took the three of them, and
> blended them all together into one form, by
> forcing the nature of difference, hard as it
> was to mix, into union with sameness, and
> mixing them together with essence.

Plato's reasoning in this sequence (if it should be called reasoning) led directly to Philo's notion that the intermediate Logos, like the intermediate World-Soul, is both ungenerated (partaking of 'that which is') and generated (partaking of 'that which is generated'); it is both the same and different from God and both the same and different from creatures.

We come now to the term ungenerated as it occurred in early Christian literature. The first of the two Christian trends regarding its use (for which Philo's _Leg. Alleg._ 3:207-8 was the prototype) was strongly represented in the writings of the second century apologist Justin Martyr.[1] Justin continually employed

---

1. Perhaps it occurred even earlier than in Justin, namely, in the _Apologia_ of Aristides, for J. Rendel
Harris translated the Syriac text of the apology's

ungenerated as one of his prime epithets for God,
usually in passages which also referred to the Son.
In three instances, however, the Son was not mentioned.
Commenting upon Old Testament passages which have God
speaking to Moses or coming down to see the tower of
men, Justin wrote, "You must not imagine that the ungenerated God himself came down or went up from any
place, for the ineffable Father and Lord of all has
not come to any place . . . ";[1] addressing himself to
false accusations brought against Christians, he said,
"None of these actions are really ours, and we have the
ungenerated and ineffable God as witness both of our
thoughts and deeds."[2] By far the most fascinating of
these passages which did not mention the Son is Justin's
account of his conversion to Christianity by an (ideal
or real) "old man." Meditating by the sea, Justin, who
at the time was still a Platonist, was engaged by the
old man in a conversation about philosophy and God.
When asked for a definition of God, Justin offered
what Robert M. Grant has called "the usual school statement": "that which always maintains the same things in
the same way and is the cause of being for all things."[3]
This launched Justin and the old man into a discussion
of two of Plato's dialogues, the Phaedrus (which discussed the immortal soul) and the Timaeus (which discussed the origins of the world), perhaps the two most
popular of the dialogues in Middle Platonism and, as
we have seen, two dialogues where the term ungenerated

first chapter as saying that "God is not begotten, not
made" (The Apology of Aristides, vol. 1 of Texts and
Studies, edited by J. Armitage Robinson (Cambridge,
1893), p. 35). Probably either ἀγέννητος or ἀγένητος
(or both) were in the Greek original, this portion of
which has been lost. In the extant version of the
Greek only ἄναρχον, ἀΐδιον, ἀθάνατον and ἀπροσδεῆ
occurred as descriptive of God (Ibid., p. 100).

1. Dial. 127.
2. 2 Apol. 12:4.
3. Robert M. Grant, The Early Christian Doctrine
of God (Charlottesville, Virginia, 1966), p. 19; the
quotation is from Justin Martyr, Dial. 3.

occurred prominently. Armed with either Stoic or
Aristotelian arguments against Plato,[1] the old man
completely undermined Justin's commitment to his
philosophic master (with the help of answers from
Justin contradictory of the _Phaedrus_ and of second
century Platonic interpretations of the master).
Toward the end of this conversation Justin articulated
a version of Platonic theology which, finally, the old
man did not attack but with which he expressed agreement. It represented "Christian" Platonism. The
version was as follows:[2]

> For only God is ungenerated and incorruptible,
> and because of this, is God, but all other
> things which come after him are generated and
> corruptible. For this reason souls both die
> and are punished: since, if they were ungen-
> erated, they would neither sin, nor be filled
> with folly, nor be cowardly and again ferocious;
> nor would they willingly transform into swine,
> and serpents and dogs; and it would not indeed
> be just to compel them, if they be ungenerated.
> For that which is ungenerated is similar to,
> equal to, and the same as that which is un-
> generated, and neither in power nor in honor
> would they be different from each other. There-
> fore, there are not many ungenerated things,
> for if there were some difference among them,
> you would not find the cause of the difference,
> though you searched for it; but, after ever
> sending your mind to infinity, you would at
> some time stop, tired out, at one ungenerated
> and say this is the cause of all things.[3]

---

1. For the first view, see Robert M. Grant,
"Aristotle and the Conversion of Justin," _After the New
Testament_ (Philadelphia, 1967), pp. 122-5; for the second
see N. Hyldal, _Philosophie und Christentum: Eine Interpretation der Einleitung zum Dialog Justins_ (Copenhagen,
1966).
2. All translations of Justin are basically those
found in ANF 1.
3. _Dial_. 5.

All things in existence besides God, on the other
hand, because they are not by nature ungenerated, are
generated and perish "on account of the will of God
(διὰ τὴν βούλησιν τοῦ θεοῦ)."[1] This includes every
soul, which partakes of life only so long as God wills
it: "The soul partakes of life, since God wills it
to live; thus, then, it will not partake at that time
when God wishes that it not live."[2] Given this strong
commitment to monotheism, to one ungenerated God, it is
no wonder that when Justin spoke of the Son in connection with God, he studiously avoided attributing ungeneratedness to him. Justin spoke of him in his
Dialogus as "the Son of the only ungenerated, ineffable
God."[3] And in his apologies he said that "through
Jesus Christ . . . we have dedicated ourselves to the
ungenerated and impassible God"[4] and that "we follow
the only ungenerated God through his Son."[5] Even when
he confessed that Christians worshipped the Son, still
he refrained from attributing ungeneratedness to him:
"For after God we worship and love the Word who is
from the ungenerated and ineffable God, since he became man for our sakes . . . ."[6] On the other hand,
Justin did call Christ the "first-born to the ungenerated God (πρωτότοκος τῷ ἀγεννήτῳ θεῷ)"[7] and the
"first offspring of God (πρῶτον γέννημα τοῦ θεοῦ)
. . . begotten without sexual union."[8] He went so far
as to write, "His Son, who alone is properly called
Son, the Word who also was with him and was begotten
before the things made, when he first created and
ordered all things through him, is called Christ
. . . ."[9] One might think the intended implication
of this last passage was a clear distinction between

---

1. Ibid.
2. Ibid., 6.
3. Ibid., 126
4. 1 Apol. 25.
5. 1 Apol. 14. Similarily in 1 Apol. 49.
6. 2 Apol. 13.
7. 1 Apol. 53.
8. Ibid., 21.
9. 2 Apol. 6.

generated things, which Justin in his Dialogus cum
Tryphone Judaeo referred to as γεννητὰ καὶ φθαρτά,
and the Son. But Justin either did not recognize a
problem here or simply refused to discuss it. The
latter is more likely, since if he denied that the
Son is generated, he would have to admit his ungeneratedness; he would thereby undermine the apologetic
argument of Dialogus 5 that there is only one ungenerated being, God. At any rate, the trend of thought
represented by Justin regarding the relation of the
Son to ungeneratedness was the trend championed by
our Neo-Arian Aetius. Moreover, it no doubt has
struck the reader that Aetius also followed Justin's
trend of thought in defining God in terms of cause
(see syllogism #2 of the Syntagmation).[1]

Nearly as heavily influenced by popular Middle
Platonism as Justin was another second century
apologist, Athenagoras. Like Justin, Athenagoras
assumed that God is ungenerated. Early in his apology
he protested against Christians being termed atheists
by saying,[2] "Surely it is not rational for them to
apply the term atheism to us who distinguish God from
matter and show that matter is one thing and God
another and the difference between them immense; for
the divine is ungenerated and eternal, and can be
contemplated only by thought and reason, whereas
matter is generated and perishable."[3] Clearly
Athenagoras had taken over the Platonic view which we
have seen him quoting from doxographical literature.
Later he used this view as a tool with which to attack
the pagan gods of the poets[4] and the divinities of

---

1. Justin, in turn, was dependent, of course,
on the Platonic tradition that went back to Timaeus
28. There Plato said, "Again, everything which is
generated by necessity is generated by some cause
(πᾶν δὲ αὖ τὸ γιγνόμενον ὑπ'αἰτίου τινὸς ἐξ ἀνάγκης
γίγνεσθαι)."
2. All translations of Athenagoras are fundamentally those of Schoedel.
3. Leg. 4:1.
4. Ibid., 19:1.

253

some philosophers.[1] In the process he admitted that
he agreed completely with the Platonists in their
attitude toward the gods, an attitude based on the
notions of ungenerated and generated:

> On this point there is no disagreement between
> myself and the philosophers. 'What is that
> which always is and does not have generation,
> or what is that which is generated, but never
> is?' Plato in his dialogues on the intelli-
> gible and perceptible teaches that that which
> always is, the intelligible, is ungenerated,
> whereas that which is not, the perceptible,
> is generated, having a beginning and an end
> to its existence.[2]

If the reader has harbored any lingering doubt that
the definition of ungenerated and generated with which
the fourth century Arians and Neo-Arians operated was
derived from the Platonic tradition, this quotation
must dispel it. Now we must ask the important question of Athenagoras. Did he belong to the Christian
trend of thinking that reserved the term ungenerated
for the high God, thus agreeing with Justin, or did he
belong to the other trend? The answer is to be found
in chapters 8-10 of Athenagoras' Legatio, where he
set out at length the details of his Christian
monotheism.

Chapters 8 and 9 of the Legatio contained arguments that God is one, chapter 8 being devoted to
arguments from reason, chapter 9 to arguments from
revelation. The basic procedure of the arguments
from reason was negative: they were designed to
demonstrate the impossibility of the notion that there
are two or more gods in the universe. Athenagoras
suggested that "if there were two or more gods from
the beginning, either they would belong to one and the
same genus or each of them would belong to its own
genus." If they belonged to one and the same genus,

---

1. Ibid., 22:3-5.
2. Ibid., 19:2.

they would have to be similar (ὅμοιοι) to each other.
But gods cannot be similar to each other, said Athenagoras, since they are ungenerated, and "whereas generated things are similar to their paradigms, ungenerated things are dissimilar, since they are generated
from no one and without paradigms." This argument
assumed the definition of a genus to be two or more
things similar to what Robert M. Grant has aptly
called "a prior model."[1] Since ungenerated things
like gods have no "prior model," they cannot be
similar to each other. And if they are dissimilar,
they cannot belong to the same genus. Hence, since
they cannot belong to the same genus, how can more
than one be God? Here was a slightly different
argument for the oneness of the ungenerated God from
the one we met in Justin, Dialogus 5. The earlier
apologist had reasoned that there cannot be more than
one ungenerated thing, since all ungenerated things
are similar to and the same as all other ungenerated
things; therefore, there would be no way to differentiate them. Having produced one argument against
polytheism, Athenagoras next took up the polytheists'
suggestion that the gods are dissimilar but of the
same genus; this can be so because they are complementary, just in the way hands, eyes, and feet are
complementary parts of one body and, hence, belong to
one genus. Assuming the Platonic distinction between
the ungenerated/incorruptible and the generated/
corruptible, Athenagoras responded that only generated
and corruptible things are composite and divisible
into parts, whereas God, since he is "ungenerated,
impassible, and indivisible," does not consist in
parts. The ploy of the polytheists did not work;
it was offensive to Platonic assumptions. So one
must conclude that if there are two or more gods,
they cannot belong to one and the same genus. But
neither can they belong to different genera, argued
Athenagoras, for he assumed that the god who has made
the world is "above" and "around" the things he

---

1. Grant, Early Christian Doctrine of God,
p. 108.

255

generated. There is no place left for any other god besides the creator. The intricacies of this fascinating argument, since they are not connected with the notion of ungeneratedness, need not concern us.[1] Suffice it to say that Athenagoras found it logical and necessary to conclude that two or more gods (1) cannot belong to one and the same genus and (2) cannot belong to different genera. Therefore, reason leads one to conclude that there is only one God, a view which is supported by biblical revelation (see Leg. 9).

Now that he has presented monotheism as the demand of both reason and revelation, Athenagoras proclaimed in Platonic fashion (Leg. 10) that "the ungenerated, eternal, invisible, impassible, incomprehensible and infinite God, who is apprehended by mind and reason alone . . . is one." Immediately, however, strict monotheism was qualified by Athenagoras' identifying this "mind and reason alone" as the Reason (ὁ λόγος) of God "by whom the universe is generated" and as "the Son of God" who is "the Reason of the Father in idea and activity (λόγος τοῦ πατρὸς ἐν ἰδέᾳ καὶ ἐνεργείᾳ)." Even though he insisted that "Father and Son are one," Athenagoras found it somewhat difficult to explicate how this is so. His claim that the Son is "the Reason of the Father in idea and activity" seems to have been essentially Middle Platonic content[2] (a mix of Platonism and Aristotelianism) poured into a Stoic-Philonic form,[3] while his explication based on scripture was just as opaque, for he contented himself with stating, "the Son is in the Father and the Father in the Son (Jn. 10:38) by a powerful unity of spirit." Nor did Athenagoras find it easy to explain how the Son is distinguished from the Father but not to be counted among the creatures. He said that if one wants to know what "Son" means, he can rest assured that it means "first offspring of the Father." This does not

---

1. See Schoedel, pp. xv, 17 n. 3, and 19 n. 6.
2. The Middle Platonist Albinus, for instance, linked God's ἐνεργεία with ἰδέα in Intr. 10:3.
3. See Schoedel, p. 21 n. 2.

mean that as such he is generated. Rather, "God, who is eternal mind, himself had his Reason in himself , from the beginning, since he is eternally rational." This Reason is called "Son" and "first offspring" because "he came forth" to provide "idea and activity (ἰδέα καὶ ἐνέργεια)" for material reality. We recognize that in <u>Legatio</u> 10 Athenagoras followed Justin in invoking the notion that the Son is God's "first offspring (πρῶτον γέννημα)," but he went beyond Justin in explicitly denying that he belongs among generated things. On the other hand, like Justin, Athenagoras was unable to bring himself to draw the conclusion that the Son is ungenerated like the Father. Probably he was conscious that if he did so, he would be obliged to find a new argument against polytheism (and, indeed, pagan Platonism) to replace the one he offered in <u>Legatio</u> 8, namely, that there cannot be more than one ungenerated being. Thus, he contented himself in <u>Legatio</u> 10 with denying the Son's generatedness and with proclaiming in ringing tones the unity and diversity of the Trinity: " . . . [we] bring forth God the Father, God the Son, and the Holy Spirit, and show forth their power in their unity and their diversity in rank." It is clear, then, that while Athenagoras has come very close to breaking out of the trend of thought regarding the ungenerated which was represented by Justin, he was still bound by it, no matter the difficulties that it provided for his doctrine of the Son.

The last representative we shall consider of the trend of Christian thought which reserved the term ungenerated for God and denied it to the Son is Clement of Alexandria. Like Philo and Justin, Clement was fond of employing ungenerated as an epithet for God, usually when he made no mention of the Son.[1] Although he insisted in one place that the Son is identical in essence with the Father,[2] thus going far

---

1. For example, in <u>Prot.</u> 6, in <u>Str.</u> 2:2, 2:12, 5:11, 5:12, 6:16, and 6:18, and in <u>Ecl.</u> 25.
2. <u>Exc. Thdot.</u> 19:1-4. Compare Daniélou, <u>Gospel Message and Hellenistic Culture</u>, pp. 366-7.

beyond Athenagoras, Clement continued to follow both
Justin and Athenagoras in being unwilling to use the
term ungenerated of the Son. He affirmed that "in
his ungenerated identity 'He that is' is absolutely
alone."[1] It particularly pleased him that some philosophers (undoubtedly Middle Platonists) confessed
that "the indestructible and ungenerated God is one."[2]
Consequently, in passages where he mentioned the Son
in connection with the ungenerated God, Clement was
careful to distinguish the two clearly. For example,
speaking of Christianity as the true "mysteries" in his
Protrepticus, Clement invited pagans to be "initiated"
and to join the choir of angels "around the ungenerated
and indestructible and absolutely only God, the Logos
of God raising the hymn with us."[3] In the Stromata,
he wrote, "Since one is the ungenerated, the Almighty
God, one too is the first-generated through whom all
things were made and without whom nothing ever was
made, for one, in truth, is God, who created the
beginning of all things."[4] Clement went on to identify this "beginning or first principle of all things"
created by God as "the first-begotten Son."[5] This
passage was parallel to the affirmation of the unnamed
ecclesiastical teachers we have seen quoted by Athanasius in De Synodis 47: "One is the ungenerated, the
Father, and one is the genuine Son from him, true
offspring, Logos and Wisdom of the Father." In fact,
it is not outside of the realm of possibility that
fourth century Arians referred to this very passage
in Clement to support their view (for the Son's generation was, after all, interpreted as creation);
perhaps Athanasius chose to quote it in a somewhat
less than accurate manner in order to allow himself
to deal more easily with it. It may even have been
especially popular with Aetius; was this the reason
Athanasius noted it? In any case, Clement represented

---

1.   Str. 6:16.
2.   Prot. 6.
3.   Ibid., 12.
4.   Str. 6:7.
5.   Ibid.

the culmination of the first Christian trend of thought regarding the use of the term ungenerated. When Aetius chose to reserve the term for God and to deny it to the Son, he had the full authority of Justin, Athenagoras, and Clement of Alexandria behind him.

When we turn from the first to the second Christian trend of thought regarding ungenerated, that foreshadowed by Philo in his Quis rerum div. heres. 205-6, we find the evidence considerably less massive. The only really clear representative of this trend was Ignatius of Antioch, who of course was quoted as such by Athanasius. Ignatius was in no sense a Platonist, so it is no wonder he did not normally employ the Platonist term ungenerated when he spoke of God the Father. When he did use the term, he used it of the Son, and really only in passing. "There is one physician," he said," fleshly and spiritual, generated and ungenerated, God in man, true life in death, both from Mary and from God, first passible and then impassible (Eph. 7:2)." Prestige has correctly pointed out (1) that there was here "no discussion whatever of the relationship of the Son to the Father" and (2) that the passage concerned only the incarnation.[1] Nonetheless, the point of the statement was crystal clear. The incarnate one was claimed to be both God and man, both ungenerated God like his divine Father and generated man like his human mother. Since Ignatius was not a modalist (a Sabellian, to use the later designation),[2] the implication of his Eph. 7:2 was that there are two ungenerated beings, God the Father and the preexistent Christ. And since the bishop had not used arguments for one ungenerated God against belief in the pagan gods or against pagan Middle Platonism, as did the later apologists, he saw no intellectual problem in affirming two ungenerates. When we inquire after Ignatius' descendants in this trend of thinking, one of the better candidates is Noetus, the modalist from Smyrna against whom

---

1. Prestige, God in Patristic Thought, p. 38.
2. See the passages cited by Kelly, Doctrines, p. 93.

Hippolytus polemized at the beginning of the third century A.D. In a passage strongly reminiscent of Ignatius, though focusing on the Father rather than the Son, Noetus affirmed that there is "one Father and God of the Universe" and that "having created all things . . . he is invisible when he is not seen, and visible when he is seen, and ungenerated when he is not generated and generated when he is generated from a virgin (ἀγέννητον δέ, ὅταν μὴ γεννᾶται, γεννητὸν δέ, ὅταν γεννᾶται ἐκ παρθένου), impassible and immortal when he does not suffer and does not die, but when he approaches suffering, he suffers and dies."[1] The major difference between Noetus and Ignatius, of course, was that Noetus was a modalist, while Ignatius tended not to be. Therefore, while the implication of Ignatius' affirmation was that there are two divine ungenerated beings, Father and Son, the Son being also generated, the implication of Noetus' affirmation was that there is only one divine being, who is at one time Father, at another Son, at one time ungenerated, at another generated. Noetus' statement, then, would be of little use to Athanasius in his attempt to prove that pre-fourth century Christians were divided about whether or not to attribute ungeneratedness to the independently-existing Son.

Were there no other early Christians committed to the Son's ungeneratedness? Paul Stiegele, the author of a study of the term ungenerated in fourth century theology, thought that he found one in Irenaeus, the famous anti-Gnostic bishop of Lyons. He wrote, "Dass der Logos nicht unter die γεννητά einzurechnen, sondern ἀγέννητος (infectus ist), sagt Irenaeus aus-drucklich."[2] The difficulty is that the passage in Irenaeus to which he was referring was not nearly so unequivocal as he has made it out to be. Irenaeus addressed man and said, "For you, man, are not ungenerated, nor do you always co-exist with God, as does his own Word (Non enim infectus es, o homo, neque

_____

1. Noetus of Smyrna apud Hippolytus, Haer. 10:27.
2. Der Agennesiebegriff in der Griechischen Theologie des Vierten Jahrhunderts (Freiburg, 1913), p. 17.

semper coexsistebas Deo, sicut proprium ejus Verbum)."[1]
Surely the words "sicut proprium ejus Verbum" were
intended to go with "neque semper coexsistebas Deo"
rather than with "non infectus es." It is possible
Irenaeus meant to _imply_ that the Son is ungenerated,
but he has not stated it unequivocally. Since in
other passages where he used the term, he used it in
precisely the same way as did Justin, Athenagoras,
and Clement of Alexandria, Stiegele's interpretation
seems most unlikely. In two of these passages, for
instance, Irenaeus employed heavy doses of Platonic
language to prove the same point that the apologists
were trying to prove, namely, that God alone is ungenerated (infectus or innatus in the Latin) and that all
else is generated.[2] In one of these a clear distinction was made between the ungenerated God and the
Logos.[3] The only support for Stiegele's view is a
fascinating sequence, again heavily Platonic, in which
Irenaeus explicated precisely what he meant when he
used the term ungenerated. Since the explication is
interesting for its own sake, it is worth quoting its
relevant portions.

> . . . everything is possible to God, because
> he is unchanging and ungenerated, but gener-
> ated things (τὰ γεγονότα), since they sub-
> sequently acquired an independent beginning
> of temporal existence (γενέσεως), on that
> very ground are bound to be inferior to him
> who made them. Objects recently generated
> (γεγενημένα) cannot be ungenerated. Inasmuch
> as they are not ungenerated, they are inferior
> to what is perfect . . . . In God are ex-
> hibited alike power and wisdom and goodness
> . . . . As generated things receive growth
> through his exceeding goodness and persist
> for an extended period, they will acquire the
> glory of the ungenerated, since God bestows

---

1. Irenaeus, _Haer._ 2:25:3.
2. _Ibid._, 2:34:2 and 3:8:3.
3. _Ibid._, 3:8:3.

261

ungrudgingly what is good. In respect of
their creation they are not ungenerated; but
in virtue of persisting through long ages
they will receive the power of the ungenerated . . . . [God] alone is ungenerated,
and first of all, and author of existence to
all. All else abides in subjection to God.
But subjection to God is persistence in incorruptibility, and incorruptibility is the
glory of the ungenerated. By this ordinance
. . . generated and created man is rendered
after the image and the similitude of ungenerated God. The Father's is the goodwill
and command. The Son executes and fabricates.
The Spirit nourishes and increases. And man
gently progresses and rises toward perfection,
that is to say, he approximates to the ungenerated. For the perfect one is the ungenerated
one, and that is God.[1]

The last few lines of this passage might possibly be
construed to mean that the one ungenerated God is
somehow three--Father, Son, and Holy Spirit--and,
therefore, the Son and Holy Spirit are equally as
ungenerated as the Father. But again, if this was
what Irenaeus meant to say, he stated his point with
extreme vagueness. This evidence, like the evidence
directly cited by Stiegele, fails to support unequivocally the contention that Irenaeus held that the Son
is ungenerated. Ignatius remains so far the only
representative of this view. The passage we have
just quoted, however, is interesting for another
reason. It reveals to us that though the term ungenerated is philologically a negative term, Irenaeus
took it in a wholly positive way. For him it meant
'perfection'. Indeed, Prestige has pointed out that
in ancient literature (1) the philologically positive
term generated was the one which actually was

_____

1.   Ibid., 38:1-3. The translation, with minor
changes, is that of Prestige, God in Patristic
Thought, pp. 44-6.

"logically tinged with a negation,"[1] and (2) the
philologically negative term ungenerated conveyed the
sense of the English expression, 'the Absolute', since
to it alone belonged inherently "omnipotence, perfection, creative power and goodness, glory, eternity,
causation, and wisdom."[2] Given that the word conveyed
such a meaning, we can well understand why the Arians
of the fourth century, especially the Neo-Arians, were
attracted to it. Now, however, we must return to our
major inquiry and ask whether Ignatius must stand
alone in his claim that the Son is ungenerated?

No, for when we turn to the great Alexandrian
scholar, Origen, we finally find company for Ignatius.
In his apologetic work against the Middle Platonist
Celsus, Origen quoted Mt. 11:27 ("No one knows the Son
but the Father and no one knows the Father but the Son
and he to whom the Son reveals him") and commented,
"For no one is worthy to be able to know the ungenerated one and the first-born of all generated nature as
the Father who begot him (knows him), nor anyone the
Father as the living Logos and his wisdom and truth."[3]
The genuineness of the ἀγένητον in this passage has
been challenged by Paul Stiegele,[4] but on generally
inadequate grounds, although one manuscript (Cod.
Anglicanus secundus) does read γεννητόν instead of
ἀγένητον. The reason that Stiegele's grounds are
inadequate is that in another passage of the Contra
Celsum Origen said that Christians offer prayers and
a righteous life to God through Jesus, "as through one
who is between the nature of the ungenerated and all
generated things."[5] Since this passage was obviously
modelled upon Philo, Quis rerum div. heres. 205-6,
where the Jewish Platonist argued that the Logos is
both ungenerated and generated, surely Origen meant
to imply the same thing in Contra Celsum 3:34 and then

---

1. Prestige, God in Patristic Thought, p. 41.
2. Ibid., pp. 46-7.
3. Cels. 6:17.
4. Stiegele, p. 21.
5. Cels. 3:34.

decided to state it explicitly in 6:17.[1] On the other
hand, although it is true that we have found two passages where Origen claimed that the Son is ungenerated,
in the overwhelming majority of cases Origen followed
the usage of Justin, Athenagoras, and Clement of
Alexandria and implicitly reserved the term for the
Father.[2] Perhaps Origen's most forcefully direct
statement of this point of view came in his commentary
on John. He wrote, "The man who is unwilling to say
that the Holy Spirit is generated through Christ must
assert that he is ungenerated . . . . We, however,
are persuaded that are three hypostases, the Father,
the Son, and the Holy Spirit, and believe that no one
is ungenerated except the Father (καὶ ἀγέννητον μηδὲν
ἕτερον τοῦ πατρὸς εἶναι πιστεύοντες)."[3] On the face
of it, Origen seems simply to have been inconsistent.
Yet, perhaps underneath he was not, for we notice that
in Contra Celsum 6:17 and 3:34 he used the term
ἀγένητον (with one ν), whereas in Comm. in Joannem
2:10 he used ἀγέννητον (with two νs). Now, up to this
point in our study we have in general translated both
indiscriminately by the English term ungenerated. And
for good reason, since, as Prestige has shown, second
and third century Christians generally did not distinguish between them.[4] Prestige concluded, "We are dealing with alternative spellings of a single word in
fact, rather than with two separate terms bearing
distinct connotations."[5] Origen, however, may well
have begun to distinguish between the two words,
meaning by ἀγέννητος 'unbegotten' and by ἀγένητος

---

1. Compare also the explication of the second of
the catena fragments of Origen on St. John (where
Origen denies that the Logos is generated) offered by
Prestige, God in Patristic Thought, p. 137.
2. For example, Cels. 6:66 and 8:14, Jo. 1:27,
1:29, 2:2, 2:14, 19:2, and Princ. 1:2:9. Compare also
Cels. 2:51 and 4:38, Jo. 13:25 and 20:33 and Princ.
1:2:4.
3. Jo. 2:10.
4. Prestige, God in Patristic Thought, pp. 41-3.
5. Ibid., p. 43.

'uncreated'; if this was so, and Prestige for one thinks it was,[1] then perhaps Origen was not inconsistent after all. Only the Father is ἀγέννητος (unbegotten), but the Son, while begotten of the Father or γεννητός, is at the same time ἀγένητος or uncreated. This may well be the solution to the apparent inconsistency in Origen, but if it is, we must hasten to add that Origen's usage seems to have had no widespread effect on other Christians; even such fourth century authors as Eusebius of Caesarea and Athanasius himself generally used the words interchangeably.[2] Only Methodius, the anti-Origenist Christian Platonist, and the unknown author of the Adamantius followed Origen's tack.[3]

However this may be, what is of primary importance to us is that in all of second and third century Christianity we have found only three indisputable passages in which the independently-existing Son was called ungenerated, one in Ignatius and two in Origen, while we have discovered that the term was reserved for God the Father in what can only be termed a 'massive' number of cases. We must conclude that Aetius had the overwhelmingly decisive weight of the Christian theological tradition on his side when he assumed there is only one ungenerated being, God the Father. It is no wonder that when he read Athanasius' De Synodis 47 and saw the homoousian bishop giving the same weight to the trend of thought which saw the Son as ungenerated as to the trend which denied ungeneratedness to him, he was outraged; to him, Ignatius, whom Athanasius quoted in his support, was simply stating logical impossibilities. Athanasius might want to take such isolated comments in the Christian tradition seriously; Aetius did not. Consequently, backed securely by the tradition of Christian

---

1. Ibid., p. 51.
2. See Prestige, "ἀγέν[ν]ητος and γεν[ν]ητός, and Kindred Words, in Eusebius and the Early Arians," pp. 486-96 and "ἀγέν[ν]ητος and Cognate Words in Athanasius," pp. 258-65.
3. Prestige, God in Patristic Thought, pp. 51-2.

philosophical (Middle Platonic) theology, he decided to cast his response to Athanasius' De Synodis in the role of a defense of tradition and to produce an all out attack on the Athanasian notion of two ungenerated beings. So, when Aetius stated in syllogism #5 of the Syntagmation that "no pious reasoning permits the same essence to be generated and ungenerated," he was tapping the fury of an outraged theological conservatism. Indeed, nearly all the assumptions which Aetius made in Part I of his Syntagmation--that the ungenerated God should be defined in terms of cause, that God is not compound but simple, that he is unchangeable, etc.--were, as we have seen,[1] traditional assumptions of Christian philosophical theology. Only two of the assumptions of the Syntagmation's first part were singled out for further argument by Aetius, namely, the assumption that ungenerated/generated language constitutes proper theological terminology and the assumption that ungeneratedness (and generatedness) pertains to essence. Since arguments in support of these assumptions occupied all of Part II and Part III of the Syntagmation, Aetius clearly considered them crucial to his position, even though he may have hoped that his disciples might not have to deal with them in order to win their disputations. To Part II we now turn.

The Syntagmation: Part II

> #12. If the term ungenerated does not present the hypostasis of God, but the incomparable name (τὸ ἀσύγκριτον ὄνομα) is of human invention (ἐπινοίας . . .

---

1. We have said least about God's unchangeability. That it was asserted by Middle Platonism is shown by Albinus, Intr. 10:7-8; that it was integral to Christian philosophical theology needs little substantiation. Suffice it to say that Aetius' homoiousian opponents assumed it: see the Ancyran synodical letter of A.D. 358 apud Epiphanius, Haer. 73:4-5.

ἀνθρωπίνης), God is grateful, because
of the invention of the term ungenerated,
to those who have invented a superiority
of name which he does not bear in essence.

#13. If ungeneratedness is externally observed
in God, those who have observed it are
better than the one observed, since they
have provided for him a name better than
his nature.

#14. If the ungenerated nature does not yield
to generation, it is what it is said to
be (τοῦτ'ἔστιν ὃ λέγεται), but if it
yields to generation, the passive experiences of generation (τὰ τῆς γενέσεως
πάθη) would be stronger than the
hypostasis of God.

#15. If the generate is by nature immutable
because of the one who generated it
(ἄτρεπτον τὴν φύσιν . . . διὰ τὸν
γεννήσαντα), then the ungenerated essence
is immutable, not because of will but
because of its essential rank (οὐ διὰ
γνώμην, ἀλλὰ διὰ τὸ ἐν οὐσίᾳ ἀξίωμα).

#16. If ungeneratedness is revelatory of
essence, it is reasonably contrasted
with the essence of the generate; if
ungeneratedness means nothing, the
term generate even more so reveals
nothing. How could nothing be contrasted with nothing? And if the expression
ungenerated is contrasted with the expression generated, silence following
the expression, it turns out that the
hope of the Christians comes into
existence and goes out of existence
(γίνεσθαι . . . καὶ ἀπογίνεσθαι), since
it rests on excellent language (ἐν
διαφόρῳ προφορᾷ κειμένην), but not on
natures as they actually are (ἀλλ'οὐκ

ἐν φύσεσιν, οὕτως ἐχούσαις), as the
meaning of names intends (ὡς ἡ τῶν
ὀνομάτων βούλεται σημασία).

#17. If the ungenerated possesses nothing
at all in superiority of essence to
the generate, the Son, being subordinate
(ὑπερχόμενος) only verbally (προφορᾷ
μόνον), will know that those who have
called him such are superior to himself,
not the one called his God and Father.

#18. If the ungenerated essence is superior
to generation, having its superiority
from its own resources (οἴκοθεν), it
is in itself ungenerated essence. For
it is not superior to generation because
it wills to be but because it has the
nature to be (ὅτι βούλεται . . . ἀλλ'ὅτι
πέφυκεν). God, then, being ungenerated
essence in itself, permits no reasoning
to invent (ἐπινοῆσαι) generation for
it, thrusting aside from generated
beings all investigation and reasoning
(πᾶσαν ἐξέτασιν καὶ πάντα λογισμόν).

The syllogisms of the Syntagmation's second part
all addressed the accusation of Athanasius and of the
homoiousian memorandum of A.D. 359 that the term ungenerated is unscriptural. They did this by focusing
on the accusation's implication that the term is an
untrustworthy guide to truth because it is human
invention, not revelation. Quite obviously, Aetius
was worried about the accusation, for his first two
syllogisms were thick with sarcasm. The sarcasm only
barely hid the fact that at base all Aetius had with
which to counter the accusation was an assumption,
namely, the Christian Middle Platonic assumption that
to call God the ungenerated is to allow him the perfection due the Absolute.[1] Syllogism #12, for instance,

1. See above, pp. 262-3.

argued that if the incomparable name of ungenerated
is a human invention and not a true description of
God's reality, God is "grateful" to those who have
invented for him a superiority which is in name only
and does not apply to his essence. Without the
Christian Middle Platonic assumption, this syllogism
would not work. Neither would syllogism #13.[1] It
pointed out that those who see fit to call God ungenerated would be superior to God himself if God were
really not ungenerated. They would be superior to
God, since ungeneratedness would not belong to God's
nature, whereas the idea of such absolute perfection
would belong to those who ascribe it to him. To
someone who absolutely refused to use ungenerated
because it is unscriptural, Aetius' syllogisms would
hold no water. But Neo-Arians could always accuse
Homoousians and Homoiousians of inconsistency if they
resorted to such a strict scriptural position, since,
after all, the term essence (οὐσία) is also unscriptural. On the grounds of scripture, the Neo-Arians'
position was as secure as their opponents'. And on
the grounds of the Christian tradition of philosophical theology, it was more secure.

Syllogisms #12 and 13, however, were not merely
pieces of rhetorical sarcasm intended to be used by
Neo-Arians against their opponents; they also introduced the issue of God's "name" and thereby help us to
understand the Neo-Arian view of theological language.
We remember that the Ancyran synodical letter of 358
discussed the problem of proper theological language
in response to the Neo-Arian claim that God's fatherly
relationship with the Son is simply a mode of address.
Then, from Basil's memorandum of 359 we learned that
between the spring of 358 and the summer of 359 Aetius
had developed the more refined position that the term

----

1. L.R. Wickham's notion, pp. 558-9 that syllogism #13 is to be interpreted in the light of Basil of
Caesarea's position (C. Eun. 2:28) that "generatedness
and ungeneratedness" are "certain cognitive properties
observed in [God's] essence" was anachronistic and,
therefore, to be rejected.

ungenerated refers to God's essence, while the term
Father designates only his will and activity--or, to
use Aetius' own word, his "power (δύναμις)." If we
view this development in the light of syllogisms #12
and 13, which raised the issue of God's "name," we
are driven to consider two passages in the early
Christian apologists Justin and Clement of Alexandria;
these apologists, as we have seen, represented the use
of the term ungenerated which Aetius accepted. In his
Second Apology, Justin wrote as follows in explication
of what a Christian Middle Platonist meant by God's
ineffability:

> For whatever name each of the angels has
> given to himself and his children, by that
> name they called them. But to the Father
> of all, who is ungenerated, no name is
> assigned, for by whatever name he be called,
> he has as his elder the person who assigns
> him the name. But these words, Father and
> God and Creator and Lord and Master, are not
> names (ὀνόματα), but appellations derived
> from his good deeds, and functions (ἀλλ' ἐκ
> τῶν εὐποιϊῶν καὶ τῶν ἔργων προσρήσεις).
> And his Son, who alone is properly called
> Son . . . , is called Christ . . . , this
> name also containing an unknown significance,
> as also the appellation God is not a name,
> but an opinion implanted in the nature of
> men of a thing that can hardly be explained.[1]

The parallels to Aetius' views are striking. God was
said to be ungenerated; the term Father was said not
to be a "name" but rather one of the "appellations
derived from God's good deeds and functions"; and
'Father' was rejected as a true name because, if it
were otherwise, the one who had assigned him this name
would be his superior. Just as striking are the parallels in a passage from Clement of Alexandria. In

---

1. Justin Martyr, 2 Apol. 5:6-6:3 (trans. from
ANF 1:190, slightly altered).

<u>Stromata</u> 5:12 Clement argued[1] in heavily Platonic
fashion that discourse about God is very difficult
because "the first and oldest principle which is the
cause of generation for all other things, is difficult
to make known." This was so for Clement, as it was
for the Middle Platonist Albinus,[2] because the first
principle or God "is neither genus nor differentia nor
species nor individual nor number." Nor does the first
principle have parts, "for the One is indivisible and,
because of this, is infinite." Hence, it is without
form and without name (ἀσχημάτιστον καὶ ἀνωνόμαστον).
Clement explained the latter claim as follows:

> And if ever we name it, we do not properly
> call it either the One or the Good or Mind
> or Being Itself or Father or God or Demiurge
> or Lord. We do not speak as though we were
> supplying his name, but accompanied by per-
> plexity we employ good names in order that
> our understanding may have them as means of
> support lest it err in other things. For
> each one by itself is not expressive of God,
> but all together they are revelatory of the
> power (δύναμις) of the Almighty, for that
> which is said is either spoken from what
> belongs to things or from their relation to
> one another, but none of these are able to
> apprehend God. Nor anymore is he apprehended
> by demonstrable knowledge, for it depends on
> prior and better known things, but nothing
> pre-exists the Ungenerated. It remains, then,
> that we understand the Unknown by divine grace
> and the Logos alone that proceeds from him
> . . . .

Again, God was said to be ungenerated in a passage dis-
cussing the problem of naming God. Clement agreed with
Justin that the commonly used names for God--names such

---

1. All translations from Clement are basically
those found in ANF 2.
2. Albinus, <u>Intr.</u> 10:4.

as Father--do not express him as he is in himself. While Justin argued that they are "appellations derived from his good deeds and functions," Clement expressed the same point by claiming that such names reveal "the power (δύναμις) of the Almighty." It was precisely this term 'power' that Aetius used (in the fragments quoted in Basil's memorandum) to describe the referent of the term Father when used of God: "The name Father is not revelatory of essence but of power . . . ."[1] Furthermore, when Clement argued that God is not "apprehended by demonstrable knowledge, for it depends on prior and better known things, but nothing preexists the Ungenerated," he was simply giving a slightly different version of the argument we have met both in Justin Martyr and in syllogism #13 of Aetius' Syntagmation. It appears undeniable that Aetius' theory of theological language was a development of the Christian Middle Platonic position present in Justin and Clement.

Aetius' version of this position, while it surely did not represent the intention of the apologists' arguments (theirs were designed to protect the claim of God's ineffability), was in harmony with the actual claims they made; Aetius' version was an interpretation of the letter, not the spirit, of second and third century Christian Middle Platonism. The Neo-Arian probably noticed that in such passages as those we have quoted, Christian Middle Platonists employed the term ungenerated of God but did not include the term among the designations of God which referred to his deeds or his power. Aetius concluded that ungenerated does not refer to God's attributes or his relations with other things (to paraphrase Clement) but to his essence. It is God's "name." On the other hand, terms like Father, which Athanasius and Basil of Ancyra preferred to ungenerated, refer only to God's activity or power. The term Father is not God's name; it does not tell us who he is in himself. If we keep in mind Aetius' development of Christian Middle Platonism and return to the language of the

_____

1. Epiphanius, Haer. 73:21.

<u>Syntagmation</u>'s twelfth syllogism, we see why the Neo-
Arian insisted against Athanasius and Basil of Ancyra
that the name ungenerated cannot in any way be a
product of "human invention." No name that is revelatory of God's very essence can be invented by man.
Aetius summarized the results of his position in
syllogism #14. If one takes seriously the name of
God's essence, and does not allow any generation to
affect that essence, then God is truly what he is said
to be. But if one follows the Homoousians and Homoiousians and allows the term Father, which really
denotes God's activity, to refer to God's essence, if,
that is, one holds that the fatherly activity of generation penetrates God's essence or hypostasis, then
one must conclude that God's ungenerated hypostasis
is not strong enough to avoid yielding to the passive
experiences of generation. God is not truly what he
is said to be or, to use Justin Martyr's terminology,
an appellation of God is confused with his name. We
see, therefore, that Aetius' arguments in syllogisms
#12-14 depended fundamentally upon the Christian
Middle Platonic tradition of theological usage.

In order to support his position that God's
ungeneratedness is independent of the inventiveness
of the human will, Aetius argued in syllogism #15
that God's ungeneratedness is even independent of his
own will. He maintained that not even God's will can
effect generation for his ungenerated essence. Since
we discussed this syllogism in our previous chapter,
we need not repeat the details here. Suffice it to
say that if the Son is willed by God to be immutable,
then God must be immutable apart from his own willing,
lest the Son be more perfect than he, that is, lest he
occupy a higher rank. And if God is immutable in this
way, he surely cannot will generation for his ungenerated essence, not the least because the willing of
generation means the willing of change. The reason
Aetius set forth this syllogism at this point in the
<u>Syntagmation</u>'s second part is evident. If God cannot
effect his ungeneratedness by his own will, how can
human inventiveness or will go so far as to effect
that ungeneratedness? Despite the absence of God's
name of ungenerated from scriptural revelation, it
cannot have been invented by man.

273

The Syntagmation's sixteenth syllogism went on to
defend the theological validity of the term ungenerated in a rather different way from that of syllogisms
#12-15. It was based upon Basil's contention in his
memorandum that while the term generated is scriptural
(it occurs in Ps. 110:3 and Prov. 8:22) and, hence,
theologically legitimate, the term ungenerated is
unscriptural and, therefore, illegitimate. Syllogism
#16a argued that only if the Neo-Arian contention is
accepted that God's ingeneracy in essence is theologically legitimate and meaningful would it be permissible
to accept Basil's view that the Son's generatedness is
theologically legitimate. For, given Platonic assumptions of course (with which Aetius always operated),
the generate is a derivative of the ungenerated; it
gains its meaning and reality from contrast with the
ungenerated.[1] But if ungeneratedness reveals nothing
about God's essence, as Basil claimed, then the entire
Platonic 'ungenerated/generated' world-view collapses:
generateness no longer has any meaning or reality;
nothing is contrasted with nothing. Section (b) of
syllogism #16 continued the same tack. It was designed to cope with the eventuality that in the throes of
disputation some Homoiousians might decide not to
follow Basil and might deny that even the Son's generatedness is a theologically meaningful concept. In
order to deal with such an ascription of all
'ungenerated/generated' terminology to human invention,
Aetius appealed to a Middle Platonic theory of language
that we find presented by the second century Platonist
Albinus.[2] Setting forth his interpretation of Plato's
Cratylus, Albinus argued that language is a mixture
of nature and convention in which "convention follows
the nature of a thing." Or to put it more precisely,
"The accuracy of a name . . . is the agreement of
convention with the nature of a thing." Furthermore,
said Albinus, because there is a "natural conformity

---

1. For a Platonist, the opposite did not hold:
the ungenerated realm does not gain its reality and
meaning from the generated realm.
2. Albinus, Intr. 6:10-11.

274

(φυσικὴν οἰκειότητα)" of names with the essences of
things, a name may be looked upon as an "instrument
(ὄργανον) which teaches and differentiates "the
essence of each thing (τῆς ἑκάστου οὐσίας)." This
does not mean, however, that everyone who uses the
conventional names of language uses them properly;
only the "dialectician," who knows "the nature of
underlying realities" is able to do this. If we assume
that Aetius held fundamentally the same Middle Platonic
theory of language as did Albinus, an assumption easy
to make given the heavy influence of Middle Platonism
on his thought, we may conclude that he was maintaining
in syllogism #16b that all conventional language, including the 'ungenerated/generated' language of the
Christian theological tradition, "differentiates the
essence of each thing." (In subsequent chapters we
shall see Aetius' disciple Eunomius developing this
theory of language in great detail.) Thus, if a
Homoiousian should claim that the 'ungenerated/
generated' language of the Christian theological
tradition is the product of human invention, he would
be denying the Christian "hope" of knowing God and the
Son by denying the very nature of language. Or, to
rehearse Aetius' ipsissima verba, "If the expression
ungenerated is contrasted with the expression generated, silence following the expression, it turns out
that the hope of Christians comes into existence and
goes out of existence, since it rests on excellent
language but not on natures as they actually are, as
the meaning of names intends" (my underlinings).
Aetius followed up this statement with syllogism #17;
here he argued that if the ungenerated/generated
distinction is simply the product of human invention,
there will be no way to distinguish the essence of the
Son from the essence of the Father, for as father and
son they will possess the same essence, even though
it is partitioned. The Son will be subordinate to
God "only verbally (προφορᾷ μόνον)." But this view,
implied Aetius, contradicts scripture, since in Jn.
14:28, to which syllogism #17 seemed to allude, the
Son clearly subordinated himself to God when he said,
"The Father, who sent me, is greater than I" (compare
also Jn. 20:17, where the Son said, "I am ascending to

275

my Father and your Father, to my God and your God").[1]
Indeed, given that the Son obviously sensed his own
subordination when he said these words, to allow
accurate knowledge of this subordination to men, who
through their ἐπινοία understand the 'ungenerated/
generated' distinction, yet to disallow such accurate
knowledge to the Son, would be the height of blasphemy:
men would be "superior" to the Son because of their
knowledge.

Finally, we come to syllogism #18 of Aetius'
Syntagmation, the last syllogism in Part II. Unlike
the preceding six, it added nothing new; it was simply
a summary of what Aetius had already established in
response to the Athanasian/Basilean accusation. Since
ungenerated essence, he said, is not superior to
generation because it wills to be, but because it has
the nature to be, its superiority to generation comes
from its own resources (οὔκοθεν); it is, therefore,
"in itself ungenerated essence (αὐτὸ οὐσία . . .
ἀγέννητος)." And if God's ungenerated essence is
even independent of his own willing, then Aetius
thought he had grounds to conclude that "God . . .
permits no reasoning to invent (ἐπινοῆσαι) generation
for [his ungenerated essence], thrusting aside from
generated beings all investigation and reasoning."
Athanasius and, especially, Basil of Ancyra were
completely mistaken when they said that the
'ungenerated/generated' language of the Christian
tradition is not theologically legitimate. In Part II
of his Syntagmation Aetius tried to provide his
disciples with the wherewithal to prove it.

Throughout his Syntagmation Aetius argued not only
that the 'ungenerated/generated' distinction is theologically legitimate but also that it pertains to the
essences of God and the Son. Perhaps more than any
claim, this one was crucial to Aetius' position. In
order to provide his disciples with a sequence of

---

1. That Aetius had the Gospel of John 14:28 in
mind is substantiated by the fact that his colleague
and one-time student Eunomius actually quoted the verse
to the same effect in his Apol. 11.

arguments intended to establish the point, should they be challenged, Aetius supplemented the syllogisms in Parts I and II which touched on this issue with twelve additional syllogisms. They formed Part III of Aetius' document.

The Syntagmation: Part III

#19. If ungeneratedness is revelatory of privation (στερήσεως) in the case of God, and ungeneratedness be nothing, what sort of reasoning would deprive that which does not have being (τοῦ μὴ ὄντος) of nothing (τὸ μηδέν)? But if ungeneratedness means being (ὄν), who would separate God from being, that is, himself from himself (τίς ἂν χωρίσειεν ὄντος θεόν, ὅπερ ἐστὶν, αὐτὸν ἑαυτοῦ)?

#20. If privations are removals of conditions (ἕξεως . . . ἀφαιρέσεις), ungeneratedness in the case of God is either privation of a condition or a condition of privation. If it is privation of a condition, how could what is not present be counted as present to God? If ungeneratedness is a condition, it is necessary that generated essence be presupposed, in order that, having thus acquired a condition, it may be named (ὀνομάζηται) ungenerated. On the other hand, if the generated [hypostasis] participated in the ungenerated essence, having submitted to the loss of its condition, it was deprived of generation. Its essence, then, would be generated, and ungeneratedness would be its condition. But if the term generate is revelatory of entrance [into being], it is clear that it means a condition, whether the generate has been remodelled from some essence or whether it is what it is said to be.

277

#21. If ungeneratedness is a condition and generatedness is a condition, the essences are prior to the conditions, yet the conditions, even though secondary to the essences, are, nevertheless, held in more honor.

But if the ungenerated is the cause (αἴτιον) of the generated, the generated, signifying its being by disclosing its cause together with its own essence, reveals an essence, not a condition. But since the ungenerated nature introduces nothing together with itself, how could the ungenerated nature be a condition and not an essence?

#22. If every essence is ungenerated like the essence of God Almighty, how will someone say that one is liable to passive experiences (παθητὴν) but the other is not liable to passive experiences (ἀπαθῆ)? If within the allotted class (ἀποκλήρωσις) 'ungenerated nature' one essence remains superior to quantity and quality and, in short, all change (ποσότητος καὶ ποιότητος καὶ ἁπλῶς εἰπεῖν πάσης μεταβολῆς ἀμείνων), and another is liable to passive experiences (παθῶν . . . ὑπεύθυνος) but is conceded to be precisely similar in essence (τὸ ἀπαράλλακτον εἰς οὐσίαν), we ought to leave the things just enumerated to chance (τῷ αὐτομάτῳ) or we ought to say what follows consistently--that is, that the essence that acts (τὴν ποιοῦσαν) is ungenerated and the one that is being changed (τὴν μεταβαλλομένην) is generated.

#23. If the ungenerated nature is the cause of a nature that is generated, and ungeneratedness be nothing, how could nothing be the cause of what is generated?

278

#24. If ungeneratedness is privation, and privation is a loss of a condition, and the loss is utterly destroyed or changed into something different, how is it possible for a condition which is being changed or being destroyed to be named (κατονομάζεσθαι) the essence of God, with the title (προσηγορίᾳ) the ungenerated?

#25. If ungeneratedness reveals a privation which does not belong to God, how can we say that he is ungenerated and that he cannot be generated?

#26. If the term ungenerated is a mere name (ψιλὸν ὄνομα) in the case of God, and the mere expression of it elevates the hypostasis of God in relation to all generated things, then the expression of men is held in more honor than the hypostasis of the Almighty, since it has adorned God Almighty with incomparable superiority (ἀσυγκρίτῳ ὑπεροχῇ).

#27. If cause is allotted to every generated thing, and the ungenerated nature is uncaused, the ungenerated does not reveal cause, but it signifies hypostasis.

#28. If everything which has been generated has been generated by something different, and the ungenerated hypostasis has been generated neither by itself nor by something different, it is necessary that ungeneratedness reveal essence.

#29. If the ungenerated hypostasis is indicated at the same time as the essence of the generate as its cause, since it is precisely similar with respect to every cause (κατὰ πάσης αἰτίας τὸ ἀπαράλλακτον ἔχουσα), it is in itself incomparable

279

essence (αὐτὸ οὐσία . . . ἀσύγκριτος),
for it does not indicate its unapproachability in relation to anything external
(ἔξωθεν), but it is in itself incomparable
and unapproachable (ἀσύγκριτος καὶ
ἀπρόσιτος), since it is also ungenerated.

#30. If the Almighty surpasses every nature,
he surpasses it because of his ungeneratedness, which is the cause of persistence
for generated things. But if ungeneratedness is not revelatory of essence, how
will the nature of generated things continue to be preserved (ἕξει τὸ
διασώζεσθαι)?

We have said that the main purpose of the Syntagmation's third part was to establish the basal Neo-
Arian affirmation that ungeneratedness and generatedness
signify the essence of God and the essence of the Son
respectively. Because the beginning of the document
defended the expression 'ungenerated God' in terms of
causation, we are not surprised that Part III accepted
the category of causation as applicable to ungeneratedness but rejected the categories of privation
(στέρησις) and condition (ἕξις) as inapplicable. Yet,
though Aetius rejected the latter two categories, Neo-
Arianism had to pay a heavy price for his employing
them at all. For Neo-Arianism's later opponents Basil
of Caesarea and his brother Gregory had in mind arguments like those in Part III when they accused the
Neo-Arians of Aristotelianism and Stoicism. While it
is true that the terms στέρησις and ἕξις were dis-
cussed--and together--by Aristotle and the Stoic
Chrysippus,[1] given that Aetius (and Eunomius after
him) rejected them in favor of cause, the Cappadocians'
accusations were unfounded.[2] The Neo-Arians probably

---

1. See, for example, Aristotle, Cat. 12-3 and
Metaph. 1022-3 and 1055, and J. von Arnim, Stoicorum
Veterum Fragmenta (Leipzig, 1903), 2:49-58.
2. That Aristotelianism and Stoicism did not

used the terms in the first place only because the
variety of Middle Platonism to which they were heir
happened to be rather open to Aristotelianism and
Stoicism, especially to their logic and dialectic.[1]

The first syllogism of Part III, #19, assumed,
as did all the syllogisms in this part, that ungenerated is a term properly applied to God. But how should
it be understood? Since the term is a negative, one
possibility is that it should be understood as a privation. A privation of what? Well, suggested Aetius,
try the most basic possibilities, non-being and being.
If the ungenerated God is non-existent and ungeneratedness means privation, the result is nonsense; how can
one deprive something that does not exist? On the
other hand, if the ungenerated God exists and ungeneratedness means privation, then the only thing that
God has of which he can be deprived is being. But
this too is absurd, for what Christian would entertain
the thought of depriving God of being? After all, the
Christian Middle Platonic tradition called him Being
(τὸ ὄν) and even scripture, most notably Ex. 3:14,
called him "He who is (ὁ ὤν)." Assuming this to be
revealed, "who," asked Aetius, "would separate God
from being, that is, himself from himself?" Now, if
we ask ourselves the question why Aetius in syllogism
#19 began with being and non-being, perhaps the reason
was that he had in the back of his mind the possibilities for understanding the term ungenerated offered by
Athanasius in his De Decretis of A.D. 350 (and even
earlier, in his Orationes). In fact, syllogism #19,
as well as a number of the syllogisms following it,

---

affect the content of Neo-Arian thought has been noted
both by Bernard C. Barmann, The Cappadocian Triumph
Over Arianism, unpublished Ph.D. dissertation (Stanford
University, 1966), p. 479 n. 100 and by L.R. Wickham,
"The Syntagmation of Aetius," p..561 n..1.

1. For a discussion of the varying attitudes of
Middle Platonists to Aristotle and the Stoics, see Reg-
inald Eldred Witt, Albinus and the History of Middle
Platonism, (Cambridge, England, 1937), p. 114ff.

may well have been first formulated in the early
A.D. 350s as a response to Athanasius, for in his
Orationes and De Decretis the Alexandrian bishop gave
the four following possibilities for the meaning of
ungenerated.[1] Ungenerated means either

(1) "what is not yet generated but is able to
be generated,"

or

(2) "what is not generated and is not even able
to be generated," the version of the
Orationes; "what does not exist and is
not able to be generated into being," the
version of the De Decretis,

or

(3) "what exists but has not been generated
from anything and has no father at all,"
the version of the Orationes; "what exists
yet has not been generated and did not
have a beginning of being, but is eternal
and indestructible," the version of the
De Decretis,

or

(4) "what has not been made but always is,"
the view of the Arian, Asterius, as
quoted in the Orationes; "what does not
have a cause of its being, but is itself
a cause of generation for generated
things," the Arian view quoted in the
De Decretis.

Athanasius claimed that he found his first three definitions of ungenerated in the Greek philosophers,[2] and
doubtless he did, since the first two were presented
in exactly this form by Aristotle in De Caelo 280b and
282a and the third, which was admitted by Athanasius
in De Synodis 47 to be legitimately Christian even
though it was adopted by the Arians (including Aetius
in syllogism #2), was thoroughly Platonic. Aetius

---

1. Ar. 1:30; Decr. 28-9.
2. Decr. 28. Compare Ar. 1:30.

robably had Athanasius' first two definitions in mind
which assume that ungenerated describes non-being)
when he formulated the first half of syllogism #19 and
ad Athanasius' last two definitions in mind--those
which assume that 'ungenerated' describes being, a
view that Aetius himself accepted--when he formulated
he second half. Thus, it is likely that Aetius
lecided to introduce Part III of his Syntagmation with
this syllogism because he expected that his devotees
might find it useful in disputations with Homoousians
and Homoiousians who were familiar with Athanasius'
works, as both groups were.

Having disposed of the notion that ungeneratedness
signifies privation of either non-being or being,
Aetius inquired in syllogism #20 whether it might
signify privation of a condition of being, an ἕξις, or
conversely, a condition of privation, an ἕξις
στερήσεως. He concluded that both of these options
are also unacceptable. If God's ungeneratedness is
the privation of a condition, that condition is non-
existent to him, and it is foolish to describe him in
terms of something that he does not possess. And if
God's ungeneratedness is a condition of privation, God
must first have been generated essence--a blasphemous
notion--in order that generatedness might be deprived
him. Aetius added that 'privation/condition' terminology not only is inappropriate for understanding
God's ungeneratedness but also for understanding the
Son's generatedness. Since he has already established
that ungeneratedness in God's case cannot in any way
be related to condition (either as a condition of
privation or vice-versa), God's ungeneratedness must
describe his essence. If this is so, the Neo-Arian
asked, what is the relation of the generated Son to
the ungenerated God? He saw two possibilities:
either the Son participates in God's ungenerated
essence or he is generated by God's will. Is privation/
condition terminology appropriate to either of these
two possibilities, Aetius inquired? Decidedly not.
At first glance one might perhaps think that the situation of participation favors the notion that the Son's
generatedness is a privation of a condition. But
further thought reveals that if the generated hypostasis'

283

participates in God's ungenerated essence and thereby
is deprived of its generatedness, one finds oneself in
the logically impossible situation, unless one gives
up on the Son's generatedness altogether, of having a
generated Son whose condition is ungenerated. Similarly, though the Son's generation by God's will might
seem to favor the idea that the Son's generatedness
is a condition, this idea also is misled. If the term
generate is revelatory only of the Son's condition of
having been generated and not of his essence, then the
Son's condition of generatedness is the condition of
some other essence besides the Son's; this other essence, through having been remodelled by the addition
of the condition of generatedness, has become the Son.
This is impious. The alternative that the term generate is revelatory both of the Son's condition of
having been generated and of his essence is, in Wickham's nice phrase, "self-stultifying."[1] Therefore,
'privation/condition' terminology is as inappropriate
for the Son as for God; God and the Son must be,
respectively, ungenerated in essence and generated in
essence.

Aetius followed the rather complex arguments of
syllogism #20 with a more straightforward one in
syllogism #21a. To an honest Christian believer,
Aetius hoped, this argument would be persuasive with
regard to the category of condition. Because all
Christians believe in the Absolute God and his Son
("We believe in one God . . . and his uniquely-
generated Son"), the Neo-Arian assumed that every
Christian must accept (1) that the ungenerated One
(which, as we have seen, means the absolute One) is
the highest good and (2) that the first one generated
by the Ungenerated is the next highest good. But if
ungeneratedness and generatedness are conditions,
there must be essences prior to the conditions, essences
which possess the conditions. This would force a
Christian to accept conditions, which are ontologically
secondary, to be his absolute God and his absolute God's
Son. Since this asks that Christians acknowledge other

---

1. Wickham, p. 562.

ods "before" their own, the notion must be rejected
as impious. Ungeneratedness and generatedness are
essences, not conditions.

This view was proven in syllogism #21b from a
different angle, that is, from the point of view of
causation. Aetius must have had great confidence in
the persuasive power of this argument, for the notion
that God is the cause of both the Son and all other
beings was explicitly stated by the Homoiousians in
their published literature,[1] and, of course, Aetius
had defined God in terms of cause in syllogism #2.
Since the ungenerated God caused the generated Son
to exist, Aetius deduced that it must have been the
Son's essence that was caused to exist as generated,
for the notion that some priorly existing essence
had been granted the condition of generatedness
seriously compromises God's ability to act as a fully
effective cause and, therefore, is blasphemous. The
ungenerated nature of God, however, is uncaused and
does not point to something else: the notion 'uncaused', unlike the notion 'caused', is non-relational--
in Aetius' words, it "introduces nothing together with
itself." But if it "introduces nothing together with
itself," God's uncaused, ungenerated nature must be
simple: it cannot be a compound composed of an essence
possessing an uncaused and ungenerated condition. Once
again, one must conclude that God's ungeneratedness
pertains to his essence.

Given the influence of Christian Middle Platonism
on Aetius, the Syntagmation's next syllogism, #22, is
most intriguing. L.R. Wickham was quite right when he
wrote that it "reads like a piece of theistic apologetic"
(though in my opinion it was originally aimed at pagan
Middle Platonists, not, as Wickham thought, "the doctrines of Democritus and Epicurus").[2] But Wickham's
guess at why Aetius included the syllogism in his Syn-
tagmation--namely, as an attack on a position held by

----

1. See the Ancyran synodical letter of 358 apud
Epiphanius, Haer. 73:3 and Basil of Ancyra's memorandum
of 359 apud Epiphanius, Haer. 73:12.
2. See Wickham, p. 563.

Basil of Caesarea[1]--is anachronistic and wide of the
mark. Aetius included it, rather, because it was an
attack on the Homoiousian position, especially the
view--assumed also in the preceding syllogism--that
God is the uncaused cause of the Son (as well as all
other things) even though the Son is "precisely similar
in essence (τὸ ἀπαράλλακτον εἰς οὐσίαν)" to God. But
first let us examine the apparent original intention
of the syllogism's argument. If the reader recalls
the conversation of the still pagan Middle Platonist
Justin with the Christian Middle Platonist "old man"
of Justin's Dialogus cum Tryphone Judaeo, he will
remember that the "old man" agreed to the validity of
an argument very similar to the one in syllogism #22.
Pagan Middle Platonists believed not only that God is
ungenerated but that all souls are. In other words,
"every essence is ungenerated like the essence of God
Almighty (syllogism #22)." In opposition to this, the
position of the Christian "old man" was that only God
is ungenerated:

> . . . all other things which come after him
> are generated and corruptible. For this
> reason souls both die and are punished:
> since if they were ungenerated, they would
> neither sin, nor be filled with folly, nor
> be cowardly and again ferocious; nor would
> they willingly transform into swine and
> serpents and dogs; and it would not indeed
> be just to compel them, if they be ungenerated.

---

1. "Why did Aetius include it? . . . a hint may
be taken from Eunomius (Second Apol. in Gr. Nyss. C.
Eunom. ii 464, I, p. 362) who argues that Basil, by
making God's priority relative to world-eras, is forced
to say either that these are eternal, in which case he
is an ignorant pagan and Valentinian, or that they are
generate, in which case he will no longer be able to
ascribe ingeneracy to God. Anti-pagan, anti-gnostic
ripostes might be useful against Aetius' opponents,
then" (Ibid. pp. 563-4).

For that which is ungenerated is similar
to, equal to, and the same as (ὅμοιόν . . .
καὶ ἴσον καὶ ταὐτόν) that which is ungenerated, and neither in power nor in honor
would they be different from each other.
Therefore, there are not many ungenerated
things, for if there were some differences
among them, you would not find the cause
(τὸ αἴτιον) of the difference, though you
searched for it; but, after ever sending
your mind to infinity, you would at some
time stop, tired out, at one ungenerated
and say this is the cause of all things
(ἁπάντων αἴτιον).[1]

It takes little perceptiveness to see that the arguments in Justin and in the Syntagmation were at base
different only in expression: they both began with the
passive experiences of those things allegedly "similar
to" God, and they both concluded that a cause for the
difference between these "similar" things and God
could not be found. Aetius' argument seems to have
been a remodelled polemic against pagan Middle Platonists, a polemic which argued for one ungenerated being,
the Christian God. Because the remodelling was only
slight, the inclusion of the syllogism in the Syntagmation is at first glance difficult to grasp. Yet,
the phrase "precisely similar in essence (τὸ ἀπαράλλακτον εἰς οὐσίαν)," the battle cry of the Homoiousians
at Seleucia, reveals to us Aetius' intent. He was
arguing that since the Homoiousians affirmed both that
the Son is generated and that he is precisely similar
to God, they must allow all generated essences to be
precisely similar to God; if one generated being is
precisely similar to God, all generated beings must be
precisely similar. But if this is so, then God who is
"superior to quantity and quality and, in short, all
change" is precisely similar to beings who are liable
to passive experiences. This is contradictory nonsense.

---

1. Justin, Dial. 5 (trans. from ANF 1:197,
slightly altered).

Only the one essence who acts but is not acted upon or changed, only the one essence who causes but is not caused, is ungenerated. All others, including the Son, are acted upon and changed, are generated and caused; therefore, they are not precisely similar to God. The Homoiousian position must be rejected: the generated Son is not precisely similar in essence to God but rather the Son is generated in essence while God is ungenerated in essence. Of course, when Aetius implied, as he surely did in this syllogism, that the Son is "liable to passive experiences" and liable to "change," he did not mean to say that the Son ever does in essence change. God wills that the Son will never realize his potentiality for change, as syllogism #15 made clear.

Before Aetius digressed into his direct polemic against the Homoiousians in syllogism #22, he had been arguing from the notion of causation. He continued this line of reasoning in syllogisms #23 and 24. In the first he used the notion of causation to prove that God's ungeneratedness cannot be a privation of being; in the second he used the same notion to prove that God's ungeneratedness cannot be a privation of a condition. Aetius was now employing the notion of God's causation, admitted by the Homoiousians, as a means of totally rejecting 'privation/condition' terminology as appropriate for understanding God's ungeneratedness. Syllogism #23 argued that if the ungenerated nature is the cause of a generated nature, but ungeneratedness signifies the privation of being, ungeneratedness is nothing; hence, it cannot be the cause of anything. Then, in syllogism #24 Aetius noted that if ungeneratedness in the case of God is a privation of a condition, and privation of a condition means that the condition is either destroyed (that is, changed into non-being) or changed into some existent different from itself, then the ungenerated is acted upon by some other cause and cannot be uncaused and ungenerated. In this case, to name God the ungenerated is without meaning. Having introduced the idea of 'naming' in syllogism #24, Aetius added one further syllogism against ungeneratedness as signifying privation, arguing this time on grounds of language, on grounds of 'naming'. "If ungeneratedness reveals a privation which does not belong to God," Aetius pointed out in syllogism #25, the language which implies that he <u>possesses</u> ungeneratedness is meaningless. Seemingly unable to bring up the problem of theological language without engaging in sarcasm, Aetius offered his disciples syllogism #26, a syllogism which outdid in sarcasm both syllogism #12 and syllogism #17 of Part II. There Aetius had said that naming God the ungenerated, when the term does not denote the actual reality of his hypostasis, elevates the men doing the naming to a position of higher honor than God; here he said that the "mere expression (ἡ ψιλὴ προφορά)" of the name is superior to "the hypostasis of the Almighty"!

With 'privation/condition' language now disposed of, Aetius concluded Part III of his <u>Syntagmation</u> with four syllogisms which proceeded from the point of view of causation to establish his main positive affirmation in this part, namely, that God is essentially ungenerated. In the first of the four Aetius noted that when one says all generated natures are caused and the ungenerated nature is uncaused, this in no way implies that the uncaused, ungenerated nature is necessarily related to caused, generated natures (even though the contrary is true). As uncaused and ungenerated, God's nature or hypostasis must be completely independent: it is not uncaused and ungenerated in relation to other things; it is <u>in itself</u> uncaused and ungenerated. Syllogism #28 said the same thing in slightly different language, language which hearkened back to the definition of the ungenerated God offered in syllogism #2. It affirmed that because every generated thing has been generated by something else, it is essentially generated; but because the ungenerated God has been generated neither by itself nor by something else, it is completely independent and, consequently, essentially ungenerated. God is even completely independent of the Son, added Aetius in syllogism #29. Surely God, the ungenerated hypostasis, is implied to be a cause by the Son's generatedness, but in precisely the same way as God is implied as the cause of every generated thing. God is just as incomparable and unapproachable to the generated Son as he is to any generated being; he is ungenerated, and

ungeneratedness does not gain its meaning from its
relation to anything external to itself, from anything
generated; it gains its meaning only from itself. So
there is only one incomparable and unapproachable
as 1 Tim. 6:16 said, from where, of course, Aetius
derived the term "unapproachable (ἀπρόσιτος)." However, despite God's complete independence of essence
from all generated beings, syllogism #30 assumed that
he still is the cause of the persistence of generated
beings. Probably Aetius was still alluding here to
1 Tim. 6:16, for this New Testament passage not only
attributed unapproachability only to God ("he dwells in
unapproachable light") but also "immortality." If it
is true that the Neo-Arian had this passage in mind,
the concern of the syllogism was not, as L.R. Wickham
assumed,[1] the eternity of "the world," but the immortality of the Son and of believing Christians.[2] Aetius
was asking whether it would be possible for the Son
and believing Christians to be caused by God to have
immortality if ungeneratedness were not revelatory of
God's essence. Aetius appears here to have assumed
that the Platonists were right when they accepted
ungeneratedness and incorruptibility (= immortality)
as inseparable. The thrust of the syllogism was to
ask whether the Son and believing Christians can be
caused to be immortal when God is not in essence immortal and ungenerated. The answer was obvious: if
God were not in essence immortal and ungenerated, he
would be in essence mortal (or corruptible) and generated, and such a being could hardly cause any generated
beings to be saved.

---

1. Wickham, p. 566.
2. Wickham (Ibid.) affirmed that this syllogism
rode on the essence/will dichotomy and implied the
eternity of "the world." This would make the syllogism
contradict the assertion of Aetius' disciple Eunomius
that "the world (τὸν κόσμον)" is not eternal (1 Apol.
22). Methodologically, it seems more appropriate to
reject Wickham's interpretation of the syllogism than
to accept a contradiction between Aetius and Eunomius,
who on all other points agreed completely.

With syllogism #30 we have come to the end of the
Syntagmation's third part. Aetius has now proven both
of the unsubstantiated assumptions of his polemics in
Part I, that is, both the assumption that 'ungenerated/
generated' language constitutes proper theological
language and the assumption that ungeneratedness in the
case of God pertains to essence. The first was proven
in Part II, the second in Part III. All that now remained was for Aetius to return to his polemic against
the Homoousians and Homoiousians. The plan of the
Syntagmation indicates that Aetius hoped the Neo-Arians
for whom the document was written would be able to win
their debates solely on the strength of the syllogisms
in Part I. But for more incorrigible opponents he provided his devotees with Parts II and III, which established the unsubstantiated assumptions of Part I. Now,
with these points covered, Aetius supplied another set
of directly polemical syllogisms. They were presumably
intended to deal with the Neo-Arians' more ingenious
and less easily persuaded opponents.

The Syntagmation: Part IV

#31.   If none of the invisible things pre-
exists (προυπάρχει) itself as a seed
(σπερματικῶς), but continues in its
allotted nature, how does the ungenerated
God, being free of allotment, see his own
essence, now second in the generate
(δεύτερον ἐν γεννήματι), now prior in
the ungenerated (προτέραν ἐν ἀγεννήτῳ),
according to the rank of first and
second (κατὰ τὴν τοῦ πρώτου καὶ
δευτέρου τάξιν)?

#32.   If God remains in ungenerated essence,
let the notion of God's knowing himself
in generation and ingeneracy be removed.
But if we concede that his essence ex-
tends in the ungenerated and the generated, he himself does not know his own
essence, being made dizzy (περιαγόμενος)
by generation and ingeneracy. And if the

291

generated received participation in the ungenerated, but remains endlessly in the nature of the generated, he knows himself in the nature in which he continues, clearly not knowing the ungenerated participation, for he is not able to have knowledge about himself as both of ungenerated and generated essence. And if the generated is negligible (εὐκαταφρόνητον) because of its liability to change (διὰ μεταβολῆς ἐπιτηδειότητα), unchangeable essence is naturally worthy of dignity (ἀξίωμα φύσεώς ἐστιν οὐσία ἀμετάβλητος), since ungenerated essence is confessed to be superior to every cause.

#33. If the ungenerated is removed from every cause, and there be many ungenerated things (πολλὰ ἀγέννητα), they will possess precise similarity in nature (ἀπαράλλακτον . . . τὴν φύσιν). For if by the allotment of nature (ἀποκληρώσει φύσεως) they have not received anything in common and distinctly theirs (τινὸς κοινοῦ καὶ ἰδίον), one ungenerated thing could not act and the other could not be generated (ἡ μὲν ἐποίει, ἡ δὲ ἐγίνετο).

#34. If every essence is ungenerated, neither of two (οὐδ᾽ὁποτέρα) will differ from the other with respect to being without a master (κατὰ τὸ ἀδέσποτον). How then could someone say that the one is changed and the other causes the change, since they do not permit God to make things exist as hypostases from non-existent essence (οὐκ ἐπιτρεπόντων τῷ θεῷ ὑφιστᾶν ἐκ μὴ ὑποκειμένης οὐσίας)?

#35. If every essence is ungenerated, everyone is precisely similar (ἀπαράλλακτος). And since the essence possesses precise similarity (τὸ ἀπαράλλακτον), one must attribute both action and passivity (τὸ ποιεῖν τε καὶ τὸ πάσχειν) to chance. And if there are many beings that are ungenerated and precisely similar (ἀπαραλλάκτων), they will differ from one another in ways not enumerable (ἀναριθμήτως), for the differences could not be enumerated either completely or in some respect, since every difference exhibiting any allotment (ἀποκλήρωσίν τινα) has already been removed from ungenerated essence.

#36. If the expression 'Ungenerated One (τὸ ἀγέννητος)', and the expression 'God' in parallel ways reveal the same thing (τὸ αὐτὸ), the ungenerated one has generated an [other] ungenerated one. But if the expression Ungenerated One reveals one thing and the expression God reveals a different thing, it is not absurd for God to have generated God, one of the two having received existence from ungenerated essence. On the other hand, if the expression 'priority to God' be nothing, as indeed it is, the expression God and the expression Ungenerated One reveal the same thing (ταὐτὸν), since the generate does not admit ungeneratedness. Therefore, he does not suffer to be spoken of alongside his God and Father.

#37. He who is in himself ungenerated God, who because of this has been addressed as the only true God (μόνος . . . ἀληθινὸς θεός--Jn. 17:3) by Jesus Christ whom he sent, Jesus Christ who both truly existed as a hypostasis before the ages and truly is a generated hypostasis, [this ungenerated God] will preserve you formidable men and women (ἐρρωμένους καὶ ἐρρωμένας) from impiety, in Christ

293

Jesus our Savior, through whom all glory
be to the God and Father, both now and
always and forever and ever. Amen.

The plan of Part IV was straightforward. Aetius
first offered two syllogisms aimed at refuting the
homoousian position and then three aimed at the homoiousian. These five polemical arguments were followed
(1) by syllogism #36, which sought to establish that
the term God is not properly applicable to the Son but
only to the one Absolute, and (2) by a benediction
which underlined this. Actually, except for some sub-
tleties in syllogism #31 and for the argument of syllogism #36, there was nothing new in Part IV. Part IV
was a re-presentation of arguments already supplied
earlier in the Syntagmation.

Syllogisms #31 and 32 were directed against the
homoousian position, the position which received the
most attention in Part I. The first sought to demonstrate that the Homoousians were logically unable to
hold that there is any difference in priority between
God and the Son; logic precluded their holding that
God is in any sense "first" and the Son "second."
Aetius argued that since invisible beings lower down
on the scale of being in no way preexist themselves
but always remain exactly what they are, exactly how
they have been allotted to be, how can the ungenerated
God, who is at the top of the scale of being, even to
the extent that he is not really on the scale at all
(he is "free of allotment"),[1] "see his own essence now
second in the generate, now prior in the ungenerated,
according to the rank of first and second"? In other
words, if there is no division in the case of invisible
beings, there can be no division in the case of their
superior. Syllogism #32 also attacked the Homoousians,
but not in a new way: it simply expanded upon an
argument we have already met in syllogism #11. If the
Homoousians' point were granted that the same essence
is present in the ungenerated God and the generated
Son, and the Neo-Arian assumption were conceded (as it

---

1. On this point, see Wickham, p. 566.

must be, see Part III) that ungeneratedness and generatedness pertain to essence, then God would not be able
to know himself, for he would lose himself in dizziness
when he tried to know himself as both ungenerated and
generated at the same time. So also the generated Son.
Since it has been established that he is generated in
essence, he can only be ungenerated by participation.
But for the same reason as God cannot know himself as
both ungenerated and generated, neither can the Son.
The last part of syllogism #32 then set forth a rather
startling statement. Following strict Platonism,
Aetius stated that generated essence, presumably including the Son, is really negligible for the believer,
since it has been caused to change (in the Son's case,
from non-being to being). Ungenerated essence, on the
other hand, is superior to every cause; it is thereby
unchangeable, and worthy of dignity in the natural
order of things. This was as close as Aetius has come
so far to saying that only the ungenerated God is to
be honored and worshipped; he would say as much again
in syllogisms #36 and 37. As we will see, Aetius
believed the Son to be religiously significant (however cosmologically significant he might be) only as
a means through which to approach the one God. Here
was radical Christian monotheism. The implication
that Aetius was seeking to promote was that the Homoousians completely scuttled monotheism when they argued
for the Son's identity of essence with God.

With the Homoousians dealt with in syllogisms
#31 and 32, Aetius turned in #33-35 to the Homoiousians.
The arguments presented were only slightly--and rather
insignificantly--different from the one in syllogism
#22. They require little explication. Attention
should be drawn, however, to two points. First, the
κοινόν/ἴδιον dichotomy, which Aetius rejected as meaningless in relation to precisely similar things, would
be picked up by the Cappadocian Fathers and made
central to their view that the Trinity is both the
same in essence and different in hypostasis. Second,
although the three syllogisms all retained the infer-
ence from the Son's alleged precise similarity to God
that all generated beings are somehow ungenerated, it
is clear from syllogism #34 that Aetius was particularly

295

concerned about only God and the Son. He used a Greek term which indicates that he was talking about only two ungenerated beings (that is, the term ὁποτέρα). And he referred to the horror that the Homoiousians had for talk about God creating hypostases out of non-existent essence; this could be horrifying to a Christian only when applied to the Son.

Finally, in syllogisms #36 and 37 Aetius sought to establish that the term God is properly applied only to the Absolute and not to the Son. L.R. Wickham's view that syllogism #36 drew the conclusion that "in one sense" the term God cannot be used of the Son but "in another sense" it can, was to the point.[1] Aetius argued that since the expression 'priority to God' is meaningless ("as indeed it is," to use Aetius' own words), "the expression God and the expression Ungenerated One reveal the same thing (ταὐτὸν)." Since 'God' is used of both the Ungenerated and the Son, it is obviously a homonymn. Aetius' position was backed up by an allusion to scripture, seemingly to Jn. 20:17. The Neo-Arian wrote, "He [the Son] does not suffer to be spoken of alongside his God and Father." Then, in syllogism #37, the Syntagmation's benediction on the Neo-Arian recipients of the document, Aetius proved his contention by further reference to scripture when he said, following Jn. 17:3, that the ungenerated God "has been addressed as the 'only true God' by Jesus Christ whom he sent." The reference to Jn. 17:3 in the benediction was significant, since it was the only absolutely identifiable quotation from scripture in the entire Syntagmation. The scriptural passage reported Jesus on the night he was betrayed speaking in prayer about salvation, "This is eternal life, that they know you, the only true God, and him whom you have sent, Jesus Christ." The Neo-Arians came back to the verse time and time again to establish knowledge of unqualified monotheism as the heart of the gospel and salvation. How could the Neo-Arians think one verse of scripture could bear so much weight? Perhaps the answer is to be found in the

---

1. Ibid., p. 568.

fourth century eastern liturgy, for the verse occupied a prominent place in the anaphora preface of the two most famous fourth century eucharistic accounts, Serapion's _Euchologium_ (Egypt) and the _Constitutiones Apostolorum_ (Syria or Constantinople).[1] By appealing to the verse in his benediction Aetius was underlining that Neo-Arian absolute monotheism was based on the authority not only of Christianity's scriptures but of her eucharistic liturgy as well. We conclude by noting that Aetius' benediction indicates, in light of the theological content of syllogisms #36 and 37, that "impiety" for Neo-Arianism meant the denial of monotheism, not the denial of the Son's divinity. It also indicates that Aetius expected that his disciples (both male _and_ female), armed with his _Syntagmation_ of syllogisms, would be "formidable" in their opposition to Homoousians and Homoiousians.

With _Syntagmation_ in hand the Neo-Arians were ready to face the theological showdown which was in store for them at the Council of Constantinople to be held in the last month of A.D. 359. However, whereas Aetius' collection of syllogisms assumed that the major opposition to Neo-Arianism would probably come from homoousian supporters of Athanasius, this turned out not to be the case.

---

1. Serapion of Thmuis, _Euch_. 13; _Const. App_. 8:12:6. Although both liturgies have been claimed to be influenced by Arianism, the verse was quoted in such a way as to avoid Arian implications. We, therefore, are probably safe in concluding that the verse was traditional in eastern liturgies at large.